Nested Scrolls

Nested Scrolls

The Autobiography of Rudolf von Bitter Rucker

Rudy Rucker

TOR®

A TOM DOHERTY ASSOCIATES BOOK

NEW YORK

NESTED SCROLLS: THE AUTOBIOGRAPHY OF RUDOLF VON BITTER RUCKER

All photographs used with the permission of Rudy Rucker, with special thanks to Hal Taylor (1959), Bart Nagel (1992), and Leslie Howle (2009).

A Tor Book
Published by Tom Doherty Associates, LLC
175 Fifth Avenue
New York, NY 10010

www.tor-forge.com

Tor® is a registered trademark of Tom Doherty Associates, LLC.

Library of Congress Cataloging-in-Publication Data

Rucker, Rudy v. B. (Rudy von Bitter), 1946–
    Nested scrolls : the autobiography of Rudolf von Bitter Rucker. — 1st U.S. ed.
        p. cm.
    "A Tom Doherty Associates book."
    ISBN 978-0-7653-2752-9
    1. Rucker, Rudy v. B. (Rudy von Bitter), 1946– I. Title.
PS3568.U298Z46 2011
813'.54—dc23
[B]
                                                                    2011024290

First published in Great Britain by PS Publishing Ltd. by arrangement with the author.

First U.S. Edition: December 2011

Printed in the United States of America

10 9 8 7 6 5 4 3 2 1

Contents

Bibliography

Death's Door

*I*n the summer of 2008 a vein burst in my brain. A cerebral hemorrhage. I spent a week at death's door, and then I got better. In normal times I don't think directly about death—it's like trying to stare at the sun. But that summer I did think about it.

It would have been easy to die. Conditioned by a zillion novels and movies, you tend to think of death as a big drama—with a caped Grim Reaper kicking in your midnight door. But death may be as ordinary as an autumn leaf dropping from a tree. No spiral tunnel, no white light, no welcome from the departed ones. Maybe it's just that everything goes black.

In those first mornings at the hospital, I'd sit on their patio with an intravenous drip on a little rolling stand, and I'd look at the clouds in the sky. They drifted along, changing shapes, with the golden sunlight on them. The leaves of a potted palm tree rocked chaotically in the gentle airs, the fronds clearly outlined against the marbled blue and white heavens. Somehow I was surprised that the world was still doing gnarly stuff without any active input from me.

I think this was when I finally came to accept that the world would indeed continue after I die. Self-centered as I am, this simple fact had always struck me as paradoxical. But now I understood it, right down in my deepest core. The secrets of the life and death are commonplace, yet only rarely can we hear them.

Sitting on that patio—and even more so when I came home—I came to understand another natural fact as well. The richest and most interesting parts of my life are the sensations that come in from the outside. As long as

1

I'd been in my hospital bed, the world was dull and gray. I'd been cut off from external input, halfway down the ramp into the underworld. When I made it back to the trees, people, clouds, and water, I was filled with joy at being alive. It was like being born.

I had a similar rebirth experience right before my fourteenth birthday in 1960. My big brother Embry and I were in the back yard playing with our rusty old kiddie swing set—seeing who could jump the furthest. The chain of the swing broke. I flew through the air and landed badly, rupturing my spleen—as I immediately told my father. I might have died of internal bleeding in less than an hour if he hadn't rushed me to the hospital to have the crushed spleen removed.

What made me think it was my spleen? I'd been studying a paperback book about karate in the hope of making myself less vulnerable to the hoodlum bullies I feared, also I'd been (fruitlessly) trying to build up karate-calluses on my hands by pounding them into a coffee-can of uncooked rice. My karate book had a chart of attack points on the body, and there was one in the belly area marked "spleen"—so I happened to make the right guess. Our doctor talked about this for years.

After the operation, I woke in the night from dreams of struggle to see an attractive private nurse leaning over me. I realized with embarrassment that this pleasant woman, one of my father's parishioners, was the unseen force whom I'd been fighting and soddenly cursing while trying to pull a painfully thick tube from my nose.

When I came home from the gray and white hospital room, it was springtime, and our back yard was sunny and green. The shiny magnolia tree was blooming, the birds were fluttering and chirping, the blue sky shone above our familiar house. I was flooded with sweetness, dizzy with joy, trembling and on the verge of tears. I'd never realized how wonderful my life was.

In the coming weeks and months, I'd occasionally brood over that blank interval when I was under the anesthetic. I drew the conclusion that someday I'd go unconscious for good, like, *bam* and then—nothing. This was my introduction to life's fundamental puzzler koan: *Here you are, and life is great, but someday you'll be dead. What can you do about it?*

2

I used to imagine that I'd live to be eighty-four, but after my brain hemorrhage on July 1, 2008, I started thinking I might not last so long. Suppose that I only had time to write one more book. What should I write? This book. My memoir. *Nested Scrolls.*

Actually, I'd already started thinking about writing a final memoir back in 2003. I'd been out backpacking that time, and I was on a rocky beach in Big Sur, with the sun going down. I was thinking about my recently deceased friend Terence McKenna—with whom I'd once led an utterly bogus but enjoyable seminar at the new age Esalen hot springs resort nearby, a three-day class called, I think, "Stoneware and Wetware."

A seagull looked at me. His eyes disappeared when seen directly head-on. Using my ever-present roller-ball pen and pocket-scrap of paper, I drew him in four or five positions. He was staring out to sea, cawing, looking at me, glancing at the shore, looking down at his feet. I don't draw especially well, but sometimes I do it as a way of focusing my perceptions, or as a way to grab a kind of souvenir. Like a snapshot.

Sulfur smell wafted from a stream raging into the restless sea. I felt lucky to be on this wild shore.

"I love you," I said to the seagull. He bowed. We repeated this exchange. Maybe the seagull was Terence.

I'd set out on my backpacking trip with a hope of deciding what to write next. And, looking at the seagull, the notion of an autobiography popped into my head. I was seeing it in terms of settling scores and taking credit. And I liked that I wouldn't have to learn anything new to write it.

But I wasn't ready. First I wanted to analyze the deeper meaning of computers, by writing a hefty volume with a long title: *The Lifebox, the Seashell and the Soul: What Gnarly Computation Taught Me About Ultimate Reality, the Meaning of Life, and How To Be Happy*. This nonfiction tome appeared in 2005, and then I got into dramatizing its new ideas in the context of three science fiction novels: *Mathematicians in Love*, *Postsingular* and *Hylozoic*. And then, unexpectedly, in 2008 I had to swing by death's door.

I'm no longer very interested in the self-promotional aspects of an autobiographical memoir. As dusk falls, however rapidly or slowly, what I'm looking for is understanding and—time travel. A path into my past.

The thing I like about a novel is that it's not a list of dates and events. Not like an encyclopedia entry. It's all about characterization and description and conversation. Action and vignettes. I'd like to write a memoir like that.

Most lives don't have a plot that's as clear as a novel's. But maybe I can discover, or invent, a story arc for my life. I'd like to know what it was all about.

Four years before starting this memoir—that is, back in 2004—I retired from my job as a professor of computer science at San Jose State University in Silicon Valley. I taught for thirty-seven years, sometimes taking a semester or two off. Although I always felt good about the social usefulness of teaching, I also regarded it as a day-job, with my writing being my *real* job. Once I was old enough to get a pension, I was happy to step away from teaching and put my full energy into writing.

Being retired felt weird at first. When you quit a job, you're losing part of your identity.

During my second winter off, in 2005, I spent a few days organizing my papers in the basement. I had a lot of stuff—reaching all the way back to a carton of papers my mother had stored—I had drawings from kindergarten, letters to friends and family, love notes to my girlfriend (and eventual wife) Sylvia, early literary efforts, volume upon volume of journals, traces of my teaching and research, novel notes—and unclassifiable late-night scribbles from me, as dogfather, creeping up from the family den to howl at the moon.

I looked at everything and organized it into four plastic boxes with hanging file holders. I physically touched all of them, and for a little while I knew where they all were.

There's something deeply melancholy about old papers. I'm kind of hoping I don't have to root around in them again. I'd rather wing my autobiography, as if I were talking to you during a car-trip, letting the important stories bubble up.

The one basement paper that I'll mention was a little journal that my mother's mother kept when she was born. On the first page I saw my mother's name and birth-year—*Marianne von Bitter, 1916*—and pressed into the journal were two of my dear mother's curls. Blonder than I would have expected, and very fresh-looking, as if they'd been snipped the day before, rather than ninety years ago. I kissed them.

I was pretty bewildered, that first month after my cerebral hemorrhage. I felt like my mind was a giant warehouse where an earthquake had knocked everything off the racks—and I had to reshelve things one by one. I was, like, "Oh, yes, that's a steam shovel, that's a potty, that's a quartz crystal, that's my first day of nursery school."

Repeatedly I remembered marrying Sylvia, and how cute she was in her white hat and veil. Somehow I was wonderstruck by the fact that humans come as males and females—and that I'd had the good fortune to marry a female. Sylvia got tired of hearing about my wonder.

"Why are you always so surprised about everything?" she said, and started imitating me. "I can't believe I have children. I can't believe I'm alive. I can't believe the world exists." Truth be told, even now, I can hardly believe any of these things. But I try not to talk about it too much.

In the weeks after my attack, smells seemed much more intense: drains, garbage, fruit, my electric shaver. When I stared at a neutral-colored object, I seemed to see its tint change in slow waves, the faint pastel hues amping up and down, as if some unseen force was diddling the world's color balance sliders.

I began writing again, feeling my way, writing up notes for the memoir project. Here's an excerpt written on July 18, 2008, that captures my state of mind.

> Today—I have to laugh—I was reading an article about the outsider artist Henry Darger—and he wrote an autobiographical tome that starts with a few pages about nearly burning down a neighbor's house when he was young, and then he segues into a fifteen hundred page description of a tornado that he saw.
>
> At this moment, I'm working on my memoir on my laptop in the Los Gatos Coffee Roasting cafe, not far from where I live. I like writing in cafes. Then I'm not so alone.

The guy at the next table has an ascetically shaved head, and he's eating an abstemious salad of greens and goat cheese. Thoroughly, carefully, he chews a single wafer-thin slice of tomato. I hate him.

"It's foggy every day in San Francisco this July," my wife Sylvia reports, studying the paper across the table from me.

A young woman at another table shakes out her hair, smiling. No health problems for her. I used to feel that way: potentially immortal. But now I'm an old man, a heartbeat away from doom.

The summer's empty days and weeks flew by. I couldn't understand how I used to pass my time. I was continually ransacking my bookshelves, looking for some wise volume to reread. Where were the answers?

I also worried that my empathy was gone. I felt like I had to force a smile onto my face whenever I met someone. It wasn't coming naturally. Had a piece of me gone missing?

But after three months, I felt like my old self. At least that's what I started telling everyone.

When he was seventy, in 1984, my father wrote an autobiography called *Being Raised*. He was a good guy, my Pop, a human, a thinker. *Being Raised* is interesting, and Pop even put in some fairly wild stories, although of course I hunger for whatever he left out. He didn't really need to hold back on *my* account. Or maybe he did. Sons are quick to judge their fathers.

I can see that I wouldn't want to record too many detailed anecdotes about unsavory episodes. And, come to think of it, I already did tell a lot of tales like that in my first version of a memoir, *All the Visions*.

I wrote *All the Visions* when I was still using a typewriter—this was in 1983, when I was thirty-seven. The book was a memory dump of tales about wild things I'd done to seek enlightenment, usually in the context of drinking or getting high.

My inspiration was Jack Kerouac's *On the Road*, and to mimic the master, I wrote *All the Visions* on a single long roll of paper. I rigged up the roll on a length of broomstick propped up behind my good old rose-red IBM Selectric typewriter. *All the Visions* was about eighty feet long when I was done.

I cut it up to send to a friendly editor at the august house of Houghton Mifflin—and he mailed it right back. Our dog Arf was a puppy then, and he dragged the book off the porch and rolled in it. It was a week before I found the manuscript in the side yard, a rain-stained object of horror to the gods.

Eventually (in 1991), *All the Visions* came out as a slim volume from a small press, bound back-to-back with poems by my far-out friend, Anselm Hollo, and with a cover by underground cartoonist Robert Williams. A cool, beatnik book.

In this, my present memoir, *Nested Scrolls*, I'm writing something more like a systematic autobiography, focusing on the main stream of my life: childhood, family, teaching, and writing. You might say that I used to write about seeing God. Now I'm trying to describe something more fundamental: What was it like to be alive?

In 1992, when my father was on his last legs, finding his way towards death through a maze of heart attacks, hospitals, strokes, and nursing homes, my big brother and my son and I were visiting Pop in a sick-room, and that afternoon I'd bought a black suit for Rudy Jr., just in case.

"Why . . . why'd you get him a suit?" asked my father.

"*Funeral!*" said my big brother in a stage whisper, pitched too low for the old man to hear. We cracked up. Times like that—what can you do? Do you cry, or do you laugh?

Birth—I want to talk about birth, but I keep circling back to death. Of course the two connect. Life is, after all, an ever-turning wheel, with the new generations rising up and the old ones cycling down.

In 2002, I published *As Above, So Below*, a historical novel about the life of the painter Peter Bruegel the Elder. As I'll discuss later on, Bruegel is a personal hero of mine. In some ways I feel that Bruegel and I had similar goals and lives. Within my family I very often call myself Rudy the Elder—and sometimes I even use this name in the wider world.

Anyway, while working my Bruegel novel, I became fascinated by the medieval concept that a person's life is like a year of four seasons—a cycle of spring, summer, fall and winter—progressing from green, muddy March towards cold, gray February.

The unanswered question is how long my life's seasons are going to last. I'd like to think that, having survived my burst brain-vein, I'm only at the start my life's winter, with a fourth of my allotted span still to run, and with plenty of time to gather with my wife, children, and grandchildren for candlelit holiday feasts.

But maybe that's not the situation. Maybe I've wandered into the wastes of winter's lees, deep into the final February, with everything sere, still and iced over.

Perhaps I'm just a step away from the gently throbbing darkness that precedes birth.

My life began peacefully in the spring of 1946, amid an oceanic sense of floating. My visual field was a network of dusky veins—beige, mauve, umber. I lived amid the rhythms of my mother's heart, the ebb and flow of her breathing—sometimes agitated, sometimes calm.

I liked it when the contractions started, molding me, pushing me down through the birth tunnel. The pressure set off sheets of light behind my eyes. And then I was out, on my own.

Instead of Mom's heartbeat, I heard clanks and rumbles. I was dying for oxygen. I stretched out my arms and took my first gasping breath. On the exhale, I found my voice. I cried without pause, relishing the fitful vibrations in my throat.

And so I was born in Louisville, Kentucky, early on Friday, March 22, 1946, the day after the spring equinox, that singular cusp of the zodiac where the world snake bites its tail, the paradoxical wraparound where death becomes life.

Can I really remember my birth? Well—I can vividly *imagine* it—especially if I'm around babies and small children. I find it wonderful to be around kids—in some ways I like them more than adults. It's great to empathize with them and see through their clear eyes. I recover a sense of how it feels to be that size. And life feels so much less harsh when I see the new shoots growing into the spaces left by the fallen old giants. The great wheel of life.

One day in September, 2008, Sylvia and I were visiting our son, Rudy Jr., his wife, and their one-year-old twin daughters. One of the little girls was toddling out the front door to the porch, laboring to make it across the bump of the threshold. She'd only just learned to walk. Watching her, I was cheering her on—and she got this proud, happy, shy look on her face, for all the world like a great lady entering a ballroom and being announced.

Welcome, babies!

Glowing Fog

My earliest childhood memories are like stained glass windows in a dark cathedral—hypnotic and mysterious. I've given up wondering why this or that scene happens to be preserved. I'm just happy for what I find, my few bright vision fragments, souvenirs of an era when time was a sea, a song, a signal—anything but a delimited line.

My first memory is from 1948, when I was two. I was fingerpainting the white expanse of my bed's footboard with the contents of my diaper. I didn't yet know it smelled bad. My fingers left smooth trails in the spreading pattern I was creating. I was proud of my discovery. I remember the morning sun slanting in, my mother appearing behind me, her cry of dismay.

A perfect start for a writer.

We lived in the countryside near the town of Saint Matthews, east of Louisville, in a big old farmhouse that we rented from the Russells, who lived on a different farm. Sometimes we'd drive in a car to visit the Russells. They were the first old people that I'd ever seen. Old Mr. Russell showed me tricks with his fingers. First he made two of his fingers into a see-saw, and then he took out his pocket knife and cut off the tip of his thumb. He slid the cut-off thumb-tip up and down his forefinger, making a squeaking noise with his mouth. I didn't like him.

When I was still two, my father had a house built for us across a field from the big farmhouse we were renting. Pop took take us to see our house frame going up, and the men nailing on plywood walls. One day we moved in. Mom pushed me in a stroller and my big brother, Embry, pulled a wagon full of his books and toys. The new house smelled like paint. Pop carried me through all the rooms on his shoulders, ducking to get through the doors.

That summer, rye grew in the field between the old farm and our new house. The stalks were taller than me. I walked through the rye, tramping down labyrinths, a little worried that I'd be scolded. But no one cared. In the fall the rye was harvested by a giant machine.

We had cats, a collie that kept running away, and a Springer spaniel named Nina. Nina birthed a litter of puppies in the garage. My parents said we could keep one. I wasn't sure if my family could hear me talk or if they could understand what I said, but I suggested that we name the puppy Muffin. Toasted English muffins with butter and honey were my favorite food. My brother and my parents laughed and agreed that Muffin was a good name. It was the first time I'd been party to a family decision. I felt shy and proud.

My father built a doghouse in the back yard, covering it in black tarpaper with shiny, multicolored speckles of sand. I liked sitting by the doghouse with Nina, Muffin and the other puppies—who stuck around for quite some time. Sometimes my brother would climb onto the dog-house roof to pick cherries from the tree behind it.

We had a wading pool in the back yard, and on Saturdays, Pop would lie in it drinking a long-necked brown bottle of beer, his knees bent so that his feet could fit into the pool too. I'd splash around in the edges, happily singing *London Bridge*, and Pop would lift his legs or bend forward to let me pass. It was good to touch his bare skin. He smelled like freckles.

After we moved, the Russells started selling off the fields around the farmhouse that we'd rented. They auctioned off the farm machinery one day in 1949, when I was three.

Our family went to the auction. I was sitting high up on a piece of machinery. It was yellow. I could see the tops of the grownups' heads. One of them smiled up at me, calling me by name.

"Rudy."

I was surprised the man knew this name. He laughed with my father. Pop's arms reached the huge distance up to where I perched on the tractor's metal seat, and he lifted me down.

A new family rented the nearby farmhouse where I'd been born. They had a boy a little younger than me. Willy.

I liked Willy. He had a citified accent, a reckless laugh, and a wild way of talking about a monster called Frankenstein, who supposedly followed Willy no matter how far he walked or ran. Willy talked about Frankenstein as if he were a real creature whom he saw all the time.

My mother had a wind-up mantelpiece clock that she'd gotten from her mother in Germany. In the house I could always hear it ticking, and every so often it would chime. Willy admired Mom's clock, and one day he snuck it home to his house under his shirt. His mother made him bring the clock back to us.

Occasionally Mom would leave me alone in our house while she worked in the garden. Besides the mantel clock and the refrigerator, I could hear a high singing in my ears. I imagined it was the sound of the Earth turning.

Sometimes I'd be sick, and I'd stay in bed all day. The doctor would arrive with a black bag and maybe a shot of penicillin. When Pop got home from work he'd come in and look at me.

"How's my sausage? Look out for the bumble-bee!"

He'd make a buzzing noise and slowly move his hand in a circle, eventually landing it on my face.

After that he'd put a nickel on the tip of his left forefinger, then snap the fingers of his right hand. The nickel would disappear up his right sleeve. He'd pretend to find it in my ear and let me keep it.

One early summer, perhaps in 1950, I learned to swat flies. I went out on our concrete back steps and swatted flies for a whole hour. More and more of them came, attracted by the bodies of their squashed comrades. I called my mother to admire the carnage. She didn't like it.

"Ugh. Don't you ever do that again."

All summer we'd run around barefoot. Our long driveway was gravel, and over the months, our feet would get so tough that it didn't hurt to walk on the gravel.

Our house was on a street called Rudy Lane, which seemed reasonable and natural to me. Only later did I realize that it was a coincidence. All summer we'd run around barefoot. Our long driveway was gravel, and over the months, our feet would get so tough that it didn't hurt to walk on the gravel. Initially we were completely surrounded by farms and fields, but then our first retail establishment appeared, a Standard Oil gas station at the corner of Rudy Lane and Route 42. My big brother Embry and I walked there.

They sold candy from large glass jars that you could reach into: caramels, bubble-gum and Saf-T-Pop lollipops with a limp loop instead of a hard stick. My brother told me that the candy was free—I guess he wanted to see what I'd do. Sure enough I took several pieces. The man running the station asked me if I was going to pay for it, and we didn't have any money, but he let us keep the candy. Embry took some of it. We'd hardly ever had candy before. It was great.

Our whole family was friends with the Keith family, who lived about a mile from us on a large farm, complete with barn, cows, horses, chickens, and a spring-house. They were good people, mild-mannered and well-educated.

Big Paul Keith was a judge, an avid fisherman who tied his own flies, and, for a time, the scoutmaster of our Boy Scout troop. He was an uncommonly good scoutmaster, calmly helping us enjoy the outdoors without any bossing or bullshit.

His wife Sally casually maintained vast beds of flowers, a smokehouse where she cured hams, and cupboards of home-made jam. She had dozens of country quilts and several shelves of cute salt-and-pepper-shaker sets that I loved to play with. I remember a girl and boy pig, a moon and a sun, a bull and a bullfighter.

The Keiths had three children: Sherry, Phoebe, and Little Paul. Sherry was loud and laughing, Phoebe wore her blondish hair in braids. They were practically the first girls I ever met. I thought they were fascinating, beautiful and sophisticated. But I was younger than them, and beneath their consideration.

When our parents would have meals together, we kids would go off together. Once we climbed into a tree house populated by daddy longlegs spiders—little orange ovals walking on skinny black legs—and they

13

completely freaked me out. Sherry, Phoebe and Embry laughed to hear me scream. Little Paul comforted me.

Other times, we'd go down to the dank stone springhouse—and Sherry would tell us ghost stories, holding a dramatic flashlight under her chin. Her spookiest story was about the . . . little . . . white . . . hands, a tale that she said had taken place in the very springhouse where we huddled.

Supposedly an old man and woman had lived in Keiths' farmhouse before them, and one day the woman had disappeared. That night, the old man heard a high, thin voice calling for him: "Help me! Help me!" He followed a ball of light to the springhouse. The light settled upon a shallow pool of water in the corner, the very spot where the spring issued. Crawling around the edges of the pool were dozens of . . . little . . . white . . . hands . . .

And then Phoebe would shriek and Sherry would turn off the flashlight, and I'd roar in terror and blunder out into the firefly-filled night.

Nursery school was held in a big room at our church, St. Francis in the Fields Episcopal. The room had grayish-black asphalt tiles on the floor, and ordinary sash windows in the walls. We played with big, hollow plywood blocks that were two or three feet long on each side. You could line them up to make paths, or stack them higher than your head. They made a nice boom when they fell down.

When I started coming there, in 1949 when I was three, one of the children took me aside and pointed out one of the others. "That's Butch. Stay away from him. He's mean." I stayed away from Butch, but I had plenty of other friends, nice little boys and girls.

We'd play a game called Rhythms where we'd dance around the room with a record playing, and now and then the teacher would lift up the needle and you'd have to freeze in place where you'd been when the music stopped. If you didn't freeze fast enough, you were Out.

I could read a few letters by the time I was in kindergarten. Printed on the porcelain of the toilet was the word, CHURCH, which made sense to me—although really I suppose it was a trademark. One day I was sitting on this toilet and two little girls came into the bathroom.

14

"Get out of here," I told them from my stall, "Can't you read? This bathroom says MEN."

"No it doesn't," they brattily insisted.

We argued and argued. It was one of the first more-or-less logical arguments I'd ever had.

In the winter, we wore leggings over our regular pants. I hated my leggings. They were hard to take off, hard to find among all the other leggings, and hard to put on.

In first grade, in 1951, I had a teacher called Mrs. Devine. She was strict. If you talked when you weren't supposed to, she'd make you stand on one leg in front of the class.

Mrs. Devine grouped the students into three tables covered with oilcloth, one red, one blue, and one yellow. I sat at the red table, and we were the redbirds. The redbirds were smarter than the bluebirds and the yellowbirds.

A boy named Lee was a yellowbird. He could hardly ever answer Mrs. Devine's questions. It was embarrassing, I felt sorry for him. But outside in the trash at the edge of the playground we found a discarded car tire that had his name on it as a brand. Lee. That was something.

In the playground I learned how to pump my legs and make my swing move by myself. It took me quite a few days to figure this out. But then I could swing really high. I often wondered if it might be possible to swing so hard that you wrapped the chain all the way around the top support.

Sometimes, instead of my mother driving me to school, I'd wait by the side of Route 42 near Rudy Lane for Barbara Tucker to pick me up and give me a ride to first grade—which, like kindergarten, was being held at our church. Miss Tucker worked at our church. She drove a nice car, a black and white 1951 Buick Roadmaster with four little portholes set into the side of the hood. At some point I stuck my fingers into the holes and determined that they were fake, in the sense that they didn't go all the way through.

Miss Tucker wore more lipstick than any woman I'd ever seen. It got all over the cigarettes she smoked. She was tidy and well-dressed and not overweight, but somehow a little odd looking. She lived with her mother.

15

She was nice and I liked her, as I found her easy to talk to. I could tell that she thought I was bright, and that made me feel good.

School was only in the mornings. I'd come home at lunchtime, and it would be just me and Mom.

I'd bring home papers from school. Sheets of one-digit sums, little dictations, and a few drawings. My writing was sprawling and uncontrolled.

For lunch, Mom would eat square pumpernickel bread and blue cheese, while I had Campbell's chicken noodle soup and perhaps a bologna sandwich. Sometimes Mom would treat me to a special meal of spaghetti and lambchop. I was fussy about food, and she worried about me eating enough.

My mother was opinionated, outspoken within the family, and quick to label things "amazing" or "disgusting"—two of her favorite words. But she was always patient and loving with me, always approving—unless I did something like smearing poop on the bedstead or swatting hundreds of flies. One of Mom's most characteristic gestures towards me was to smile and then nod encouragingly.

After lunch I'd sit on her lap and she'd hug and kiss me. "Yes," Mom would say. "Good Rudy."

Muffin would whine, looking dog-mournful. "Look at Muffy," I'd say. "Muffy feels left out." Then I'd pat Muffin and take my nap.

Sometimes I wouldn't actually sleep, I'd just lie on my bed for awhile. My mother would lie down in her room, reading or napping. Once I wanted to get up early to play, and I went to ask her if it was okay. She seemed to be asleep, so I knelt down next to her bed and prayed that she'd let me go outside. Suddenly noticing me there, she sat up, surprised.

"What are you doing?"

"Praying that you'll let me go outside."

"Of course you can go outside. You don't have to pray for a thing like that."

My mother got me into a driving group with some of the other kids at the St. Francis School. The school went up to the third grade. I liked one of the girls that I rode with: Polly. She had a nice voice, and a calm, casual way of talking. She was almost like a boy.

In the winter of 1952, when we were on the playground, I was mad because Polly had pushed onto the seesaw ahead of me. As she rose up past me, I grabbed her leg and bit it. For the rest of the day I was waiting to be punished. Very slowly I realized that, as Polly was wearing leggings, she hadn't felt the bite. And nobody else had noticed.

I got to go play at Polly's house a few times. She had a game called Cootie that I liked. You'd roll dice to get plastic pieces that you assembled into a brightly colored model of an alien insect—and you won if you were the first person to finish making a complete cootie.

Another girl I hung around with was Barbie, who lived on a big farm with horses. My parents knew her parents from church. They had a patch of gooseberries, which I'd never seen before—fat, striped berries filled with slimy, sour seeds.

Barbie got me to play a game where we were separated lovers who'd been looking for each other for years and we walked right by each other in a snow storm, missing each other by only a foot, but not seeing each other in the fog of ice-crystals. This enactment was taking place in a pasture on a sunny September afternoon on her farm.

Another time, Barbie got me to play a game where we pulled down our pants and ran around in a circle, with her chanting, "I see a little boy's popo," and me chanting, "I see a little girl's popo." She was worried that her two older brothers might see us doing this. I felt uneasy to be on this odd girl's team instead of her brothers' side.

The thing I liked best at Barbie's house was an amazing toy circus that she and her brothers had upstairs in their play room. There were dozens of little tin animals and acrobats, a little ring, a tightrope and a tiny trapeze. I used to dream about that circus a lot, over and over, especially when I'd have a fever.

I'd be in a circus big top—and, in a way, it was like a spaceship. I'd be sitting in the bleachers off to one side, watching the thin, bright shapes that spun above the center. These acrobatic beings were like flames, like twisting neon tubes, and the other seats were populated by moving lights as well, with tiny little creatures scuttling around my feet.

17

I'd imagine that I myself was a creature of light, and that the flame people were planning to push me down beneath the bleachers, down into the world of ordinary humans, to mingle with them and find out what they're like. Eventually I'd incorporate this early vision in my science fiction novel, *The Secret of Life*.

Once, perhaps in 1952 as well, a driving-group mother started grilling me about Mom's accent.

"She's from Germany," I told the woman.

"Oh," she said, sweetening her voice. "Is she a war bride?"

"I guess so," I said, having no idea what that meant.

At home my mother explained that a war bride was a woman who'd married an invading soldier, and that she herself would never do something that tacky. Mom had come to the U.S. before the war. She'd come as an art student, and had met my father in Philadelphia. And the woman who'd been questioning me was a catty old bag.

Later I'd come to understand that three of Mom's sixteen great-great-grandparents had been Jewish, which could eventually have doomed her family to Hitler's camps. This precise racial calculus was characteristic of the time. My Uncle Franz would tell me that the family had been eager for Mom, the youngest child, to make it out of Germany in time.

Among Mom's other ancestors was the famous philosopher Georg Hegel. I remember the relationship under the rubric, "three greats," that is, I'm Hegel's great-great-great-grandson. When my mother left Berlin before World War II, she brought with her Hegel's schoolboy diary—a treasured family memento. Written mostly in Latin, the little book covers the period 1785 to 1787, when Hegel was fifteen to seventeen years old. Eventually my mother lent it to some scholars who translated it into German.

In later years I'd find a favorite passage where Hegel is excited about a rumor among the local peasants that an army of dead souls had ridden by the night before. Shades of a UFO sighting! As it turns out, the peasants had been deceived by the lights of passing carriages from a late party.

"*Ei, ei!*" Hegel exclaims in his diary, falling into German. "Imagine people still thinking like this in the year of 1785!"

18

My guess is that the human mind will never fully modernize. Our myths express something deep about our situation in the world, and we'll always have a place for fantastic tales.

The Suburbs

On the lot next to us, a man named Jones started building a house in 1952. When I went over to inspect the project, one of the carpenters teased me.

"Look out, boy, here comes the chicken!"

Hearing a wild squawking and cackling, I climbed up the exposed two-by-fours to the rafters. Getting away from that chicken. The workmen had a good laugh at me.

Behind our house, beyond the old rye field, bulldozers and earthmovers began carving the Russell farmlands into a big subdivision. The suburbs were coming to swallow us.

As a child I wasn't nostalgic. I never thought of revisiting that old farmhouse where I'd been born, even though it remained standing on a side road of the growing development.

One day two boys with Mohawk haircuts appeared in our front yard. My brother Embry got into a fistfight with them, and drove them away.

Another day, Embry and I saw a very strange aircraft fly over our yard—an airplane with no fuselage or tail. Embry said it was a flying wing. He said that maybe the boys with Mohawks had come from it.

Our lot butted right onto Rudy Lane. We had two acres, an expanse which my brother was proud of—he said we should call our estate "Twakers," but nobody else in the family picked up on that. Embry always had this sense of being a noble, but that worldview of his never caught on with anyone we knew.

Across Rudy Lane the Merrifield subdivision appeared, with about fifteen houses. In 1953 when I was seven, a family with two boys the ages of Embry and me moved into Merrifield. Jimmy and Paul Stone.

Their mother, Faith Stone, was a sexy, vivacious woman. She had red hair, big breasts and an infectious laugh. Once a year she'd get depressed and get electroshock therapy, and then she'd tell stories about it at dinner, laughing about her memory loss. She seemed artistic and exotic, not like a typical Mom. Sometimes Faith would tell off-color jokes that I couldn't understand. I remember one that took me weeks to figure out:

"Did you hear about the cannibal who passed his brother in the swamp?"

The father, Jim Stone, was witty and worldly-wise. He and my father used to call each other Dad and Duke. They'd drink bourbon together. Old Jim had gone to Harvard. He liked to tell the story of how he and some college pals had gotten hold of a red Communist flag with a hammer and sickle, and before dawn after a night of revelry, they'd hauled it up on a flagpole in front of the State Department in Washington, D.C.

Once when I was over at the Stones' house playing with Paul, I really had to go to the bathroom, but I put it off too long, and when I got there, a turd shot out of my butt and landed on the tile floor next to the toilet. I figured it wasn't my affair to deal with this, so I refastened my pants and went back into the yard to play.

A little later, Paul's mother came out and looked at me with a strange expression. "Rudy—were you in the bathroom?"

"Um, yes."

"Did you have an accident?"

"It popped out," I said, wanting the conversation to end. "I couldn't help it."

"Can you go in there and clean it up?"

I was a little outraged at this request, but grudgingly I did the dirty work. The other boys found out and laughed at me.

Paul Stone had a devil-may-care attitude that I admired. He and his brother watched Abbott and Costello on TV. Paul wasn't at all interested in school. When his father pointed out the bright dot of Venus above the horizon, Paul imitated him.

"Look, boys, there's a weenis in the sky! Psss."

Paul had a lot of pocket money and once he paid a neighbor girl to show him her naked butt.

"What was it like?"

"She had freckles."

While Paul was cool and sleepy-eyed, his big brother Jimmy had a florid, volatile personality. It wasn't unusual for Jimmy to have a fit of anger, or to burst into tears. He and Embry looked down on Paul and me.

Once Jimmy was angry at me and he yelled, "Your parents spoil you rotten. They wouldn't care if your big brother got run over by a truck!"

I weighed this in my mind, feeling a little guilty, but also enjoying the thought that maybe my parents did like me best. Why wouldn't they? Actually, it wasn't till I was about fifty that I realized that my parents really had loved my brother as much as me.

Sometimes Paul and Jimmy seemed to be alone in their house—or maybe it was that their mother was napping. Things could get wild.

One time Jimmy had a bright idea that could have killed Paul and me. He and Embry more or less forced us younger brothers to get inside a trunk in the basement, which they closed and latched. They said it was a game, they said they were playing kidnappers.

And then Paul and I were in the dark trunk, cramped and worrying about having enough air. Jimmy and Embry went totally hyper, running all around the house, upstairs and down, whooping and roaring, fully knowing they were in the wrong. Finally they came back and let us out. I never obeyed Jimmy again.

For one of his birthdays, Embry got an air-pump BB gun. It came with a Safety Oath inscribed on the butt of the gun, and I saw Embry reading this oath aloud for my father.

But pretty soon he got tired of shooting at cans.

We got together with the Paul and Jimmy and hid in a cluster of trees beside Rudy Lane at the bottom of our long front yard. Jimmy had a pellet-gun pistol. He and Embry took turns shooting at passing cars. It was great.

Eventually a pickup truck stopped, and a man jumped out. We four boys ran terrified up the long yard and hid behind our house. After a half hour went by—and the truck was gone—we made our way back to our hide-out amid the trees. The guy in the truck had left a note, tucked into Paul's shoe, which had dropped off in our frenzied retreat.

"Boys, I know all your names and where you live. I'm going to report you to your parents and to the police."

Horrors! The Stone boys slunk home, and Embry and I mooched around our house, quietly waiting for doom. In the end, nothing happened. The man had been bluffing. But we didn't shoot at cars anymore.

Paul and Jimmy's father owned part of an island in the Ohio River near Louisville. It was called Four Mile Island. He pastured some cows there. The only way to get to the island was via a rickety ferry made of wood planks and empty barrels.

The ferry's pilot was an aged hillbilly with most of his teeth missing. He was voluble and cackling. I was scared of him; I wasn't used to being around strangers.

On the island, the air was filled with the racket of the seven-year locusts, oversized flying grasshoppers the length of a man's finger. Paul and I found the empty amber shell of a locust clamped to the bark of a tree—they repeatedly shed their skins as they grew.

I brought the locust shell back home with me, carefully guarding it as we rode the ferry back across the mud-brown Ohio River. I treasured it for years.

My mother befriended some of the other women who moved into the Merrifield homes. Once she took me over to Mrs. Holland's house for a visit. Mrs. Holland's husband had given her a large box of candy for her birthday. He worked at General Electric. Mrs. Holland told me that I could pick one of the candies and eat it.

While my mother and Mrs. Holland chatted in the living-room, I studied the box of candy in the hall. It was the first box of chocolates I'd ever seen. It bothered me that I couldn't see what was inside the cores—so I had the idea of gnawing off a corner of one, just so I could peek inside. It looked like it had strawberry jam inside it, which I didn't want, so I gnawed off a few more corners, finding green mint goo, pink cherry paste, caramel, and eventually one that was filled with chocolate. I ate that one.

When Mrs. Holland offered the box to my mother, the women noticed the gnawed corners. I was in disgrace. My big brother loved this story. He always liked when I did something completely uncouth.

It wasn't so much that Embry wanted to see me get in trouble—it was more that he liked to see social norms being flouted and undermined. One of his favorite stories was about a little boy on the radio who'd been asked what he got for Christmas—and the little boy said, "Garbage."

Embry was in some sense destined to be a 1950s-style juvenile delinquent, and from the very start he was getting into trouble at school. He seemed to change schools every couple of years.

Most days our dog Muffin would wander all around the neighborhood. One night in 1953, she didn't come home for dinner. My parents and my brother kept saying that Muffin would be fine. But I was sure she was in danger. I almost thought I could hear her.

I cried and fretted so much that finally my father got Mr. Keith to go out with him with a flashlight and look for Muffin. They found her swimming in the septic tank of that big old farmhouse we'd once rented. The wooden cover of the tank had rotted away, and Muffin had fallen in. For hours she'd been dog-paddling around, yelping for help. I really had heard her. I had better ears than the others.

We sprayed Muffin with the hose in the back yard, and fed her a big meal. She shook off the water and rubbed against us, vibrating with joy at being alive, with pleasure at rejoining our pack.

Saturday mornings, I'd listen to the "Big John and Sparky Show" on the family radio. My brother and my parents weren't interested in this show, so I'd listen to it alone, lying on the wood floor next to a gently breathing heater vent, sometimes with Muffin at my side.

The show was "for the young and the young at heart"—and even then I suspected that, in this context, "young at heart" meant "simple-minded." Big John was a square Dad type, and Sparky was a shrill elf. They'd acoustically transport the listeners to the "land over the rainbow"—*wheee!*—and the show would begin, the air around us shimmering in veils of pastel color.

I remember one particular radio play that they aired, "The Odyssey of Runyon Jones." It was about a kid who travels across the galaxy, looking for

24

his dead dog in "curgatory." I really liked that story. It might have been the first science fictional tale that I absorbed.

*I*n the early 1950s, my father owned a business called the Rucker Corporation—his men made inexpensive coffee tables and end tables which he sold through distributors in Chicago. Every so often he'd take the train to regional furniture fairs with a sample table in tow. When Pop had to take a trip, he'd tell me that he was going to the Fat Man's Convention, and I believed him. Not that he was actually fat—he was in fact quite fit—but he was certainly the biggest person I knew.

Over time he began doing most of his business through a pair of brothers named Reinisch, from Chicago. One time these two visited Louisville, and they came to our house for a meal. Mom didn't like them, because after dessert they belched and picked their teeth. And I think the Reinisches played some part in driving the Rucker Corporation into bankruptcy fairly soon after that.

But Pop quickly rose from the ashes with a more limited kind of company, Champion Wood Products. Rather than manufacturing entire pieces of furniture, Champion made small wood parts, which they whole-saled to furniture makers. They might produce two thousand drawer-backs, for instance, or ten thousand of the little rectangular wood blocks that are glued into the join where a drawer back meets a drawer bottom.

As Champion Wood's business involved making custom wood parts of specific sizes, they were called a *dimension manufacturer*. The term is a nice prefiguring of what I'd later end up doing myself—as a writer of science fiction and popular science books involving the fourth dimension.

The men who worked in Pop's plant were wild and intimidating, almost like they were from a different race. Their skins were pale, pale white. They had missing front teeth, prominent chin-stubble, oily black hair, and mad, intent eyes. Their Kentucky and Indiana accents were so baroque that it was hard for me to understand them.

The few times I visited Pop's plant, I imagined that the men looked upon me as soft and pampered. The bathroom there had intensely obscene graffiti, some of it directly aimed at the boss's family and, by extension, at me. Just to show the men I wasn't a prissy Lord Fauntleroy, I wanted to emerge from the john yelling all the curse words I knew. Of course I never actually did this, but perhaps something of this attitude carried over into my writing. Like—how can anyone dismiss me as an ivory-tower intellectual if my books have bad words in them?

When Pop got home from work every day, we'd have a family dinner around our shiny wooden dining table. Often he'd start the meal with one of his standard jokes.

"Did you boys hear about the big explosion today?"

"No," we'd say, playing it straight.

"The wind blew up the Ohio River!"

One time Embry and Mom worked out a trick to play on the old man. Mom had gotten a long string of plastic snap-together Pop-It beads—a new fad in the 1950s. They were shiny and creamy-white, vaguely resembling pearls. At dinner, Mom wore her new necklace and asked my father if he liked it. As we'd expected, he said something about it being a little long.

"All right!" cried my mother. "I'll throw it away!" She unpopped the necklace into five or six pieces and threw them on the floor. We boys cackled in joy,

"What is it with you weisenheimers?" asked my father.

On Sundays we'd have roast beef, gravy, and rolls. Before carving the roast, my father would sharpen his carving knife. I loved the sound of this. Pop had a special bone-handled carving set, with a matching sharpening stick.

Sometimes I'd take out the bone-handled steel sharpening stick and play with it. It had a powerful aura, like a scepter. With the tool in hand, I'd hide in a corner of the living-room behind my father's armchair, feeling safe and strong—possibly with some stray thoughts of taking down the old man.

Back to the dinner table. I loved eating rolls with butter and the plum jam that my mother and her friend Sally Keith made. One time Embry and my parents weren't paying attention to me, and the basket of rolls was next to me, and I ate them all.

From then on, Embry liked to glance over me during meals and ask, "More rolls, Rudy?"

I didn't usually pay that much attention to the table conversation, I tended to be off in my own world. Once Embry and my father suddenly got into such a big argument that Pop smacked Embry and knocked him out of his chair. But Pop never raised his hand against me, even after I grew as rebellious as my brother. I think Embry wore him down.

Pop was a great story-teller; sometimes after our Sunday dinner or evening meal, he'd spin tales for my brother and me. The stories were always different, but they usually involved dwarves. Pop would always give me and Embry special looks just to make sure we understood that we ourselves were in fact the dwarves he was talking about.

One event would flow into the next in a logical yet unpredictable fashion—and sometimes a story would run over from one day to the next. Pop prided himself on making up his stories as he went along. He said that if you just kept on talking, the ideas would come. Later, when I became a writer, I used this lesson.

Sometimes at the end of the meal, my mother would bring out an apple pie. We had a triangular silver spatula for serving pie slices. Pop would ask us boys to fetch it from the sideboard.

He'd say, "Can you bring me the shovel?"

Once, in the richness of his wit, my brother had the idea of instead running out to the garage and fetching a gardening shovel. We pulled this routine several times over the years.

Pop always wanted to have a piece of cheddar cheese with his pie, but Mom didn't like to see that. She thought it was tacky to eat pie that way. Nobody had eaten cheese with pie in Berlin when she was growing up. So Pop would go out to the kitchen and fetch his slice of cheese himself. We boys didn't dare ask for any.

*I*n 1950, Mom took Embry and me on a trip to Germany to visit her parents and her brothers. We went by air, via a series of planes that stopped in New York, Newfoundland, Iceland, and Ireland on the way. In Germany, World War II was still not so far off, and a lot of the buildings on my grandparents' street were just piles of pink bricks. You weren't supposed to climb on the bricks because the piles might collapse, and there might be some unexploded bombs under them.

My grandfather, Rudolf von Bitter, taught Embry and me to play chess. And then he pitted us against each other in a play-off match. The prize was a ball-point pen, the first such pen we'd ever seen. It smeared when you wrote with it, but we both wanted it. I was four and Embry was nine. Embry won the match.

My grandmother, Lily von Klenck, had a big box of painted metal zoo animals and a board with a picture of roads and cages. I played zoo in her dark hallway. Often we'd walk through the woods to the real zoo, the first zoo I'd ever been to. I loved seeing the strange animals, most of all the elephants and the hippos.

I was very fond of my grandmother. Unlike most adults, she spoke to me as an equal. And she had a playful side, always ready for little tricks and games. I remember sitting next to her on a park bench, and when a toddler stumped over to us, Grandma drew a face in the walkway's sand with the tip of her cane.

While we were visiting Germany, we went to visit some of my mothers' relatives who lived on a farm outside the city. Times were still tough, and it was rare treat to get salami. My great-aunt offered me some.

I didn't like the way the meat tasted, but I liked the bits of peppercorn that were tiled into the slices. I picked out the peppercorns, ate them, and hid the meat under the couch cushion. Later my great-aunt found the meat of course.

They were cutting the hay that day, and my brother got to ride on top of a giant wagon of hay, tiny and triumphant. I wanted to go up there, too, but they said I was too little and that the hay would make me sneeze. I had such a tantrum that I had to lie down on the ground to cry harder.

And then I started pulling my cousin Hedwig's pigtails.

My German relatives still talk about what a brat I was.

Three years later, in 1953 when I was seven, Mom took Embry and me to Germany again. This time we rode across the ocean on a ship, a tramp steamer called the *Karl Fisser*. There were only four or five passengers in all.

I didn't like most of the food on the ship, it wasn't like any food I was used to. My mother prevailed on the cook to make me spaghetti and, above all, pancakes. The crew got wind of this—probably they were intrigued by my attractive, aristocratic mother—and they began calling me *Prinz Pfannkuchen*. Prince Pancake.

The toilet paper on the ship was too stiff, so I threw it out the bathroom porthole onto the deck. It rolled around in the wind and festooned everything. To find soft toilet paper, I took to sneaking up to the captain's plush bathroom.

During the trip, the crew painted the ship's railings, and Embry and I climbed on them while the paint was wet, for which we were scolded.

The trip took a long time. We saw dolphins and flying fish, and a waterspout. There were any number of passageways and gray steel decks with narrow stairs leading among them. Embry and I got into playing a dangerous game. I had a tight, red knitted hat, and one of us would pull the hat down over our eyes and let the other boy guide him around, like, "Walk forward, turn left, turn right," and so on.

We began talking about the terrible possibility that one of us might get the other to walk unsuspectingly onto a downward flight of steps. And then I decided to do it to Embry before he did it to me.

"Step forward," I said, giggling—not really expecting him to hurt himself.

The ship pitched as Embry stepped into the empty space above the steps. He fell forward and slid down the whole flight on his stomach, banging his mouth, bloodying his front teeth.

I felt horrible.

B ack in our suburb of Louisville, Kentucky, my absolute favorite reading materials were the *Donald Duck* and *Uncle Scrooge* comic books by Carl Barks. Once a week I'd accompany my mother to the A & P Supermarket, and she'd give me a nickel for a comic.

I loved the irreverence of the ducks and the energetic, abbreviated way in which the narratives hopped from one frame to the next. I learned a lot from those comic books, including authorial tone, story construction, and vocabulary. When grown-ups would ask me how it was that I knew the meaning of some unusual word, I enjoyed telling them I'd learned it from *Donald Duck* comics.

By now some of my school friends had televisions. One boy lived within walking distance, and at his house I saw a *Howdy Doody* show. It was the first TV show I'd ever seen.

I could hardly believe how great television was—the creamy black and white shades, the hiss of static, the announcer's rounded tones, the jerky scan across the children in the *Howdy Doody* audience, the hilarious commercials for Ipana toothpaste.

There were some great ads for Jell-O as well. In one Jell-O ad, a warm housewife voice would sing-song, "Busy day, busy day," as her cartoon icon hurried around. And then would come the punch-line: "Jell-O tonight!" Another Jell-O ad had the tag line, "Chinese baby very happy"—the happiness came when the baby was given a spoon instead of chopsticks for eating his Jell-O. I loved that baby. I'd never seen a Chinese person in real life.

I didn't actually like the puppet Howdy Doody himself—he disgusted me, with the awkward waggling of his lower jaw. And I hated his conniving friend/enemy Clarabelle the clown. Nor did I like the show's smarmy host, Buffalo Bill. But near the end of the show came the payoff: they'd air a cartoon. The cartoons were paradise.

My brother and I worked on our parents, and eventually they agreed to get a TV set. We went to a department store in downtown Louisville, and Pop negotiated with the salesman for nearly an hour. Embry and I watched a cowboy show on the dozens of display TVs, the horsemen eternally riding down a sandy road beneath dry, spindly trees.

We went home with a Dumont set, a small tube in a cubical yellowish cabinet that might have been particle-board. You could get two channels in Louisville, 3 and 11. And at 4 p.m. on Saturday afternoons I'd get to watch *Cartoon Circus*.

I worshipped that show. To make it even better, when I watched *Cartoon Circus*, Mom would give me my one soft-drink of the week, orange soda in a pale green anodized aluminum cup.

Everything about the cartoons was wonderful. The exultant blare of chase music, the high slangy voices, the xylophone sound of sneaking footsteps, the moany-groany graveyards with twisting ghosts, the sarcastic ducks, the battles and stratagems of the cats and the mice.

One Saturday afternoon my father for some reason wanted to take me for a drive in the car.

"No, no! I have to watch *Cartoon Circus*."

"Oh, don't worry, we can hear it on the car radio."

I wasn't quite sure if watching cartoons on the radio would work—and then, of course, it turned out that there wasn't any cartoon radio show at all. But I didn't nag my father on it. He seemed a little sad and distracted. Perhaps he and Mom were having a fight.

My parents were friends with the Graves family, who lived in a shiny log cabin even further out in the country than us. Grant Graves was the church organist, quite a musician, and Lillian Graves was my teacher in second and third grades They were cultured, pure people, who appreciated my mother—in these postwar years, some people still harbored a dislike for Germans. But Grant had studied in Germany and had played a concert in a cathedral there. He had a poster for it on his wall.

One time in 1953, the Graves family had a house party and my family was there, enjoying ourselves. I was talking to some big kids, telling them I was in the third grade, and one of the older girls said she was in the tenth grade. I was stunned. I had no idea the grades went up that high.

Around this time, my father, my mother and I drove out to a well-to-do friend's country retreat to get big flat river rocks for Mom to put into her rose garden.

"What do you want to be when you grow up?" the landowner asked me.

"A businessman," I replied, wanting to be like Pop. He seemed to get a lot of pleasure out of his little furniture company.

"Oh, don't be a businessman, Rudy," said my father. "You can do better than that. You're *bright*."

"Then I'll be a scientist," I said.

My parents tended to send me to bed before I was really tired. So I'd play mental games while I was waiting to fall asleep. I developed a little repertoire of fun things to think about: fantastic powers like shrinking, or breathing underwater. Perhaps all along I was meant to be a science fiction writer.

Some of these imaginings still stick in my mind. One evening, perhaps in 1954, I imagined being an inch tall and walking around my room. The space beneath my bed was like a dim, dusty hall. The mouse that sometimes invaded our house was there, the size of a horse. He could talk, and he was friendly. I rode the mouse into the kitchen and got us two slices of apple pie with chunks of cheddar cheese. It was more than we could possibly eat, but we tried.

I made myself still smaller, the size of one of the dust specks I sometimes noticed floating in the air. I drifted across the kitchen, through the grill of the window screen and into the night. A gentle breeze set me down upon a blooming, luminous flower at the top of our magnolia tree. I took a swim in a dewdrop resting on the flower's petals. Music chimed from the palace-like structure at the flower's center.

Other times I'd imagine an endless stream of bare-breasted women walking into my room. They'd pose in the light from the hall, smile at me with lipsticked mouths, and move on. I didn't understand yet why I liked to think about them. But they lulled me to sleep.

I often had flying dreams—in the dreams I'd launch myself by hopping backwards, and instead of crashing to the ground, I'd angle upwards and float on my back as if I were in a swimming pool. Taking off from our house's front yard, I might shoot up through the clouds and follow the light to downtown Louisville where the big buildings were. I'd fly still higher to where the air was cold and thin.

And then—as so often happened—I'd lose the ability to fly. So long as I believed flight was possible, I could stay aloft, but the minute I doubted myself, I'd began a long tumble, with the air beating at my face.

At this point, I'd usually wake up and lie there, thinking things over. I remember once, still half-asleep, I managed to sculpt this recurrent dream into a happy outcome. I was still falling, but there was a hole in the ground below me, so I didn't have to crash. Yes, I was falling into a bottomless shaft that went down forever. In the dream again, I looked around, enjoying myself. Lava dripped from the distant rocky walls, small goblins peeped at me. I would fall forever and a day, on and on, world without end.

Schoolboy

*I*n the fourth grade, that is, in 1954, I switched from the idyllic St. Francis School to the boys-only Louisville Country Day school. I hated Country Day for all of the five years that I attended it.

Why was I there? My big brother Embry had gotten into trouble at his latest school—he'd called one of his teachers "Miss Gumwad" to her face, and he'd kicked a hole in the building's outside wall. So my parents were sending him to the private school most favored by Louisville's elite. I was following in his wake.

We wore a kind of school uniform: blue corduroy coats, gray chinos, white shirts, blue and gray striped ties—but as a group we were somewhat motley, for our parents could buy our prescribed garments wherever they liked. Mine were hand-me-downs from Embry, who was four grades ahead of me. Mom would shorten his old shirt sleeves by sewing folds into them. With my sloppy necktie and ill-fitting jacket, I looked like a waif, a circus worker, an immigrant scientist.

Backpacks were still unheard of. We boys toted heavily-laden leather satchels from one class to the next, and used them to lug home the books we needed to study from. The satchels had a single handle at the top, and their soft sides opened like jaws. My satchel was a medium tan, and it was nearly new. I liked it. It smelled nice.

We got a hot lunch at Country Day, all eight grades sitting on benches along the shiny maple-wood tables that we also used for study hall. A teacher sat at the head of each table, supervising. The food was dreadful, but only once did I have a table-master who cared if I cleaned my plate.

33

That guy was an unpleasant red-haired guy with an Australian accent and stained teeth. He called himself Colonel Sands. In study hall, I'd draw pictures of low-flying airplanes firing machine-gun rounds into him.

I was younger and smaller than most of the boys in fourth grade. Some of the others were snobs and bullies. Many of them seemed to know each other from before. I was immediately in the low range of the pecking order. I never really questioned this—children tend to accept life's indignities as inevitable.

But, looking back, how could those other kids already think they were better than me—in the fourth grade? Of all the outrage. Maybe it was because my parents weren't in the Louisville Country Club, or because I was dressed like an immigrant circus worker, or because I was prone to staring off into space while I thought about things.

From the earliest days, I've had a tendency to get deeply involved in the sights and sounds around me, to study the patterns and colors of stones and walls, to track the gentle movements of air-tossed leaves, to ponder the changing curlicues of the clouds, or to savor the sliding flow of water.

My mother had a frightening German book from her own childhood that she'd half-jokingly read to us. It was called *Struwelpeter*, and was filled with intriguingly detailed and old-fashioned color drawings.

In nearly all of the book's six or seven adventures, a child's misbehavior is punished by death. In one story, a boy named Robert opens an umbrella in a storm, the wind carries him into the sky, and he's never seen again. In another tale, Kaspar won't eat the food his mother serves, so he shrivels away to a stick and dies, his grave marked by a stone soup tureen. And Hans Stare-in-the-Air gazes too much at the clouds while walking, so he falls into a river and nearly drowns.

I was, and still am, Hans Stare-in-the-Air. I like clouds much more than sidewalks.

So anyway, my status was low at Louisville Country Day, but there were some boys further down than me. Sam Manly, for instance, liked to carry his satchel outside to the vacant lot where we had recess—he used it as a defense weapon, swinging the satchel like a mace when the meaner boys tried to prey upon him.

There was even a boy whom the senior boys had stuffed into a canvas duffel bag which they'd thrown all around the locker room, letting him thump against the floors and walls.

And ferret-faced Jimmy Vale was so peculiar that hardly anyone but me would even talk to him—he was full of wild, confusing stories about sex. Vale came from a large family living in a small house, and he knew about bodily functions from close up. Once when I clumsily spilled some pee onto my pants in the bathroom, Vale sniffed me appraisingly and said, "You smell like a baby." You could learn a lot from a guy like Vale.

One day in 1955 when I was nine, Mom was driving Embry and me back from school and, peering ahead of us from the car, I said, "Look at the hay wagon!"

Mom and Embry began to laugh. "That's a school bus," said Embry. I'd mistaken the mounded yellow shape with its black lettering for—a cart of hay with bars around it.

"You have to get glasses," said Mom.

I was uneasy that the other boys would tease me for wearing glasses, so I selected a pair with pink semi-transparent frames, supposing that frames like this might blend into my skin and be unnoticeable.

It was a revelation when I stepped out of the store onto Fourth Street in downtown Louisville. With my glasses on, I could see the fine features of the tops of buildings. I'd never realized before that I was near-sighted. It was wonderful to see so much detail.

Most of my Country Day teachers were unjust and incompetent.

Mr. Murden, the perpetually aggrieved history teacher, would give us pop quizzes, grade them on the spot, and announce "goose egg" when handing back the papers that he'd graded zero. Once he showed up at school with a bruised cheek and a black eye that he said he'd gotten from a hitchhiker. We boys were quietly exultant.

I well recall the red-faced Mr. Flagg, but not which subject I had him for—as he never actually taught anything. He'd spend every class period holding forth about his resentments towards rich people, towards "pansies," towards barbers who raised their prices, towards intellectuals, and towards his neighbor who'd tried putting a move on Mr. Flagg's pure flower of a wife while Mr. Flagg was in the john during a drunken party last Saturday night.

My fifth-grade math teacher, Mr. Viol, once assigned us the wrong page number to study—the page he named was a blurred, gray photograph of shoppers at a New York City fruit-stand. I suppose the illustration was meant to dramatize the value of arithmetic in daily life. Taking revenge upon us for his error, Mr. Viol gave us a quiz with questions like, "On the page you studied, what was the price of apples per pound? What kind of fruit was resting on the scale? How many shoppers were present?"

Although I was becoming less and less interested in my studies, I did learn one memorable thing at Country Day: how to diagram sentences. I'd never realized it was possible to dissect a sentence into the component parts of subject and predicate, of nouns and adjectives, of verbs and adverbs—with prepositional phrases veering off on little alleys with labels: for, by, of, into, from.

Mr. Herrick, who taught me about this, enjoyed discussions about the fine points of diagramming. He was a lean man, somewhat world-weary and cynical. He had a permanently bloody spot on his dimpled chin where he cut himself shaving every morning.

His English class was almost like an anatomy class, with our language presenting ever new forms to be mapped. And when we were assigned a homework project of composing and diagramming sample sentences, I had my first taste of literary creativity, crafting sentences with fancy words and dramatic situations.

"After placing his latest victim's head into the simmering kettle, Bloody Bill dragged the rest of the body into the basement, where he interred it beside the others."

Good old Mr. Herrick never tried to staunch my creativity.

One afternoon a classmate and I were out riding bikes, and on some random subdivision street, we encountered Mr. Herrick putting away his lawn-mower. It was strange to see him out of context, living an ordinary life. He asked us if we'd like to come inside for a soda.

"No, no," we said, embarrassed—although then we regretted our modesty, wanting the free soda, and we circled around in front of his house for ten minutes, to no avail.

The other good teacher I had at Country Day was my seventh-grade math teacher, a colorless man called Williams. You wouldn't remember seeing him if you passed him on the street. The spectral Williams showed us how to use these strange little pamphlets of tables that listed the logarithms of numbers, also their sine and cosine values. You could do some amazingly complicated things with these pamphlets—and to make it more exciting Williams taught us a method of so-called interpolation for guessing, say, the sine of an angle that didn't actually appear in the table, basing your guess on the values of the sines of the next larger and next smaller angles. And one day Williams really went wild and taught us how to calculate square roots by hand, without using the logarithm tables, but by instead using an intensely paper-and-pencil method somewhat like long division.

Probably I was the only boy in the class who understood what was going on, but I didn't realize this. By then I was discouraged and beaten-down, both by the bullies and by the generally poor teaching. I no longer thought of myself as being bright, or a good student.

One particular boy at Country Day, a Peter Bunce, picked on me the most—this would have been in 1956 when I was ten. Bunce called me, "Suck," perhaps because it rhymed with my last name, a name which was my cross to bear through all those years of middle school. Peter Bunce would lean over me, his voice a mocking falsetto, crooning, "Suck's a big boy now," as if I were a toddler learning to walk. I didn't understand why he hated me.

He had a burr haircut, slightly waxed in front to produce a tiny, cocky pompadour. When he wanted something from a grown-up he'd put on a sweet voice and act like an angel.

Meanwhile my father was getting more involved with the St. Francis in the Fields Episcopal Church, and he taught Sunday school class there. One Sunday afternoon Pop started talking about a bright, lively boy in his Sunday school class, almost sounding like he wished I were more like this personable wonder-kid. As the conversation continued, I realized—with despair and disgust—that the old man was talking about my nemesis. Yes, Peter Bunce had been kissing up to my Dad at Sunday school. Maybe he didn't have a father of his own, and he wanted mine?

I tried to tell Pop what a horrible person he was dealing with.

"He's a good kid," said my father, not understanding. "I'm sure you could be friends with him."

The next day at school, Monday morning, Peter Bunce slugged me in the stomach. I found my big brother in the halls and explained the situation.

"I know that kid," said Embry, narrowing his eyes. "I'll talk to him."

After lunch, Peter Bunce returned from recess with a bloody fat lip. He never bothered me again. I thanked Embry, but he thought the matter was hardly worth discussing. It was dog-eat-dog at Country Day.

Like a convict in a prison, I settled into life at Country Day, making friends among the lower echelons. Often the bullies and the older boys would leave us alone, and we could just be silly kids—chanting nonce words, making toys from folded paper, playing tag—small fry in the pond.

I have a clear memory of one winter afternoon, chilly and with dusk almost falling. I was waiting at the front entrance of Country Day for my mother to pick me up. The entrance porch was a simple slab of shiny concrete with brown-painted steel poles holding up a flat roof. We boys liked to dance from one pole to the next, swinging around them, hooting to each other, kicking our satchels across the pavement like shuffleboard pucks.

A few yellow leaves stuck to the damp pavement. Supper was cooking at home and the lights were going on. The sky felt cozy and low.

I realized that I was happy, and I had the strange knowledge that in later years I'd remember this particular moment.

Another good time was a birthday party for a boy whom we called Haystack Lampton—after his messy shock of uncut reddish-blonde hair. Haystack lived in a two-story brick farmhouse in our neighborhood. His family owned a parrot, which perched in one of their trees, screaming

38

the family members' names. They had a black cook who lived in a shack on the premises, and Haystack claimed he'd crawled under the floor to peer up through the cracks at her underwear, and that she'd only laughed when she'd noticed him.

For a special birthday party entertainment, Haystack's parents had set out a large black rubber lifeboat. Its sides were inflated like a giant inner-tube, and the bottom was smooth rubber. The idea was to get inside it and bounce off the fat edges. But then someone found a grease gun in the barn and had the idea of squirting grease onto the raft floor so that we could slide around in our party shoes.

Some of the kids hung back, perhaps not wanting to risk spoiling their clothes, perhaps realizing we were doing something wrong. But I was fully into it. I grabbed hold of the grease gun and squeezed the stock, pushing out additional coils of shiny black lubricant. I was sliding all over the life raft, whooping. And then Haystack's mother descended. I got all the blame.

O n Christmas Eve, we'd go to church and there'd be a Christmas pageant.

In 1957, I was Joseph, and I had to spend twenty minutes in a robe staring into the Holy Cradle, which was a cardboard box with a light bulb in it. I passed the time by mentally calculating the volume of the Hi-C cans that had once filled the box, and comparing this volume to the full volume of the box.

The best part of the pageant was when some men of the church would play the Magi, walking up the aisle singing verses of "We Three Kings of Orient Are." At first I wouldn't be able recognize them in their robes and makeup, and then I'd realize I knew them. It was exciting and mysterious to see everyday people transformed.

Afterwards we'd go outside and the sky would be black with twinkling stars, the air crisp, and Christmas almost here.

On Christmas mornings, Mom would arrange a fan of books around the base of the tree for Embry and me. Some of the books were science fiction. Embry plowed through any and all the books—he was an omnivorous, inexhaustible reader. But it was I who cherished and pondered the SF.

I recall being absorbed by Lee Sutton's *Venus Boy* with its deadly humming-birds, Andre Norton's *Star Man's Son* with its radiation-tainted ruins and telepathic Beast Things, Robert Heinlein's worldly and colloquial time-travel extravaganza, *Door Into Summer*, and by his countercultural *Revolt in 2100*, complete with sexual innuendo and paranormal powers. I felt quite sure that someday I'd master telekinesis.

Mom regularly took me to the downtown Louisville Free Public Library, and I'd pore over their slim SF holdings—which filled but a single shelf. I remember marveling over the riches to be found in a book like *The Best Science Fiction of 1949*.

I recall one story that was written backwards, that is, it had a section called "The End," followed by "The Middle," and "The Beginning." When I read "The End," it seemed like a standard happy ending, but by the time I got through "The Beginning," I realized that things had really gone wrong in "The Middle." None of the stories in our school English anthologies were ever this wild and experimental.

*T*he inner walls of the toilet stalls in the library men's room were covered with sexual graffiti, seemingly by a single author who wanted to be the "sex slave" of a young man. It was hard for me to understand the writings, as they were filled with unfamiliar slang words. Naive as I was, I wasn't quite sure if they'd been written by a man or by a woman. I was intrigued by the graffiti, and excited. It was like discovering a wall of hieroglyphs in an Egyptian tomb.

The little that I knew about sex, I'd learned from boys like Vale at school, and from a book that the children's librarian had given my mother to give me—the book was mostly about flowers and mice. I wasn't at all clear on what a woman's crotch looked like. Upstairs in the children's room at the library stood a stone statue of a goddess, and I'd actually crawled under the statue to try and see up her skirt—much to my brother's embarrassed amusement.

*B*y 1957, the developers were building tract homes on the old Russell farm behind us. They drained a pond, and Embry found two giant snapping turtles in the exposed mud, big fellows a couple of feet across. He and the Keith kids brought the turtles to our house. Embry wanted to keep them as pets, or perhaps to sell them.

We had some ditches in the corner of the yard where Embry, the Keiths, the Stone brothers and I had done some excavating, initially digging for buried treasure, and then planning to build a fort with a system of tunnels. Embry's first plan for the turtles was to fill our ditches with water, and to let the giant turtles live there. But the water sank into the dirt, and Mom didn't want him to run the hose all day long.

So Embry found a couple of battered old metal garbage cans and filled those with water, throwing in some mud so it would look like pond water. He tried sticking the turtles in there. One of them was willing to tolerate this, but not the other.

Embry set the rebellious turtle into one of the damp trenches. It looked like it wanted to crawl off, so he used his beloved electric drill to make a hole in the edge of the turtle's shell, and he chained the shell to a corky little stink-tree.

In the morning, the chain was bitten in half, and both the turtles were gone. We never saw them again. I hoped they'd found their way overland to some watery new home, perhaps to one of the streams that coursed through the Keiths' pastures.

As Embry was five years older than me, we didn't play together all that much, but we'd definitely bounce off each other a few times a day.

He was agile and flexible, and he was able to administer powerful pinches with his feet, that is, he could use a big toe and the toe next to it like the pincers of a crab claw. Often, after dinner, he'd loll on the living-room floor near the hallway door that led to our bedrooms. And when I'd try to make my way past him to do my homework, he'd wallow across the floor and grab my ankle or my wrist with his toes. I'd scream for Mom. It was fun.

Embry himself didn't like doing homework. He was smart, but he never developed the nose-to-the-grindstone kind of attitude that schools want to drum in. He had a Zippo lighter that he was proud of, and in the evenings, when he was supposed to be studying his Latin book, he'd squirt lighter fluid onto the glossy pages, fire it up, and tend the little flames so that the fluid would burn away without seriously charring the page.

He preferred thinking about get-rich-quick schemes, and every now and then he'd enlist me as his helper for one of his projects.

For instance, in 1957, I became the head rancher of Embry's white mouse farm. He'd bought a pair of them from a kid at school, and his plan was that we'd breed them, sell baby mice to other kids, and make a fortune.

Mom helped me get supplies for the mice. They lived in cages in my bedroom with pine shavings in the bottom. I liked them; I named two of them Moose and Meese. They couldn't run all that fast, so it was fun to set then down on the floor and watch them mosey around, perhaps guided by maze-walls of building-blocks. You had to be careful about sticking your finger into a mouse's face, as he'd mistake it for a carrot and bite you, drawing blood.

The school craze for white mice faded, and we couldn't sell any more of them, or even give them away. Embry totally lost interest. I set a few of the mice loose outside or in the houses under construction behind us, but I didn't like to do this, as I had the feeling the mice wouldn't survive on their own. Sometimes I'd go back to an empty house where I'd left a mouse, bringing along some food and water just in case, and I'd find the creature pathetically roaming around the endless blank wood floors, its bottom a little gray from sweeping up dust. And meanwhile the litters kept on coming. It was an impossible situation.

Finally Mom sold all our mice back to the pet store. We used our small profit towards getting started with tropical fish instead—guppies, neon tetras, zebra fish, and swordfish. The aquarium lived in my room. I liked the quiet buzz and bubble of the aerator, and the weightless way the fish would hang.

Another of Embry's businesses was selling cinnamon toothpicks—you could buy oil of cinnamon at a drugstore, soak toothpicks in it, and sell six of them for a nickel at school, wrapped up in a tinfoil pack. They were hot and delicious, especially if you used the higher-quality round toothpicks instead of the cheap flat ones. But then our school banned cinnamon toothpicks.

On Derby Day, I'd help Embry to sell people bunches of mint to use in their julep drinks. We'd trudge door to door among subdivision houses.

Some of the people who answered the door were drunk, according to Embry, although I couldn't tell.

Embry knew about such things. He said that once he and Mom had been in an elevator, and a really drunk man had gotten in and had repeatedly muttered "Blackmail." I liked that story a lot. I hoped that someday I'd see some really drunk people, or even get drunk myself. I was also curious about the "dope pushers" that the papers were always talking about. Where could I meet them?

The most disastrous of Embry's businesses was when he answered an ad in *Popular Mechanics* that committed us to selling five dozen packs of greeting-cards. The cards were ugly and overpriced. We trudged around the neighborhood houses for a few hours selling but a single pack—to a lonely woman had us in for lemonade and cookies. Finally Pop had to phone up the greeting-card sales company to get us off the hook.

W hat did Embry and I need money for? One of our main outlays was for items from the fabulous Johnson Smith Catalog of novelties and gags—the same items that we'd see for sale on crowded pages in comic books, goodies such as: college-style pennants with the names of prisons on them, the wind-up joy-buzzer, itching powder, stink bombs, a trick guillotine that would cut a carrot but not your finger, Whoopee fart-noise cushions that we loved to sneak under Pop, soap that made your hands turn black, X-ray glasses that let you see people's skeletons, silk rollers that turned one-dollar bills into tens, a handkerchief that changed from red to green, rings shaped like skulls with red glass eyes, bull-whips, switchblades, hot-air balloons, ventriloquism mouth-chirpers, the secrets of the pyramids, and a beanie attached to a pea-shooter that curved down to my mouth—or would have, except that, in my excitement, I tore the beanie in half while ripping open the package it came in.

Gambler that he was, Embry once ordered a Johnson Smith Mystery Bag which was guaranteed to contain $10 worth of merchandise for only $1. His Mystery Bag contained a comb, a pencil, an extra-thick rubber band, and a pamphlet describing how to paint your house.

He also ordered a complete set of gambling supplies, including a small roulette wheel, loaded dice, and a deck of marked and stripped cards. The "stripped" aspect meant that the cards were slightly tapered, so that if you pulled out a card, rotated it, and stuck it back into the deck, you could readily find it again.

Embry was generally friendly or neutral towards me, but sometimes he'd turn callous. I didn't like it when my parents would go out and leave him to baby-sit. Once, or instance, I had a blister on my thumb, and he formed the idea that I should let him pop the blister with a pin.

"Pus is poisonous," Embry intoned, not that the blister was actually full of pus. It was full of something more like water.

I locked myself into the bathroom so he couldn't get at me. I was planning to stay in there until my parents returned. But then something slid under the door. A firecracker! I heard the strike of a match and the hiss of the fuse.

I freaked out, screaming in terror. In the tiled confines of the bathroom, the explosion deafened me, making my ears ring. When I calmed down I realized that in my thrashing around, I'd in fact popped the blister myself.

So as not to be punished for his misdeeds against me, Embry took to telling my parents that I lied a lot. "Rudy is always making things up," he'd say out of the blue, paving the way for future outrages. "He imagines things."

*I*n 1957, as soon as Embry turned sixteen, he wanted a car, and my father managed to find him a 1930 Model A Ford in someone's barn. Embry bought it for about $100, and spent a lot of time fixing it up. Being such an early model, the car's inner workings weren't all that complicated. And you could still buy parts for it at a dealer—after all, it was less than thirty years out of date. Embry used fiberglass to patch the rusty spots, painted the body red, and, to start with, constructed a roof from a sheet of particle board mounted on four dowels.

He sometimes drove me to school in the car, which I enjoyed. We'd ride high up off the ground, and people would look at us and wave. The car had an arcane control called a "magneto," and by jiggling it, Embry could get the engine to backfire. Sometimes he'd ask me to steer, which was fun, but then he'd drive faster and faster, yelling at me, "Slow down," as if I were controlling the speed as well. Once I lost control and veered off the road through somebody's yard, scraping the bottom of the Model A on some of those concrete pyramids that people set along the edges of their lawns to deter cars.

Eventually this particular Model A caught fire. Some sparks escaped from the exhaust manifold and set the thing's wooden floor alight. I worried that I myself had made the holes in the exhaust pipe by running over those concrete lawn-pyramids, but Embry didn't seem to blame me. He acquired a second Model A, red and with a nice cloth roof. He never did stick with one car for long. By now we're old men, and I imagine that he's owned fifty cars with more to come.

*P*erhaps the most annoying thing Embry that ever did to me involved a motor-powered model plane that I built in 1957. I'd received it as a birthday present, it was called a Stuntmaster. The kit was very basic: tissue paper and some sheets of balsa wood with pieces you could pop out.

It took me weeks to glue all the struts together to make the wings, to glue the tissue paper over the wings, and to paint the thing. I bought a reel with lines for it, a little fuel-powered engine with a propeller, and with a special spark device for getting the engine to start.

Finally the great day arrived when I would fly my Stuntmaster. At this point Embry got interested in the project. Now that he was working on his car all the time, he was deemed the family expert on engines. Mom said I should let Embry start my plane's engine, as he'd be better at it than me.

So fine, Embry started the little airplane engine, but then he insisted on holding the controller and being the first one to fly the Stuntmaster. The idea was that you'd turn around and around as the plane flew in a circle. The tricky bit was to tilt the reel left or right so as to make the plane fly higher or lower—there was a system of pulleys and levers on the plane to make this work.

Embry tilted the controller the wrong way, and my Stuntmaster crashed into the ground, snapping off the wing. From where I was standing, the damage didn't look too bad, and I was already making plans to glue the wing back on. But Embry totally lost control—he burst into tears, ran over to my plane and jumped up and down on it, irreparably smashing it.

I couldn't believe my eyes.

"Poor Embry," said Mom.

"What about me?" I cried.

"Be nice to him, he feels terrible."

To make it up, Embry privately gave me a switchblade knife and some playing cards with pictures of bare-breasted women—special treasures drawn from a little metal lockbox he kept in his room. Actually his gifts to me had to stay in his lock-box, lest Mom find them, but Embry now entrusted me with the box's combination.

I could never stay mad at him for very long. And, after all, I was the one who'd made him fall down those steel stairs on the ship. Come what may, we were brothers.

Mom signed me up for art lessons with a Louisville artist named Lennox Allen. He was an eccentric young man from a wealthy local family. I remember seeing an exhibition of his seascapes at a local pottery warehouse, and he made portraits of people—in fact my parents once hired him to do a color pastel portrait of me.

He took what seemed to me like ages on the portrait, going on and on about how hard it is to depict a nose. Mom didn't mind how slow he was— I think she and Lenox enjoyed being around each other. Each of them was, in their own way, a fish out of water in 1950s Louisville, Mom as an aristocratic German expatriate, and Lennox as an impractical artist.

Lennox always wore a suit, but with smears of paint on every part of it. He had a scraggly beard and a rapid-fire, breathless way of talking. When a few other kids and I would have our art lessons from him at one of our houses he'd tell us crazy stories.

For instance there was a recurring dream that he had about his dead mother. A voice would wake him in his bedroom in the family mansion, calling him to hurry and come outside. He'd walk down the long hall, heading towards the grand staircase, with a pale green light shining ahead. And then, when he'd reached the marble balustrade of the stairs he could see the source. It was his mother's head, grown to the size of an automobile, resting on the front hall floor, luminous, with her blank eyes staring at him.

Even though we were a co-ed group, Lennox would tell us smutty stories, too. Like about the time when he'd noticed a woman stopping her

46

car and going down a path near a country bridge. "I had a feeling about what she was up to," gloated Lennox. "I followed her, and—sure enough—she was taking a pee. I got a real eyeful." He cackled, his Adam's apple bouncing in his paint-smeared neck. What a guy. In retrospect, it occurs to me that he resembled Jack Kerouac.

I was in the choir at St. Francis in the Fields Church from 1954 to 1957. I enjoyed choir, as it threw me together with a different group of kids than school. And it was nice to be doing something with girls, and to be however tenuously involved in their intrigues.

One of my friends at choir was a wry kid called Roger Smith. He had a crewcut, heavy frames for his glasses, and a sarcastic attitude that I admired. There was this one hymn we were rehearsing, with the chorus, "Jesus loves you, why not serve him?" And Roger would make his voice sweet and gentle, and sing an obscene variant.

In those days, if a boy farted, you could yell "Pokes," and begin counting, and he had to yell "S.O.E." This supposedly stood for "Save Our Ends." If you were the first to yell "Pokes," you got to punch the farter in the arm for as many times as the number you counted to before he called, "S.O.E." Once at choir practice, a truck on Route 42 outside made a huge, gaseous noise, and I shrilled, "Pokes!" and everyone laughed, especially Roger Smith.

"You're great, Rucker."

But our choirmaster, Mr. Graves, was mad at me, maybe not *mad* exactly, more like stern and disappointed, while at the same time forgiving me and expecting better.

One summer, Mr. Graves got my parents to send Embry and me to choir camp. Before each meal the campers had to sing a particular song that went: "Hey-ho, nobody home. Food, nor drink, nor money have we none. Fill the pot, Hannah!"

I disliked the song, as its heartiness seemed so . . . uncool. And who *was* Hannah? The cook who worked in the kitchen?

Inevitably, we boys began thinking of "fill the pot" in a vulgar way. At first this was funny, but as we continued having to sing the song before every single meal, the joke became a burden, overlaying the serving dishes with chamberpot images.

Instead of a swimming pool, the choir camp had a pond. I'd walk out onto this one particular fallen tree, and jump into the sun-filled green water. It was lovely.

But some of the older boys claimed they'd seen copperheads and water moccasin snakes in the water and on the banks. I worried about those snakes a lot. If you saw one kind you were supposed to dive under the water, and if you saw the other kind, you were supposed to climb out, but I couldn't remember which was which, and I didn't know what those kinds of snakes looked like anyway.

M y mother played only classical music on our hi-fi set. But in our driving groups, the mothers often had the radio on, and thus I began to learn about popular music. I was glad to be soaking up knowledge of the modern world. In the car we heard singers like Dean Martin and Doris Day.

Even though we were in Kentucky, I don't remember hearing much country music at all—although later, in high-school, Embry got hold of some bluegrass records that I loved. In those mid-1950s years, pop music was pretty much Tin Pan Alley corn—but then came Elvis.

The night that Elvis made his first appearance on the Ed Sullivan show—this would have been September 9, 1956—my family was having dinner at some friends' house in an older part of Louisville. It was a hot and humid autumn evening, and we kids were running around the front lawn, catching lightning bugs under low-hanging trees, and putting them into jelly jars. You could shake up your jar and all the bugs would flash at once. We didn't worry much about how that was for the bugs.

The grown-ups called us when Elvis came on. Everyone had been talking about his impending appearance. He sang "Don't Be Cruel." The grown-ups were variously disappointed and outraged—but we kids could see that Elvis was great.

Embry began wearing pink shirts and black pants, and affecting a hill-billy accent. He said he was a hood, a bad ass, an outlaw. He went to see Bill Haley's *Rock Around the Clock* at the Vogue movie theater in Saint Matthews and—he claimed—helped to start a riot that brought the police. I wished I'd been there.

*T*he tract homes were still growing up behind our house, with two houses butting onto our lot now, one of them done, one still under construction.

One gray spring afternoon in 1957, I noticed a boy solemnly playing around a large sandpile in the unfinished house. He was wearing a knit wool cap. He looked thoughtful and lonely. I was too shy to talk to him.

A few weeks later, Pop got me to go out back to throw the baseball, something we almost never did. But Pop had a plan. The new boy in the house behind us appeared in his yard, eying us. Pop handed his glove to the boy, and set us boys to playing catch together. The boy's name was Niles Schoening. We were both ten years old. He was going to public school.

After Pop went inside, Niles and I set down our gloves and talked. Neither one of us was much interested in baseball. We kept on talking through that summer and through the coming years, up until high-school graduation would separate us.

On My Own

All during 1957, Niles and I spent our Saturdays exploring the new houses under construction in our neighborhood. The workmen took Saturdays off, so we had the houses to ourselves. We'd search for the metal slugs that were punched out of the electrical boxes, hoping to pass them off as nickels in Coke machines. We'd feed discarded lunches to Muffin until she threw up. We'd pee on the blueprints. We'd climb around the giant mounds of dirt from the basement excavations, and throw clods at each other.

Once we climbed a long ladder to the half-shingled roof of a new house. I went second, and when I hopped off the ladder onto the roof, the ladder teetered and toppled to the ground. Niles and I were stranded and the sun was going down.

A neighborhood kid we called Danny Dogbutt chanced past.

"Push up the ladder, Dogbutt," called Niles. "We're stuck."

Danny offered no response whatsoever. He stared at us as if he were deaf, the sun glinting off his thick glasses.

A little later my father appeared, walking down the road in his shirt-sleeves. Dogbutt had squealed on us. But Pop thought our predicament was amusing. He pushed up the ladder, gently admonished us not to climb on roofs again, and led me home.

We were glad it wasn't Mr. Schoening whom Danny had fetched. Niles's father was stricter than mine.

———

Once, in the summer of 1957, Mr. Schoening got quite worked up when he found Niles looking at pictures of naked women in his attic. He burned the pictures in the furnace, even though it was summertime. I'd loved one of those pictures in particular, of a long-haired naked woman holding a violin.

Niles and I had found the pictures at a quarry that was a couple of miles from our house. This was a fascinating place, with sheer limestone walls over a hundred feet tall. It wasn't much in use, so we could poke around there as much as we liked, particularly on weekends. There was a good path to the quarry along a stream that ran through the Keiths' pasture.

When we were at the quarry, Niles loved to sit on the bulldozers and cranes and pretend he was driving them. He'd slam around the gearshift levers and make motor noises with his mouth.

The dirty magazines on the site had been left there by the workers. It may have been that they were tearing out pages for toilet paper. Niles and I salvaged a few dozen good photos. I was scared to bring any of the pictures home, as my Mom knew every square inch of our house at all times. But Niles, whose mother was equally observant, had taken the reckless chance of keeping the precious documents in his attic.

One day, coming back from the quarry, Niles and I made our way up one of the cliffs and found a new way home. We passed through an amazing, spooky zone that we never managed to revisit again—as it was so difficult to get there.

In this curious region, the limestone had been irregularly eroded so that we were walking as if in a labyrinth, the smoothly worn walls reaching up to our chests or even over our heads, the passageways branching and merging.

"This is so cool," I told Niles. "It's like science fiction."

For Christmas in 1957, Niles and I both got Erector Set kits, red metal boxes filled with struts, little nuts and bolts, wheels, and a real engine that you could plug into the wall. The kits came with instruction pamphlets filled with detailed drawings of things you might construct. After some preliminary projects, both of us set to work on the largest item in the book: a Parachute Ride, which was something like a merry-go-round, but with dangling seats.

We had endless consultations over the details—which weren't all that clear from the pictures. Eventually I managed to build a Parachute Ride just like the one in the pamphlet, but Niles wasn't quite so patient as me, nor so inclined to follow detailed instructions, and his looked a little—different, not that it didn't work just as well. I was intrigued by the evidence that you could in fact ignore instructions and still get something to work.

Niles and I also spent a lot of time playing games: Parcheesi, *Mensch Ärgere Dich Nicht* (a German game similar to Sorry), and, above all, Monopoly.

We'd keep a Monopoly game going in Niles's room pretty much all the time. When I had to go home, he'd slide the game under the bed, out of the way of his younger sister and his two younger brothers. Niles always had a strong sense of the ironic, and when he'd get on a winning streak during a Monopoly game, he'd begin trumpeting and making *oompah* sounds, and he'd chant, "Get on the Schoening bandwagon!" Inevitably, his luck would change after he started doing this—so much so that "the bandwagon effect" became part of our vocabulary.

Niles and I joined the Boy Scouts together. Although we shared a rebellious attitude towards the Mickey-Mouse goody-goody aspects of the Scouts, we enjoyed learning camping lore and, above all, going on camping trips, led by Mr. Keith. Some other misfits joined forces with Niles and me, and we made our own patrol, which we called the Porcupine patrol.

Nothing ever went the way it supposed to on the camp-outs. Sometimes it would rain, and most of the tents would leak. Other times there might be a cold snap, and we'd have to huddle over our camp-fires—fires which, always, we had great difficulty in lighting.

As long as Mr. Keith was the scoutmaster, it was fun, but later some more officious guys took over, and we drifted out of Scouts. Near the end, one of the boys' fathers insisted on coming along with our patrol on our campout, and it turned out he wanted to order us around. Niles and I refused to do some make-work task that he'd dreamed up. To pay us back, the unwelcome father wouldn't let us have any supper. Niles and I stole a can of tomato soup and heated it over a tiny fire on the fringes of the encampment, feeling like bums, savoring our bitterness.

———

As well as science fiction, I sometimes read the boy scout magazine, *Boy's Life*, although, even then, I could tell that the *Boy's Life* stories were written by hacks who thought their readers were stupid children. A lot of the stories were about Catching the Big One—they were almost like a pornography of fishing.

My father liked fishing, and he had a tackle box that fascinated me. It was made of bare gray metal, with rows of little shelves inside. He had quite a range of fishing lures that he called plugs. They were about an inch long, painted in garish, iridescent greens and reds, with sparkles in the paint, and with dangling triple hooks at the front and the rear.

He took me fishing in the woods or at ponds a few times, although there was never much prospect of Pop and me Catching the Big One. If we caught anything at all, no matter how small, we were happy.

Occasionally we'd fish or swim at a faded country club called Sleepy Hollow that Pop had joined—I doubt if the dues were more than thirty dollars a year. We didn't have the money to join the fancy Louisville Country Club or the classy Boat Club on the river.

Sleepy Hollow featured a funky concrete dam that had created a swampy lake. They had some rotting rowboats that you could maneuver into the overgrown waters. A deserted club house from the 1920s loomed over the dock, with empty wood-paneled halls and ballrooms—and no staff on duty. When we'd play shuffleboard on the shining wooden floors, I'd sense the ghosts of flappers and bootleggers.

One of Pop's pet peeves when fishing there was that he'd lose his pricey fishing plugs by having them snag on submerged trees and logs. The problem was that if he pulled hard enough to be sure of dislodging his plug from the log, he was likely to break the fishing line.

Pop had studied civil engineering in college, and he had some facility at designing and producing things. As a solution to the lost-plug problem he invented a special device that he called the Retrieve-O-Ring.

The Retrieve-O-Ring was a weighty doughnut of metal with a slit cut into it, and with a hole drilled through it. The accompanying twine was tied to the ring via the hole, and the slit was there so you could slide the ring onto your fishing line. The idea was that you'd let the Retrieve-O-Ring slide down your line to clunk against the snagged plug, and hopefully one of the plug's hooks would snag onto the ring. And then you could use the sturdy twine to yank the plug loose, with no danger of breaking the line.

We had several hundred of these items in our basement, each in a box with a coil of twine and a printed sheet of instructions. Pop placed tiny ads for his Retrieve-O-Rings in *Field and Stream* magazine, managing to sell a few dozen of them by mail order.

Unfortunately, more often than not, the Retrieve-O-Ring didn't work. It would fail to engage the plug or the snag, or the twine wouldn't be long enough, or the ring wouldn't slide all the way to the trouble spot. Nevertheless I was proud of my dad for having an invention to his credit.

And it was handy throughout my childhood to have all those rolls of shiny unused twine in the basement. Niles made fun of the Retrieve-O-Ring, but I liked to imagine that, deep down, he, too, was impressed.

*I*n 1957, Embry and I were in a Country Day driving group, along with Paul and Jimmy Stone from across the street. It was often interesting when their mother Faith would drive us, as she rarely stopped talking. She nursed a grudge against Mr. Sauter, a new English teacher at Country Day.

"What is wrong with that man! He wears his hair so long and slicked up. I think he's a fruit!"

I wasn't sure what a fruit was, or why Faith was against them. I didn't necessarily go along with everything she said, as by now I'd come to realize that she thought I myself was an oddball—I suppose our estrangement went back to the time when I'd accidentally left that turd on her bathroom floor.

As it happened, I didn't mind Mr. Sauter's class. He'd gotten us to do dramatic readings of some absurd educational plays he'd found in multiple printed copies. One of the plays featured The Parts of Speech as characters. I played the part of The Adverbs.

There was a strange collection of boys in the driving group. An older boy named Kenny was something of a thug, always wanting to pinch and slug the rest of us. He talked about how, on the day after school had ended last year, he'd lined up his Latin and Algebra textbooks and shot them with his .22 rifle.

Another boy, saddled by his simpleton parents with the nickname Skeeter, was a radio buff, and one day in October, 1957, he entered Faith's car in a state of high elation. He'd been listening to the radio beeps of Sputnik, the tiny new satellite that the Russians had put into orbit.

"It's so . . . spooky and wonderful," rhapsodized Skeeter. "To hear that little thing calling down to us from up above the sky." My mind drifted off with Skeeter's, contemplating the miracle of a human-made object floating in outer space.

"Ow!" yelped Skeeter.

Kenny had swung his plastic trigonometry triangle like an axe, bouncing its corner off the boy's short-haired scalp.

One of the things that Country Day did, by way of being a college prep school, was to have all of us students take huge batteries of aptitude and achievement tests every spring. That way, by the time we got to the standardized college-admission tests, we'd be used to them.

I didn't see the point of these tests for the first few years, and I didn't do very well. I'd stop halfway through, wander off to sharpen my pencils, or, even worse, skip a question but forget to leave that answer-row blank, thus ending up with most of my answers in the wrong-numbered slots.

When I finally did manage to successfully complete one of the annual batteries of tests, the principal called in my parents and me to demand why my grades were so poor, when clearly I had the ability to do better.

"It's because you're not teaching us anything interesting," I wanted to say.

Niles loved science fiction every bit as much as I did. We read all the SF books in the Louisville Public Library, and we even bought some SF paperbacks at the Woolworth Five and Ten Cent Store. We were excited about Sputnik, and we felt it was our duty to help the US to catch up with the USSR.

So we two started building half-assed rockets. We didn't even waste our breath trying to talk our parents into buying us good stuff like powdered magnesium, potassium perchlorate, or steel rocket tubes. Instead we used recipes we'd invented or that we'd heard at school.

For our first rocket, we harvested the little red heads from about ten packs of matches, and stuffed them into a pointed plastic tube that had once held a flower. The fuel flared up wonderfully, spewing a fierce beam of flame. But instead of taking off, the plastic tube simply melted.

Niles and I usually had a small stash of firecrackers that we'd brought home from family vacations through the South, or that we'd buy from friends. To fuel our second rocket, Niles and I emptied out the powder from a whole pack of firecrackers, unrolling the layers of newspaper dense with wonderfully alien Chinese characters. We funneled the powder into a hollow rocket-shape we'd molded from Reynolds wrap, and lit it off with one of the firecracker fuses. The tin rocket raced around the ground in a widening spiral, spraying Nile's leg with sparks.

This was too big a waste of firecrackers, so we switched to a more efficient technique for launching things. Niles figured out that we could get a rocket-like effect from a single firecracker by making a mortar from two tin cans, each can with a single lid removed. One can was a little smaller than the other, so you could nest them together, enclosing a small space. For our launches, we'd set the larger can on the ground with its open end facing up, drop in a lit firecracker, and quickly set in the smaller can with its open end facing down. *Whoosh*, the little can would fly thirty feet high.

As a variation on mere rocketry, we dug a shovelful of gravel from our driveway, soaked the rocks in gasoline, lit them, and tossed the shovelful high into the air, loving the movie-disaster look of the flaming pebbles. This was good, so we did it a few dozen times in a row.

Alarmed by our pyromania, Mom bought me a safe rocket, a red plastic Alpha-One, which was powered by something like baking soda and vinegar—although the instructions called these the fuel and the oxidizer.

The Alpha-One was quite well designed, and we enjoyed many successful flights, often a hundred feet high. The thing was in fact still working twenty years later, when I unearthed it from a box of boyhood mementos and started launching flights with my own children and a chemistry professor friend.

*I*n some ways my mother was a hypochondriac. She definitely set too much store in doctors. Since I'd sometimes get red-eyed when I was around freshly mowed lawns or plants with a lot of pollen, she took me to an allergist in downtown Louisville.

The doctor's office was in the Starks building, the closest approximation of a skyscraper that Louisville had. The Starks building had a news stand in the lobby, marble halls and a bank of elevators. It was the first elevator I'd ever been in.

The doctor pricked my back, my arms, and my legs with trays of pins that had various serums on them. The idea was to see which spots got red. When we were done, the doctor announced that I was allergic to cuttlefish and to black walnuts—neither of which were likely to show up on Mom's menus. But, yes, I had hay fever as well, with goldenrod and ragweed being a particular problem. Goldenrod was, at that time, the Kentucky state flower.

The doctor prescribed some powerful antihistamine pills that made me feel sleepy and dead inside. For a couple of months, Mom forced a pill into me with my orange juice every morning, but finally I was allowed to stop.

As I was sometimes wheezy when my attacks of hay fever would hit, the doctor also gave me an asthma inhaler, which was something I enjoyed a lot more. The inhaler was an intricate plastic device, a so-called nebulizer with a rubber squeeze bulb. It looked very scientific, and I liked using it, not that I actually had asthma very often. Whenever I'd go to spend the night with a friend, I'd bring along the asthma inhaler, and my mother would explain it to the other parents, and I'd feel important.

My most severe asthma attack occurred one cold Sunday afternoon when I was playing in the front yard. I wanted to get into the house, and I realized that my parents had locked me out. Or maybe it was just that I couldn't get the balky front door to open. My parents were nowhere to be seen—perhaps they were lying together on their bed, resting and cuddling.

Of course I had to be a brat about the door, pounding on it and screaming that I was having an asthma attack. When I saw the unhappy, worn expression on my father's face as he came to the door, I somehow dialed up the intensity of my wheezing to the point where I really did seem to be in a serious state.

They drove me to the hospital and I got a shot of cortisone, which immediately cleared my chest. Perhaps a glass of cold water in my face would have done the same. But Rudy's dramatic asthma attack became enshrined in the family mythology, and my condition was now viewed as a serious problem.

In 1957 and 1958, when I was eleven, I became increasingly unhappy with my life at Louisville Country Day. The endless snobbery and bullying was getting me down. What with puberty about to kick in, I was in a shaky emotional state.

Something that just about put me over the edge was a scary TV drama that I happened to watch alone one evening in the basement. In the show, a second-rate pianist had cut off a dead pianist's hands, and was planning to somehow wear them so as to perform better. But the hands got loose and started crawling across the floor. I totally freaked out, ran upstairs screaming, and I couldn't stop thinking about those disembodied hands for days.

I'd be riding on my bicycle and imagine the hands flying along right behind me, about to choke me. As chance would have it, the wonderfully crazy daily comic strip *Dick Tracy* was just then running an adventure about a killer who imagines a pair of disembodied hands following him. So maybe the hands were real?

One night at bedtime, I told my mother about my fear of floating, crawling hands, and she was very soothing. Feeling safe, I went on and explained about the pecking order in my class at Louisville Country Day. I had it quite well mapped out. Only two other boys were below me, I was third from the bottom. I don't think Mom had ever realized before quite how bad it was for me at Country Day, and she decided that something had to change.

Combining her desire to get me out of Country Day and her worry about my asthma, Mom came up with the idea of sending me for a full year to a boarding school in the Black Forest of Germany. For me this would be the eighth grade.

Going to Germany wasn't as far-fetched an idea as it sounds, as my grandmother and two of my uncles lived there, and they were eager to get to know me. So the plan was set into motion. The German school year ran from spring to spring, and so, in 1958, just before my twelfth birthday, I went to Germany for a year.

Niles didn't like the idea of his best friend leaving town. He sang a sarcastic ditty, making his voice reedy and dumb. "We go to Germanyyyyy—to see the King!"

As it happened, I enjoyed my time in Germany very much. The language came easily to me. My classmates were friendly. I liked the little intrigues with the girls in my co-ed classes, in fact I had my first girlfriend, not that we actually talked to each other more than once or twice.

Her name was Renate Schwarzwälder, and her father and brother were watchmakers. Renate had long, braided blonde pigtails. Eventually, our flirting increased to the point where she plucked one of her extremely long hairs and dropped it near my desk—glancing back a few moments later to observe me picking it up. But that was about as far as it went.

Something I loved about the Black Forest was the vast network of informal trails. Back in Louisville, it seemed like all the open fields were fenced in, but here you could stroll through pastures, along tiny streams, and under the tall pines of the woods. It was natural to wander about, and nobody cared.

Sometimes the other boys and I would collect pine cones and have a war, hurling them at each other. Other times we'd gorge on blueberries, or build secret forts.

Away from my horrible life at Louisville Country Day—and away from my role as the goony baby of the family—I realized that I wasn't weak or dull. I was a kid like any other kid, and I had the ability to cope with life on my own. I fought a bit with the German boys at first, but quickly I won my way in. There wasn't an unbreachable wall of snobbery like at Louisville Country Day.

My German relatives were excited to see me. Grandma in particular was as much fun as ever. For a lark she taught me to knit, not that I got very far with that. And she showed me an art book that would mold my taste forever, *Das Bruegel Buch*. It was filled with the paintings of Peter Bruegel the Elder. I really liked these pictures a lot. Some of them, like *The Triumph of Death*, resembled science fiction scenarios, others, like *Netherlandish Proverbs*, were filled with delightfully arcane symbolism, subtly suggesting the world around me was itself a clever puzzle filled with deeper meanings.

I'd arrived in Germany in March, 1958, and that summer when I was on break from the boarding school, my Uncle Conrad drove me, his wife, and two of his children to Belgium in his VW bug to visit the Brussels World's Fair. Back in those days, world's fairs loomed large in the public mind, or at least in my mind.

The Brussels fair was known for its huge, sculptural Atomium—a three-hundred-foot tall construction in the shape of a cube resting on one corner, with a sixty-foot-wide chrome sphere at each corner plus one more sphere in the cube's center, and with chrome tunnels connecting the spheres to each other. It amazed me to see a pristine mathematical object that big.

Something else at the fair that amazed me was a short black and white experimental film in one of the pavilions. The film showed a woman, perhaps a movie star, repeatedly puckering up and blowing kisses at the camera. I could hardly believe how sexy she was.

The Black Forest school I attended, the Zinzendorf Gymnasium, was run by members of a minimalist Protestant sect, the "*Herrnhüter Brüdergeminde*." They called each other Brother and Sister.

We boarders were grouped by age. Initially I was with the Sparrows, a group of boys slightly younger than me. We were under the watch of Sister Schütze, a short, strict lady who confiscated my *Time* magazine for having a photo of a movie star in a negligee, and my *Boy's Life* for having some pages of color comics inside it. Sister Schütze was high-strung, brittle and prone to screaming fits that we boys would weather in anxious, stone-faced silence. Half the time I didn't understand what she was talking about. There was one boy whom Sister Schütze would always pick on when we took our weekly shower. Dieter Gorlacher. Sometimes she had him come into her room in the evening—the rest of us were glad it wasn't us.

Soon I was allowed to move up to be with the Foxes, a group of older boys. That was more fun—although our counselor, Brother Resas, made a point of slapping me very hard in the face on one of my first evenings under his tutelage.

"Do you understand why?" he asked intensely.

"Yes, yes," I said. Sure I understood why. He wanted me to be afraid of him. After this little ordeal, the other boys in the Foxes' communal dorm room greeted me in a friendly fashion. I was one of them now.

The food wasn't much to my liking—the worst of all was a cabbage soup we'd get on alternate Saturdays. It looked and smelled as if it had been made by boiling water in a garbage can. I had the nerve to complain to one of the counselors about the food, and at the next meal, the house overseer announced, "We have a gourmet among us, Rudy Rucker. As our food isn't good enough for him, he'll eat bread and water for a day." It was a classic European boarding school experience.

But all in all, I was feeling cheerful and energetic. We boys carried little wallets with stamps in them, and we traded them on the playground—I'd collected stamps back in Louisville, but it had never been so dynamic and social. And I had a little Voigtländer camera that my grandmother had given me; I was having fun taking pictures.

During the week-long fall break at the Zinzendorf Gymnasium, most of the boarding kids went home to visit their families, but I was one of the kids who stayed over during that particular vacation. Two of the counselors took us stay-on kids for a huge group hike, sleeping at youth hostels. The counselors would cook stew for dinner, and we'd wait in line for our servings, playing the part of wild savages, singing a song with the chorus, "*Umba umba!*"

The food was delicious in the woodsy air. Each of us would only get one portion—we never really got enough. I thought about food a lot that year. In the Foxes group, I was allowed to keep the copies of *Life* magazine that my mother sent me, and it was with deep longing that I'd study pictures of things like hot-dogs, hamburgers, and chocolate bars.

It began raining a lot towards the end of that fall-break hike, and the puddles had yellow dust in them. I wondered if it was fallout from the atmospheric atomic bomb and hydrogen bomb tests that the U. S. and other countries had been conducting. It even occurred to me that World War III might have happened while we were off in the primeval pines, and that I'd return to find everything gone. That would be sad and horrible— but in a way it would be cool. It would mean that ordinary life had turned into science fiction.

For some reason, the biggest holiday of the year for the people running the school was the First of Advent. This was the one day when good food was served in our dorm, starting with white-bread rolls and salami for breakfast. In preparation for the First of Advent, each of us boarders had to make a little work of art to be displayed in our common rooms. The most popular projects to make were stellated polyhedra—I myself made a humble tetrahedral pyramid with a narrow point glued to each face, but the older boys made exceedingly intricate models, networks of a hundred or more squares, triangles, pentagons and so on, with specially folded paper points growing out from each of the polygons. I felt an intense longing to understand how the more complicated patterns worked.

At Christmas, my mother came for a visit with Grandma and me at Gradma's apartment, bringing a number of the plastic airplane model-kits I liked, also an algebra textbook. I'd been very concerned that I was missing out on my first year of algebra—back home, they started algebra in the eighth grade, and I'd been looking forward to it for several years, even though I didn't exactly know what algebra *was*.

After Christmas, it was back to the Black Forest for a few more months. Spring came early, and we went on lots of hikes. I became pals with a boy called Joachin. We'd walk faster than the other hikers so we could get out in front and find a nice little glen where we could sprawl by a stream and relax—looking at the waterbugs, building a little dam, maybe playing a game of cards. All the boys my age were into a pinochle-like game called *skat*.

Joachin liked reminiscing about his life back home—about eating fresh, white rolls with jam and all the milk you wanted. Basically, he was home-sick. I realized that, for my part, I'd begun enjoying life on my own. I liked being in this pack of boys, a kid among kids, the equal of the others.

I became quite fluent in German over the year—the down-side was that my English acquired a German accent. So when I got back to Louisville in the spring of 1959, the snobs and bullies at Louisville Country Day had another reason to pick on me.

Returning to my family was of course comfortable, but it was constraining as well. The four of us had certain set roles, and I wasn't that happy with playing the youngest kid anymore. I hadn't missed the tensions between my parents and between my brother and me.

Another problematic thing was that Niles and my schoolmates had started going out with girls—and even kissing them. They were miles beyond my shy flirtation with Renate Schwarzwälder. While I'd been tramping around the Black Forest, my friends had segued into puberty. I was way behind the curve.

I told my parents that I absolutely couldn't stand Louisville Country Day for another year. I wanted to go to a co-ed public school like Niles. But they were dead set against the Louisville public schools—perhaps for reasons of social status, or perhaps because they thought the schools to be bad.

Given my talent at taking aptitude tests, a large private school called Atherton was willing to let me attend, but only if I skipped the ninth grade—their lowest grade being the tenth. But I refused to do that. And then somehow my parents hit upon the idiotic idea that I should try a brand new private boys' school that was opening in the fall: *Catholic* Country Day School. And we weren't even Catholic.

Because the American students had started algebra while I was in Germany, I got some tutoring that summer to make up for what I'd missed. My algebra mentor was a charming, sophisticated woman named Gigi. She was married to Hal Taylor, a new assistant minister at our church, St. Francis in the Fields.

Hal and Gigi were a breath of fresh air for our community. They were both arty, with lots of their paintings in their house, and a whole table covered with soft little clay sculptures made by them and their Bohemian out-of-town guests—mostly grotesque images of heads.

Hal had prematurely gray hair, a flat-top haircut and two motorcycles. When he preached, he talked about Kierkegaard and existentialism, which greatly interested Pop. Pop had an itchy fascination with these new philosophies. On the one hand, it seemed as if the ideas might be bogus, on the other hand, Pop didn't want to miss out on the latest developments in theology. He was becoming more interested in religion all the time.

For her part, Gigi was getting a Master's degree in mathematics at the University of Louisville. She was the very image of a Fifties hipster woman, dressed in slacks and a blouse, wearing little or no makeup, and with her flowing hair pinned into a bun or a pony-tail. She had a casual can't-be-bothered manner of speaking, and she addressed me as if I were an adult. She was brilliant at explaining the essential parts of algebra—laying bare the simple truths buried within the fusty textbook that I'd lugged back from Germany.

Seeing my progress, Embry signed up for math tutoring too, but really he just wanted to be near Gigi. He didn't care about the math at all. Although I thought Gigi was attractive, I was young enough that I didn't fully see her the way that Embry did. Soon she dropped him as a student. But Hal let Embry stick around to work on his motorcycles.

Embry was exultant about the fact that one of Hal's bikes was an Indian Blackhawk from the early 1950s. He even got Hal to let him ride it around town. So—Embry was playing Marlon Brando, and I was learning about solving polynomial equations.

The summer of 1959, my last summer before high-school, was a peaceful time for me. I still had a sense of self-confidence from my year in Germany, and the social struggles of the teenage years hadn't really kicked in. I'd taken a lot of photos in the Black Forest—mostly of my friends but sometimes of lakes, mountains, buildings or ruins. Many of the other boys had taken photos, and we'd liked comparing and discussing our shots.

In order to get some real skill at photography, I wanted to shoot a lot more, but it was expensive getting the rolls developed. So I decided to develop my negatives and make my own prints. I didn't take a class or anything, I just read about darkroom techniques in a library book—which isn't actually a good way to learn such a hands-on craft.

Mom took me for repeated trips to a darkroom-equipment store down-town to amass the necessary chemicals and equipment. I liked being around this store's staff and customers. These characters were from a completely different world, a land of shape and shade, where academic studies didn't matter.

I converted our basement bathroom into a darkroom, with great worries about whether it was truly light-tight. Whenever I stayed in there long enough, I'd start seeing dim gleams from the corners of the black-painted window or from the cracks where the bathroom's walls met the basement floor. I was always slapping on more tape.

I also had problems with the intricacy of the process of turning a roll of film into a pile of prints. I had to use up to six distinct baths of photochemicals, each of which came with tissue-thin folded-up instruction-sheets covered with thousands of words in Bible-font type. I couldn't discern which of the many variables really and truly mattered.

Why were my blacks so gray? Did I really need to worry about the temperature of the developer bath? And how could I keep the damned prints from curling up? Working in a darkroom is a prolonged introduction to the willfulness and recalcitrance of the physical world.

Nevertheless I pressed on, and got a used enlarger from Hal and Gigi Taylor, practically for free. I'd vaguely imagined that an "enlarger" might be some kind of science fictional matter-control device, but it was little more than a vertical slide-projector, arranged to beam images of my negatives onto a table-top where I'd lay out good-sized sheets of photographic paper.

Now and then, I'd get a lucky hit—I remember a yellowish, low-contrast enlargement of gangly Embry sitting by my desk, looking very much like himself—and one gorgeous print of Mom in the garden, smiling over a bowl of fresh-picked cherry tomatoes, her eyes warm and happy. Pop loved this picture.

But overall, my results were spotty. It wasn't so much that I had a primitive camera and that my darkroom technique was poor. The deeper problem was that I didn't yet understand how to take a good picture. It would be ten or fifteen more years before I could begin reliably to *see* the pictures embedded in my surroundings.

And now I had to survive high school.

Curved Space

After my parents signed me up for my freshman year at Catholic Country Day school in 1959, their football coach—the formidable Coach Kleier—wrote us that, as the school was still so small, all of the boys in the high-school would be required to go out for the varsity football team. The new school didn't even have an eleventh or twelfth grade yet, so it was the freshman and the sophomores who had to play. The summer football training sessions were to begin two weeks before the academic classes.

"I don't think I'm varsity material," I told Pop. But he liked the idea of me playing football. He'd been on his college team, and he loved telling stories about it. Never mind that I weighed 115 pounds. The experience would be good for me.

I was one of our team's two left offensive guards. The other left guard wasn't much bigger than me. Coach Kleier would repeatedly send us in to substitute for each other, so that we could carry play suggestions to our quarterback, Tommy Veeneman, a likeable screwball who often regaled us with tales of his success with the ladies.

"I spent Saturday night under a blanket with Betty-Anne playing nookie," Veeneman might tell us in class on a Monday morning, while our ancient teacher was out in the hall smoking a cigarette and having a cup of coffee.

"What's nookie?" I'd ask. But Veeneman never gave a straight answer.

Although I wasn't particularly good at blocking the opposing players, they weren't very skilled at rushing past me, so most of the games went okay. But I do remember a time when a guy kept sacking Veeneman. He and the fullback gave me a pep-talk in the huddle. "You can do it! Rudy Rocket!" I managed to dig in and hold the tackler back for a few plays.

Coach Kleier played his role to the hilt. He was a solidly built, earthy, aggressive and blue-chinned. When discussing our play, he always said "hat" to mean "helmet." Thus, if talking about how to tackle, he'd say, "You gotta stick your hat in there."

We played a full season against teams fielded by other private schools, and we lost every one of our games. I especially liked the away games, where we'd drive in a caravan of cars, sometimes quite a distance, down rainy two-lane Kentucky and Indiana roads, with stops at roadside restaurants for wonderful greasy dinners, and lots of manly joking at our table.

Right before Christmas vacation, we had a sports banquet, and we all got letter sweaters. Coach Kleier made a speech in which he said there was one person here who exemplified his idea of courage: Rudy Rucker! Pop was proud and thrilled, he talked about this event for years. He said I was so small that when I stood up from my chair to get my letter, my height barely changed.

I was glad the season was over, but in the spring I had to play varsity baseball, which was even worse. You can't hide in a pack when you're playing baseball, the ball is unpleasantly solid, and gung-ho psychos throw it at you as if they want to kill you. Fortunately, I was so ineffectual at baseball that I hardly ever had to go out on the field during a game. Coach Kleier was satisfied if I did my part by keeping up the bench chatter and jeering at the other team's pitcher.

I made a new friend at Catholic Country Day, a boy called Michael Dorris. Dorris's father had died in a jeep accident in the army. Mike lived with his mother, his aunt, and his grandmother. He managed to evade his football duties with a trumped-up medical excuse about a sore leg. Coach Kleier made him a team manager.

Mike and I enjoyed talking things over and gossiping about the other boys in our class. We talked on the phone every night, giggling and confiding like a pair of girls. Being a product of Catholic parochial schools, Mike had some strange notions about sex—for instance, he thought masturbation was a sin and that you should tough it out until eventually you'd achieve release via a sexual dream. I kept mum about my own practices.

Although Mike wasn't very good at math or science, he was great at the other subjects—English, Latin, and history. He and I were very competitive with each other. When he'd do badly on a math test he'd always say that he'd known the material, but that he'd had a mental block.

For my part, I did poorly in our history class. One problem for me was that the history textbook seemed tainted, in that it contained a special version of history written to conform with the worldview of the Roman Catholic Church. On the title page, I could see where a couple of high-ranking ecclesiastics had signed off on the book: It read, *Imprimatur* and *Nihil obstat*—meaning, *Let it be printed* and *Nothing to object to*. Although I was already suspicious of my school books, it was weird to see censorship and mind control made so obvious.

The bigger problem was that our history teacher was a vain and ignorant man. His name was Stulz; he had short red hair. The historical era we were studying included the Protestant Reformation, and Stulz would go into vitriolic diatribes against Calvin, Luther, and all the Protestant religions. Other times he'd go on about how successful his ugly new baby was going to be—we knew the baby was ugly because he'd showed us pictures. Or he'd spend a whole period expatiating on crackpot John Birch Society theories about Red China. I hated Stulz, and did as little as possible for his class.

In later years, when I was working as a mathematician, people often made a point of telling me that they'd hated all of their math teachers. For whatever reason, I had that feeling about all of my history teachers. Perhaps I really did have poor teachers, or perhaps it was because my history classes were about battles, kings and politicians—all of which are topics that bore me. Only in my thirties did I learn that history can be about things that matter to me, such as mathematical ideas, literary movements, philosophical concepts, or styles of art.

In any case, Mike Dorris loathed Stulz too, so that wasn't a problem between us. Now and then we'd argue about religion—the infallibility of the Pope was an issue—but generally we were more interested in talking about our schoolwork, about literature, and about our dreams of eventually getting to know some girls.

*O*n the girl front, Mom had enrolled me in a weekly dancing class held at the Louisville Country Club—they called it the Cotillion. A certain spritely spinster had been running the Cotillion for a zillion years. To get me up to speed, she gave me a simple lesson on the box-step in her living-room. She felt light as a feather, like a nimble wraith.

On Cotillion night—I think it was every two weeks—we'd all put on our best clothes—which meant coats and ties for the boys, and shiny colored dresses for the girls. The girls would line up along one wall of the Country Club ballroom, the boys along the other, and a guy would play the piano: waltzes, foxtrots, now and then a jitterbug, and once per evening, the Mexican Hat Dance.

It was up to us boys to walk across the floor and ask girls to dance. There was no way out of this—the Cotillion employed athletic young men to strong-arm us into acting civilized. One of these enforcers actually worked as the Algebra teacher at Catholic Country Day. He was a pretty good guy, handsome and with a burr cut. He taught me a trick for factoring quadratic polynomials that stood me in good stead for the rest of my career.

Back to the Cotillion, given that I *had* to ask some girl, it was better to go across the floor earlier, as then I'd have a chance of finding one whom I might like. Not that the initial choice was all that important, as we'd swap partners with the nearest couple every few of dances or so. If you were alert, you might maneuver to be near a couple you wanted to swap with.

I often ended up dancing with this one particular girl named Debby. She was cute and perky. She often wore a bracelet made of exotic kinds of seeds and nuts, and this formed a reliable conversation topic.

"What's that one?"

"A yamayama bean."

Conspiring with one of her girlfriends, Debby invited another boy and me over to her house for a cook-out in the spring of 1960. As it happened, the house she lived in was none other than the former home of my boyhood friend Haystack Lampton, the place where I'd squirted grease into the black life raft. But the place was much more fixed-up now. Debby's mother was quite the decorator. She was the well-off daughter of a big Louisville jeweler—where her patrician husband now worked.

Oddly enough, Debby's mother arranged to have a photographer from the *Louisville Courier Journal* at our cookout, and our picture appeared in the society pages a few days later. I recently found the clipping among my mother's papers in my basement. I look eager and innocent, attired in madras Bermuda shorts, a short-sleeved button-down oxford cloth shirt, white wool Adler socks, and Bass Weejuns loafers. A lamb led into battle.

More parties followed. Finally at one of them, Debby and I started kissing. We were lying on the lawn out of sight behind a bush. It was early summer, with thunderstorms in the distance, the air still and charged. Kissing Debby was even more pleasant than I'd expected.

I ended up dating her until the end of my junior year in high school— over two years. An ongoing issue with Debby was that she idolized Doris Day and the virginity-first characters whom Doris played in her movies. Maybe she'd learned caution from the fact that her older sister had ended up pregnant and in a shotgun marriage with a stable-hand. Debby's family never talked about the strayed sister—I heard about her from my brother.

To confirm that Debby and I were going steady, in 1960, at the end of my freshman year of high-school, I presented her with my von Bitter signet ring, and with my Catholic Country Day football letter sweater. The latter was a bulky item, I brought it to her house stuffed inside a brown paper shopping bag. She wasn't very thrilled about the sweater. A Louisville Country Day letter would have been another story—but Catholic Country Day... *eccch.*

Debby left the sweater in its brown paper bag on her house's back porch. "Oh!" exclaimed her mother, finding it, and immediately understanding what it was. "This is a sweater! I thought it was the garbage."

Every few weeks, Pop would drive Debby and me on a date. We'd sit in the back seat together, as if he were a cab driver, and he'd ferry us into town to see a Doris Day movie. Of course Pop insisted on talking to us. He thought Debby's mother was cute; apparently the mother had sat on Pop's lap at some party in the inconceivably distant past.

Debby always called Pop, "Sir," which just slayed him.

The summer of 1960 was my brother Embry's last few months at home before going off to Kenyon College in Ohio. To be further from my parents' scrutiny, he'd moved his dwelling into the basement of our house. He had shelves of hot-rod magazines, copies of *Dig* magazine, a set of bongo drums, and dozens of back issues of *Evergreen Review*. Niles and I began spending time in Embry's lair, even when he was there.

Niles thought the hot-rod magazines were absurd. "Look at this ramshackle jalopy," he said, dismissively tapping the picture of a championship dragster. "What a piece of crap."

"That car goes a hundred and sixty miles an hour," Embry testily responded.

"Sure," jeered Niles. "Off a cliff."

*I*n the fall of 1960, Pop took it into his head to become ordained as an Episcopal minister. He was forty-six. Over the previous few years, he'd covered the required course work by independent study, and had passed the required academic, theological and psychological exams. And now he became ordained, first as a deacon, and soon thereafter as a priest. We in the family could hardly believe he'd gone through with this.

My mother in particular wasn't thrilled by this turn of events. "I would never have married a minister," she remarked.

I never did understand precisely why Pop became a priest. He didn't talk a lot about religion to me. Certainly he was committed to being kind to people, to doing good, to helping the less fortunate—not only because it was the right thing to do, but also because it made him feel good about himself.

Another factor was that Pop enjoyed being a leader, a person who stands out from the crowd. With his businesses and his inventions, he'd always been looking for a life-changing big score. Becoming a priest was a definitive move for breaking loose from the herd.

But there was more to it than Pop's personal needs. When he was standing before a congregation, he'd acquire a numinous glow, as if filled with divine power. He plugged into a higher force and—whatever his personal flaws—he made a positive difference in many people's lives.

This said, my mother, brother and I did tire of hearing how wonderful Father Embry was. Later in Pop's career, when I was around thirty, he started giving his parishioners buttons that read, "Embry Says I'm Perfect"—and they loved it. I was often in a resentful frame of mind in my midlife years, and those buttons got my goat. I didn't feel like Pop was regularly telling *me* that I was perfect. But, in all fairness, often he did. No matter what, he generally tended to treat me with acceptance and love.

Another of Pop's saving graces was that he never took himself too seriously. Once when he was interviewed on a Louisville TV show called *Pastor's Round Table*, they asked him why he became a minister so late in life. With a straight face he answered, "Well, I couldn't make a go of anything else, so I thought I'd give this a whirl."

In reality, Pop held on to his Champion Wood dimension manufacturing business even after he became a priest, although now he delegated much of the management work to his employees, his partners—and eventually to my brother Embry. The company prospered, and Pop was fairly well-off during my high-school and college years.

After my freshman year at Catholic Country Day, I switched to an all-male Roman Catholic school called St. X, for St. Francis Xavier, and I was there from 1960 through 1963. Why another Catholic school? Well, my friend Michael Dorris was switching there, and he convinced me it was a good idea. And, according to an article in the *Louisville Courier Journal*, St. X was supposed to be have the best science classes in Louisville. The feeling in my family was that I was going to be a scientist. And the tuition at St. X wasn't very high.

I went by the office, took an aptitude test, and the vice-principal, Brother Bosco, said I'd gotten a very fine score and that they'd be happy to have me.

From Country Day, I already knew I was good at taking standardized tests, but my score on this latest test set me to wondering if I were a genius. Certainly I wanted to be a genius—and never mind my indifferent grades.

I found a book about intelligence on my parents' bookcase, and looked up "genius" in the index, which led me to the following observation: It's not enough to get high scores on intelligence tests—geniuses are people who've created something significant, whether it be in science, art, literature, politics, cooking, sports, or whatever. The moral: To be a genius I'd have to *do* something. But I had no idea what.

In any case, it meant a lot to me that the St. X vice-principal viewed me as a desirable student to have. Right through the end of the ninth grade, I'd been a fairly mediocre student. My teachers hadn't expected much of me, and I hadn't had much interest in pleasing them. In a nutshell, I hated school.

But the academically rigorous environment of St. X would prove to be a stimulus, and a challenge that I'd rise to. By the time I finished at St. X, I'd have the highest grade point average in my class.

The teachers at St. X were all Xaverian brothers, with a status something like monks. They'd taken vows of poverty, chastity, and obedience, and they lived together in a dorm. They wore long black robes with rosaries dangling from the waist.

When I started at St. X it was in an old brick building on Louisville's version of Broadway, and I recall that in 1960 we leaned out the windows to watch when Richard Nixon went by in a motorcade. He was running against Jack Kennedy for the presidency. Mike Dorris and his family were big Kennedy supporters, but my family was for Nixon. How odd this seems in retrospect, given how liberal my father later became. But at this point he was still partly in businessman mode.

As for *me* opposing Kennedy—maybe it was simply a result of my ongoing rivalry with Mike Dorris. Or maybe it had to do with Kennedy being Catholic, and me being in a tiny minority at a Catholic school, where I often felt like I was having that religion shoved down my throat. We started each class with a recitation of the "Hail Mary" prayer. I had to sit in and listen to the weekly religion class.

Being a Protestant hadn't seemed to matter that much at Catholic Country Day, but the boys at St. X were a little more rough-edged. A kid named Richards referred to me as "the Jew"—which was, in his tiny mind, equivalent to being an Episcopalian. I didn't really mind this—Richards was a funny guy, and it seemed cool to be called the Jew, not that I was sure if I'd ever met one. A less friendly pair boys wanted to "baptize" me, meaning they planned to drag me into the men's room to soak me with water or piss. But I faced them down. I didn't want this to end up like Louisville Country Day, with me at the bottom of the pecking order. I held my own and kept my status.

Mike Dorris and I were in a lot of the same classes, and we formed a small driving group, with Pop ferrying us into the school in the mornings.

We'd get the bus back out to where Mike lived, and his mother would give me a ride the rest of the way home. Mike's mother always gave us a glass of milk and a piece of cake at his house. She had a spinsterly face that could stop a clock, but I was fond of her.

One thing that impressed me about St. X was that we boys were allowed to smoke cigarettes at recess, which was in an asphalt courtyard behind the school. Sometimes I'd bum—or buy—a cigarette from another boy. Some of these guys were real hoods. All of us wore windbreakers with the collar turned up.

There was one flamboyantly weird student called Rocky, who was forever hanging around by the urinals staring at penises. He'd leave a book on the shelf over the urinals, and act like he'd forgotten it, and then come in to fetch it, his eyes goggling, not that there was a hell of a lot to see. Rocky was about six and a half feet tall, and seemingly a little off in the head. It was horrifying to see the way he ate a hot-dog, his eyes darting around to see who was watching. The hoods were always yelling things at Rocky, but the Brothers tolerated him.

*I*t came as a true liberation when Mike Dorris got his driver's license in 1961. I'd double-date with him in his mother's powder-blue Chevy. Sometimes Debby would dig up dates for Mike, sometimes he'd find a girl on his own.

The most debauched night I remember in this company was when Mike brought along an allegedly hot girl named Michelle, and the four of us went to the drive-in to see a racy movie called *Not Tonight Henry*. The film had a historical theme, with Henry, the hapless hero, imagining women like Cleopatra or Lizzie Borden or Betsy Ross taking off their clothes— not that you could see much more that the upper regions of their breasts.

Mike was neither the smoothest of operators nor the most macho guy, but he was on fire that night. He wrapped his arms around Michelle and bent her backwards, scoring kiss after kiss. I was glad to see my awkward, horny friend having such a good time. For her part, Debby was uneasy and embarrassed, and we made numerous trips to the snack-bar.

Eventually Mike became a professional writer, just as I did, and he achieved considerable commercial success. He was best-known for his novel, *A Yellow Raft in Blue Water*, and for his nonfiction book, *The Broken Cord*.

I remember being fairly envious of Mike's acclaim, self-centered writer that I am. At least for me, our high-school competitiveness carried over into later life. I'm sure that if we'd been seeing each other regularly, I could have gotten over that. But it's a big country and we were travelling down different paths.

The very last time I saw Mike was around 1989, when he came to California for a book tour. At that time, he seemed distracted and unhappy, and it was hard to talk to him. He was in a shell, unresponsive. Later I'd come to understand that he was suffering from clinical depression. And in 1997, I heard the terrible news that, worn down by family troubles and his depression, he'd killed himself.

That broke my heart. As the years go by, I sometimes think of how much additional life that Mike has missed. But here and now, I'm thinking about him as I knew him in high-school, alive and happy, in the eternal sunshine of the past.

M any of the teachers at St. X were very good. I had one particular guy for chemistry and for mathematics two years in a row, a Brother Emeric. He was a sharp-witted, sleek little man, fond of geeky jokes—but proud and irritable. When the dumb kids got tired of having to learn things, one of them would ask, "Why should we have to learn this stuff, Brother Emeric? Math isn't really good for anything." And that would turn the Brother's face red. He'd set off on a thirty or forty minute rant, while the dumb kids grinned and winked at each other.

I got perfect grades in Brother Emeric's classes, and he'd joke with me now and then, but I had the feeling he didn't like me. I think he thought I was a know-it-all because I'd once corrected him in the chemistry class. He'd said there were no chemical compounds involving the noble gases, such as helium, neon, argon and xenon. I proudly told him that I'd just read in this week's *Science News* that scientists had synthesized a noble gas compound in the form of xenon tetrafluoride, or XeF_4. Brother Emeric hadn't liked this.

My physics teacher, Brother Antonio, was much more congenial, and he helped me carry out an intricate science fair experiment in which I fed radioactive food to some poor goldfish, then dissected them and measured the radiation accumulated in their skulls and livers.

In way, my favorite teacher was my English teacher, Brother DePaul. He once mentioned that he always smoked cigarettes when he was typing in his room, and to me this gave him an air of authenticity. He had us write a little essay every week, and we accumulated our works in special folders. He encouraged me and told me I was good writer, although I myself wasn't excited about any of the things I was turning in.

Well, there was one assignment that I enjoyed—Brother DePaul told us to craft satiric fables, and, in 1963, when I was a graduating senior, I once made up an anti-clerical science fiction story. Jesus comes back to Earth and encounters some nuns having a picnic. The nuns are addled by their belief in the doctrine of transubstantiation, that is, the belief that communion wafers are in some very real sense the actual flesh of Christ. So, in my short story's climax, the nuns eat Jesus.

Somehow I'd thought Brother DePaul would appreciate my story for it's craft. But he looked weary and sorrowful. I felt ashamed, and at the same time rebellious. I still felt that, as a construct, my story worked. But I was seeing that, if something is offensive enough, the readers ignore your artistry.

As a result of the extremely constrained range of allowable topics and modes of expression, I had a lot of trouble writing assigned essays in high school and in college. I'd always find it hard to come up with the required number of words. And sometimes I'd rebel.

Let it be said that some of the Xaverian brothers who taught at St. X were very tough customers. At the end of one class period I once saw the raw-boned Brother Cassian beckon an obnoxious student back into the room—and drop him to the floor with a punch to the jaw.

But it was more typical of the Brothers to consign a malefactor to Jug, that is, to an hour of detention at the end of the school day. While in detention you invariably had to write an essay titled, "Why I Am in Jug." In 1962, in the fall of my senior year, I got in trouble for writing an obscene stream-of-consciousness piece for my Jug essay. I'd imagined the Brother presiding over detention would toss my paper out without reading it—so for once I felt free to write something that interested me. But the guy read it, and I had to go see the vice-principal Brother Bosco in his office.

"You're not a mule, Rudy. I can reason with you, can I not?"

"Yes." I knew what he was hinting at. The man was a master of the veiled threat. If you really acted up, Brother Bosco would take you out to the gym and paddle you. A boy had told me about it at lunch one day. *He carries that paddle hid under his robe. You can hear it bangin' on his goddamn leg.*

"Because I would rather not have to treat a good student like a mule," continued Brother Bosco.

"You can reason with me," I assured him, suddenly on the point of tears. "I understand. I'll act better."

One of the odder things at St. X was that we seniors had to attend monthly sex lectures by the demented Father Panck.

"I tell the mothers in my parish to be on the lookout for contraceptives in their sons' rooms," Father Panck once told us, pacing before five hundred boys like a colonel addressing his troops. "And I've heard that some of you fellows are too smart for that. Oh, I know all the tricks. Yes, there was one boy who kept his prophylactics taped to the inside of his car's rear hubcap. I said Mass at his funeral last February. For, one snowy night, he was out there in the street, with a tire iron in his hand, and his pants around his ankles, and . . . "

We all enjoyed imagining the scene—visualizing the dark-haired girl in the back seat, with her wool skirt hiked up, and her panties glowing like magnolia petals. Some of the less articulate boys might lose control of themselves and begin hooting during Father Panck's talks. Bony Brother Cassian would wade into the crowd and slug them.

*I*n the summers, Niles and I would mow lawns all around our neighborhood, which had become a dense patchwork of suburban homes. We'd hoard our money all summer, saving up for a massive blow-out at the Kentucky state fair on the outskirts of Louisville.

The great attraction at the state fair was, of course, the midway, with the huge, clanking rides: the Ferris wheel, the Tilt-A-Whirl, the Wild M rollercoaster, the Round-Up, the bumper cars and so on. There was tasty junk to eat, carnie games to gamble on, side-shows, and mechanical peep-show machines with flip-books from the 1940s.

The louche Kentucky fairground crowd fascinated me—the soldiers from Fort Knox, the teenage hoods in pink shirts and black suits, the drunks and the hillbillies, the fat men and their skanky women with permed peroxide hair, people in polio braces, and the furtive, angular carnies running the booths and rides. I remember a guy who was sporadically reading a science fiction paperback while controlling the Ferris wheel—when things got busy, he'd tuck the book into the hip pocket of his jeans. I dreamed of someday writing an SF novel that hipster carnies might buy.

I'd bragged to Niles about my trip to the Brussels World's Fair, and we set our hearts on visiting such a fair together. And so, when we were sixteen, we took the train all the way from Louisville to the west coast to visit Seattle's 1962 World's Fair.

It was a wonderful trip, rich in incident. We changed trains in Chicago, and proceeded through marvelously Wild West places like Missoula, Montana, with a huge painted sign for Bluff Tap Liquors. Niles jokingly proposed that we hop off the train and bluff our way to the tap. I met an unaccompanied girl on the train and sat with her for a few hours in the scenic observation dome, shyly talking about—the mathematics of group theory, which was the most interesting thing I'd learned at school that year.

My father had a friend in Seattle called Mr. Heath, and we stayed with him for a few days, and then in a student hostel downtown. Mr. Heath was a kind man and a good host, but Niles of course made fun him, referring to him as The Magnificent Heath. Niles was both self-deprecating and radically deflationary of any pomp that he observed. The Magnificent Heath had an eager-beaver son called Jeffrey, and Niles found the boy deeply uncool. Niles developed this alarming comedy routine that he'd deliver in a wheedling hillbilly accent.

"I'm sorry about little Jeffrey, Mr. Heath. We didn't really mean to butcher him up that-a-way. But it'd be a sin to waste that meat. We've got Jeffrey a-roastin' on a spit out back. It's the fittin' way to say goodbye, like how we do it in Kentucky..."

Niles would be, like, mumbling this to me while we were riding in the back of the Magnificent Heath's car. I was relieved when we made it into the student hostel in the city.

A high point of the world's fair trip came when Niles and I managed to get into a burlesque show. You were supposed to be twenty-one to see the show, but we'd doctored our driver's licenses.

Perhaps to look more official, the Kentucky licenses at that time were made with white print on black paper. There was a certain car magazine which printed numerical specifications in just the same size, and in that same white on black font. Niles and I had replaced the final numerals of our birth years with zeroes, making ourselves five or six years older. The carnie running the show waved us in.

It was thrilling to be inside with the seedy crowd of gawkers. A comedian came out and told jokes involving complex double-entendres that I barely understood—like interchanging "*C'est si bon*," and "Shave zee bone." From time to time he'd break off and wheeze asthmatically into the microphone, saying, "Hear the roar of the crowd?"

A heavy-set woman called Baby Dumpling appeared, wearing spangled shorts and pasted-on nipple-covers with dangling gold tassels. By rhythmically hunching her shoulders, she was able to set the tassels to twirling—in opposite directions. "Ah, the breeze from the mountains," she cooed.

For the final act, an aging woman slunk about the stage with ostrich feather fans—you were supposed to imagine that, behind the fans, she was naked, but it was hard to be sure. She was intensely sucking in her stomach so as not to look fat, which brought her ribs into horsey prominence. Be that as it may, we were ecstatic to have seen burlesque.

There weren't actually that many carnival-type rides at the World's Fair. But I did manage to win a two-foot-tall chrome Space Needle cigarette lighter by tossing a penny over a railing onto a polished sheet of painted plywood. Miraculously my penny came to rest entirely within one of the dots painted on the sheet, and not just within any old dot, man, I hit the single grand-prize-winning *red* dot. I proudly brought the lighter home for my mother to display in our living-room. In a few weeks it migrated to my dresser, and then to the basement.

The world's fair exhibit that impressed Niles and me the most had to do with Einstein's Theories of Relativity. We'd heard of the Special and General Theories in our science fiction books, but we had little understanding of what they said.

One part of the exhibit was about the notion of spacetime as a unified four-dimensional continuum—which is a central concept for the Special Theory of Relativity. To illustrate this, they'd made an enormous sculptural model of the Moon's path around the Earth, including the time element by depicting both of the celestial bodies as trails in space. The Moon's worldline was like a helical vine twining around the vertical worldline of planet Earth.

I looked at it and—*bam*—I got the picture. That is, if I were to move a plane from the floor to the ceiling, I'd see the moon-line's cross-section as a dot circling the stationary dot of the Earth-line's cross-section.

Kicking things up a level, you could stack up the successive states of our full three-dimensional universe to create a four-dimensional spacetime block universe—and you could animate it by moving a cross-sectional Now from the Past towards the Future! You could model time as the fourth dimension.

The General Relativity display consisted of a large curved funnel that was rotating inside a railing. It was a model of the solar system. The funnel's downward curve towards the center represented the curvature of space, a curvature which was induced by the mass of the sun. We could toss balls into the turning funnel to see how the centrifugal force from the spinning balanced off against the central pull.

Fun to play with, yes, and here came another insight. If gravity amounted to a stretching of our space, what direction did our space get stretched in? The fourth dimension! But, wait, if time was going to be the fourth dimension, then I'd probably want to bend space into the direction of the fifth dimension, or ... ?

My mind was sizzling with burlesque and general relativity, alive with curved space.

Following The Beats

*I*n the spring of 1962, at the end of his sophomore year, my brother Embry parted ways with Kenyon College. His grades were minimal, and he'd gotten in with a group of bad apples. After a night of heavy drinking, they'd phoned in a fire alarm. When the firemen arrived outside, one of the boys began sniping with a .22 rifle—supposedly he was only trying to shoot out the truck's tires, or maybe to ring the bell hanging above the hood—but the school dean took the opportunity to get rid of the troublemakers.

I was glad to have Embry at home that summer, if only to take my side in the dinner table conversations with Pop. The old man had begun taking exception to ordinary turns of phrase that Embry and I might use, phrases as innocuous as, "a lot of food."

"What do you mean *a lot*?" he'd demand. "A lot is a piece of land. And what is this disgusting phrase 'make out' that I heard one of you use? You make out in a business deal, fine. But to say you make out with a girl? That's slimy, boys. Common."

Embry and I would look at each other and laugh. We were going to talk however we liked. Language marches on. Pop was out of it.

My brother hung around the house for a few weeks, until one day Pop said, "Embry, come downtown with me, there's a guy I want you to meet."

The guy turned out to be a recruiting officer for the U. S. Army—which didn't really seem all that outrageous to Embry. Growing up indoctrinated by World War II movies, we boys all expected to end up the army some day. For that matter, given the jail movies that I'd seen, I expected to serve some time in a penitentiary as well. Those were all things that you did when you grew up: went to college, joined the army, got married, had children, got an office job, went to prison.

As the Vietnam War hadn't started yet, Embry got a good deal. He went to the Army Language School in Monterey, studied German, and ended up stationed near the East German border, billeted in a room over a beer-hall, and assigned to eavesdropping on the East German military radio. And eventually he finished college in night school.

*I*n the fall of 1962, with Embry off in the army, I spent more time in his basement room, studying his eclectic library. Realizing that the *Evergreen Review* magazine had curse words in it, I began combing through Embry's back issues—looking for pornography. But that wasn't exactly what I found. Instead I found a career.

One particular excerpt of William Burroughs's *Naked Lunch* utterly blew my mind, it was about junkies and hangings and weird sex, written in a hilariously in-your-face dead-pan tone, utterly contemptuous of any notion of bourgeois propriety. Burroughs was a banner to salute, an anthem to march to, a master to emulate.

The *Evergreen Review* stash was a treasure trove—I found poems by Allen Ginsberg, journals by Jack Kerouac and, somehow the most heartening, story after story by Beat unknowns. Men and women writing about their daily routines as if life itself were strange and ecstatic.

Next I found an anthology in the library called *The Beat Generation and the Angry Young Men*, and this was where I first saw Ginsberg's *Howl*. Niles and I read that amazing poem out loud to each other, reveling in the wild language and the bad attitude, exulting in the sense of liberation. From here it was a short hop to Kerouac's *On the Road*. This book spoke to me like none I'd read before. To be out in the world, free as a bird, drinking, smoking, meeting women and yakking all night about God— yes!

Niles also found a book on Zen Buddhism by Allan Watts, loaded with itchy koans. And in a slightly different vein, but even more importantly for me, he discovered Edwin Abbott's *Flatland*.

"It's this weird flat world where the people are lines and triangles and other shapes. The main character is called A Square. They slide around like scraps of paper on a tabletop."

"How does it rain?"

"The rain is a band of water that slides across the world. Never mind that. The neat part is that A Square travels up into our space. And then he goes back and tries to teach the Flatlanders about the mysterious third dimension, and the High Priest throws him in jail."

Although I didn't realize it right away, the point of *Flatland* is to guide its readers towards trying to imagine the fourth dimension. Just as the third dimension is a mystery for a flat being in a plane, the fourth dimension is baffling for us humans in our three-dimensional space. In the future, I'd spend months and even years working out the details of this analogy—but initially, all I got out of *Flatland* was an increased sense of excitement about higher dimensions.

I didn't see how to fit all my new literary influences together until good old Mom happened to give me a paperback copy of *Untouched By Human Hands*, a collection of science fiction tales by Robert Sheckley.

Somewhere Vladimir Nabokov writes about the "initial push that sets the heavy ball rolling down the corridors of years," and for me the push was Sheckley's book. I thought it was the coolest thing I'd ever seen. Not only was Sheckley's work masterful in terms of plot and form, but it also had a jokey edge that—to my mind—set it above the more straightforward work of the other SF writers. There was something about Sheckley's style that gave me a sense that I could do it myself. He wrote like I thought. Starting in 1962, I knew in my heart of hearts that my greatest ambition was to become a beatnik science fiction writer.

I happened to read an article about modern French novels in a magazine, and finding none of these books in the public library, I pestered my parents into ordering me some of them through the University of Louisville bookstore. My favorite was Jean-Paul Sartre's existentialist novel, *Nausea*, in which the alienated and neurotic main character develops a sense of disgust at the insistent physicality of the world. In a climactic scene he's freaking out from staring at the gnarly trunk of a chestnut tree.

I thought it would be cool to perceive the world that intensely, and then to write about it. I talked about *Nausea* a lot to Niles and my other high-school friends. Generally they enjoyed hearing me wax philosophical.

One main thing that I was picking up from my readings was that there probably wasn't any kind of afterlife at all. I was increasingly concerned about the inevitability of death. Although my parents regularly ushered me to church, I wasn't feeling satisfied by what I heard there.

Niles and I often talked about the meaning of life and the problem of death.

"Time keeps passing, Niles. In a couple of years we'll go off to college, and before we know it, we'll be dead. Can there really be *nothing* after death?"

Niles and I formed a theory that some kind of life force energized us, and that when a person dies, their life force returns to a central pool. The theory became very clear to me one cold winter day when we were walking in the Keiths' pastures.

The stream was frozen over. We squatted and watched the bubbles beneath the ice. The gelid surface was patterned in ridges and blobs, clear here and frosty there. Toward one bank, the ice domed up. A lone, large bubble wobbled there, braced against the flow. Smaller bubbles kept arriving to merge into that big bubble, and it, in turn, kept growing and sending out tendrils, silver pseudopods that pinched off into secondary bubbles that were swept further downstream.

"That's what it looks like," I exclaimed. "The pool of life force is that big bubble under the ice. And each of us is a little bubble that can merge back in. The key thing is that once a little bubble joins the big one, the little bubble is *gone*. Your life-force is preserved, but your personality disappears!"

"Hubba-hubba," said Niles. "I done lost my life-force up Laura's crack."

Music always seemed like a way out of alienation, a way of plugging myself into the wider world. From Elvis on, I'd always enjoyed hearing pop music on the radio. At night, as I did homework, and later in my bed, I'd stay abreast of the Top Forty, listening to WAKY on my little radio with its glowing tubes and faint smell of heated plastic.

Sometimes I'd do the box-step to one of the slow, sentimental songs like "Angel Baby" or "You're a Thousand Miles Away," imagining that I had a girl in my arms.

My favorite musician of all was Bo Diddley—the only LPs that I actually owned were Diddley's, and I'd play them good and loud when I was alone in the house. I worshipped his rueful song, "Crackin' Up," about a guy whose woman is always yelling at him. Listening to this song, I'd look at myself in my mother's full-length mirror, imagining that someday I might be cool and hen-pecked and rising above it all. Bo Diddley made the pain of living into sweet, plangent art.

*I*n Louisville, quite a few of the high school boys banded together into fraternities. The most elite of these was the Athenaeum Literary Association, whose members were mockingly called Shakers, due to their businessman-like tendency to shake people's hands. The Chevalier Literary Society was just a bit behind Athenaeum, along with Dignitas and Fidelian.

Being out of circulation in the brainiac track at St. X, I probably wouldn't have been asked to join a fraternity, but Embry had been a member of Chevalier—and thus I was invited in. I was happy to join—it made me feel important, and I already knew many of the boys from my early years at Louisville Country Day.

We'd have meetings once a week, often in a spare room at a church. The main purpose of the meetings was to socialize and to share information about the weekend's parties. There were some goody-goody types who wanted to run our meetings as if we were a board of trustees, but solemnity never lasted long. I remember a fat guy called Whale throwing a rubber dog-poop-pile into the aisle and calling out, "Mr. Chairman, there's a movement on the floor!"

Although it was mainly for good public relations that the fraternities called themselves literary societies, we each published a little magazine once a year. Chevalier's was *The Pegasus*. These professionally printed, digest-sized journals contained photos, jokes, drawings, and a story or essay by each member. Now, looking back, I realize that quite a few of the articles were plagiarized. In any case, they were nice-looking magazines, with a certain buzz attached to them, and we sold a decent number of copies to other students. Plus we got parents and local merchants to chip in for ads.

In the spring of my junior year, 1962, I wrote my very first science fiction story, "The Miracle," for *The Pegasus*. In this story, some spaceship aliens pose as angels so as to bring peace to the Earth, and while this is happening, the main character gets drunk. And in the fall of senior year I wrote a Beat piece for *The Pegasus*, called "Bus Ride—December 20, 1962," an anomie-filled first-person description of what I saw and thought while riding the bus home from St. X one day.

At this point, writing down my actual thoughts was a very rare and unusual activity for me. In the coming years, I'd get the hang of this style by writing letters to my friends during summer vacations and after college. In typing out those letters, I'd slowly learn to write like I talk—in my opinion, that's a key part of having a pleasant literary style.

By now, of course, thanks to years of practice, writing has become all but effortless for me. When I'm at the keyboard, the words flow out through my fingers as if by telepathy. In some ways, writing is easier for me than talking. If anything, I wish I could talk as coherently as I write.

O ne of the side-benefits of being in Chevalier was that it enabled me to purchase beer and hard liquor, that is, I could ask one of the older members to buy me something after one of our Saturday evening meetings—not that any of us was actually twenty-one, but there was one guy in particular who was very good at scoring. He was already out of high school and going to the University of Louisville, but he still came to the Chevalier meetings, lost soul that he was. He wore a tweed jacket and smoked a pipe.

One of the first times I got drunk was in the fall of 1962, when I drove to a party alone. I'd broken up with Debby, and I was between girlfriends. I chugged two beers on the way to the party, listening to the spacy instrumental song "Telstar" on the radio. People were still excited about every satellite that went up.

During the party, I went outside and drank a third beer, and that was enough to make me utterly bombed. Normally I was shy and quiet in groups, but now I was talking to everyone, telling them about the beatnik ideas I'd been nurturing, going on about the life force and the universal one mind. People listened to me, interested and laughing. I felt wonderful.

That time, I managed to get home and into bed without my parents even finding out I'd been drinking, but in the months to come this would become harder and harder. They'd wait up for me and make me kiss them good-night so that they could sniff my breath. If I'd been drinking I'd be grounded for a week or two.

"He who calls the tune must pay the piper," my father once intoned.

From his vantage point, Pop could see something that would take me years to internalize and to act upon: I was fated to have a drinking problem. Beer and liquor had an unnatural appeal for me. From the very start I was fervently scheming about how to get drunk on the next weekend or maybe on the weekend after that.

As it happened, Niles shared my fascination with alcohol. We'd often drink together on our double dates—which wasn't much fun for the girls. But I did notice that when I went out together with Niles I could often get a better class of girl to come along. Niles had grown to over six feet tall. He had blonde hair, blue eyes, and he was a star on the swimming team.

Niles usually drove, as he was a lot better than me at keeping it together when he was tanked. He'd joined a fraternity called Sigma, on the basis of their sodden rush parties.

"Hell, Rudy, those guys weren't drinking any piddly little half-pints. They were runnin' around wavin' fifths!"

On Derby Day, 1963, in the spring of my senior year, some of my younger Chevalier friends and I went over to the house of a boy whose family had a house high on a hill above a winding gravel driveway. His parents were off at the Churchill Downs racetrack, their fridge was full of beer, and they had a capacious liquor cabinet. I got wasted. And then it was time to go somewhere else.

On this day, I was the one driving. I had my mother's cute little blue VW bug with the sunroof. On the way down the hill I started showing off, veering the car to the left and right, making it skid. And then suddenly the steering wheel was twisting in my hands like a live thing. I'd lost control. The car slammed into a tree. The collision was a blaze of white, a sense of being twisted through space. I was unconscious for a minute, and I awoke tangled in a fence. I'd flown out of the car. If my head had hit the tree, I never would have woken up. Death would be like a light-switch turning off.

In the coming weeks, I thought about this a lot. It was the same teaching I'd been shown when I ruptured my spleen, and the same fact I'd encounter again when I had my brain hemorrhage. It seemed like, when the end came, all my theorizing about the life force wasn't going to be much use. What to do? Be more careful. Stretch out my span on Earth for as long as I could. And enjoy it while it lasts.

I asked Mom if she believed in heaven and hell. "I think we make those things for ourselves while we're alive," she said. "I don't know about anything after we die."

Mom had reason to think about heavy things herself, as she'd been having some health problems. The scariest had been her abrupt onset of diabetes, signaled by a sudden coma. Now she was giving herself insulin injections several times a day. And she had a problem with maintaining a good balance between the insulin and her diet, with the upshot that every so often or so her blood sugar would get so low that she'd have a so-called insulin reaction.

At these times, Mom would become confused, slur her words, and stumble. The cure was simply to force some food into her, but often she'd perversely resist, insisting that she didn't want her blood sugar to get too high. She tracked her blood sugar very carefully, even obsessively, measuring it many times a day.

The insulin reactions were harrowing experiences for the rest of us. We always had extra tension at our holidays, as our festive dinners inevitably came a little later than the precise noon moment when Mom normally had lunch. She was unwilling to adjust her food and insulin intake to take this into account, and when the mealtime approached, she'd often be in a daze. My father would beg her to have some orange juice, his voice breaking, and she would argue with him. It was terrible and sad.

The worst was when, once or twice a year, Mom would go into an insulin reaction while she was asleep. She'd start thrashing and moaning, which would wake up my father, and then he'd get us boys to help. In the throes of a night reaction, she'd be too far gone to be able to drink any orange juice, and one of us would have to give her an injection of a special drug that would restore her blood sugar levels.

Pop was always imploring Mom to be more careful with her food and her insulin, but she stubbornly insisted on working as close to the edge as possible. She said that if she didn't keep her blood sugar low enough, she might get gangrene or go blind. At the time, it was hard to be sure what was right.

By the time I was in college, Pop had begun to serve sherry and champagne to all of us before the Sunday and holiday meals, and that seemed to make things better—the alcohol helped Mom's blood sugar, and, since we were all getting a little tiddly, we didn't worry about the reactions anyway. For quite a few years, drinking with my parents was convivial and unproblematic—although eventually alcohol would become a problem for my father, and then for me.

Even though my heart was with the beatniks, the existentialists, and the science fiction writers, I'd developed a facility for jumping through academic hoops while at St. X. I enjoyed my well-designed and challenging classes there. I got top grades, and I won a National Merit Scholarship.

Which college to attend? This was a sticky wicket. Each college application required the student to write a brief essay, and I committed the error of writing what I considered to be the truth: (a) life is essentially meaningless because we're all going die; (b) whatever career I picked made no real difference, so even being a truck-driver might be okay; and (c) I planned to spend my years living as authentically and ecstatically as possible.

I was too pigheaded to change my essays even when my parents suggested that I should. I imagined that the wise academic administrators would share my disdain for the status quo! Fat chance.

My first-choice school was Harvard. I remember going downtown to the office of a local Harvard alum, a stockbroker and a college football fan. He could hardly believe what he was hearing from me. "These existentialists you're going on about, that Sartre fellow, how old is he? Has he ever met a payroll?"

My second-choice college, Swarthmore, an elite private school near Philadelphia, was on the point of rejecting me as well. My father phoned up the admissions office with something like tears in his voice. "My son has a National Merit Scholarship. I thought—I thought that meant he could go to pretty much any school he liked."

I was furious and embarrassed at the old man's meddling. But it worked.

*I*n the summer of 1963, I started refusing to go to church. Given that my father was an Episcopal minister by now, this caused some family arguments—although eventually my weary parents just dropped the subject.

In many ways, Pop was proud of me, but in other ways I was getting to be a pain in the ass. There's a reason why you send your kids away from home and off to college.

Niles and I were getting drunk as often as we could, and endlessly bull-shitting about the meaning of life. Before I'd quit going to church, I'd sometime officiated as an acolyte, so I knew where the communion wine was stored. Every now and then I'd go and steal a bottle of that. But by now Niles was pretty good at buying bottles in liquor stores.

I didn't have a steady girlfriend, and I fell in with a younger girl named Susan. I met her at a party at some Kentucky mansion where she got my attention by stealing my glasses off my face. She was impressed by my literary aspirations—I gave her a copy of the Chevalier *Pegasus* with my stream-of-consciousness story about riding the bus home from school.

Susan's father was an overweight psychiatrist who strongly disapproved of me. Having read my Chevalier story, he told his daughter, "Rudy will be unhappy for his whole life."

But he didn't understand that when an author complains in his writing, he might actually be happy and having a good time. I was already coming to learn that whining on paper always puts me in a better mood.

This said, I was indeed anxious about my unknown future and sad to see my childhood years coming to a close.

In September, 1963, the same month that I was to go to Swarthmore, Pop took a job as the rector of a church in Alexandria, Virginia, a suburb of Washington DC. He'd been working as an assistant at St. Francis, but now he wanted a congregation of his own. He and Mom called the movers and put our house up for sale.

I was headed for a liberal, intellectual, co-ed college, and Niles was going to Columbia University in New York City—everything was working out just as we'd wanted it to. But we felt like condemned men. Our familiar lives were disappearing.

"Instead of saying goodbye, we should hit each other in the face with pies," I suggested to Niles.

"Great idea. Genius."

So I bought two frozen cream pies and let them thaw out overnight in our kitchen, and the morning before my parents and I were to drive off towards Northern Virginia, I met Niles at the strip of grass where his back yard met mine.

The pies looked flat and cold and dreary. We didn't bother shoving them at each other. We just said goodbye.

Sad to say, Niles and I hardly ever saw each other again. With both of us at college and my family no longer in Louisville, we were on diverging paths. With the best of will, it was rare that we managed to reunite. I've come to realize this often happens. The winds of life toss us about like tiny specks. No blame.

My Louisville years were over.

Spring Blossoms

On the morning in September, 1963, when my parents dropped me off for college in the little village of Swarthmore, Pennsylvania, Pop bought me a copy of Edwin Abbott's *Flatland* in the corner drugstore—the same book that Niles had been talking about the year before. Pop was into *Flatland* as a metaphor for personal salvation, rather than as tool for visualizing the fourth dimension. He saw A Square's trip out of the plane as a metaphor for a human being's contact with the higher reality of God.

An exalted start, but it's not like the guys in my dorm were budding philosophers. We used to have huge water fights that raged from floor to floor, people ambushing each other with waste-baskets filled from the faucet. There was one feisty little character who, when cornered, would put his hands up like fins and say, "Careful. I know karate."

In reality, none of us Swarthmore students was particularly tough—far from it. Even if we liked being wild and silly, everyone was smart. It was a real change from high school—as if I'd traveled to a different planet.

A lot of the students were New Yorkers, and nearly everyone was a big talker. We'd stand in the hallway of my dorm, discussing everything. Like—one of the older boys in the dorm got a chain letter saying that if he sent a dollar to the top person on this particular letter's list of ten people, removed that top name from the list, added his own name to the bottom, and then copied the new letter to ten people, within a few months he'd receive a fortune.

With relish we dissected the proposal. A upper classman, a political science major, pointed out that you'd do just as well to write the new letter without sending anyone a dollar at all and that, while you were at it, you'd do better to send the letter with your name on the list to *twenty* people instead of ten. I observed that ten to the tenth power was ten billion, and that ten billion was considerably larger than Earth's current population, so it was in fact impossible for our chain letter to parasitize enough victims for us to get returns.

"So we'll put our names close to the top," suggested the Poli-Sci major. But nobody wanted to bother writing out the letters.

My roommate was Kenneth Turan—tall, friendly, thick-lipped, and wearing heavy black-framed glasses. He came from a tough part of Brooklyn and sometimes he acted like an old man.

"Push that desk over there, Rudy. I'm sorry I can't help you, I've got a bad back."

We got in the habit of having long talks in the dark after we went to bed. We were both such provincials—each in our own way—that we were fascinated by each other's strange accents and curious cultures. Kenny had an insatiable appetite for facts about the Southern high-school scene, and in return, he'd tell me about his gritty life in Brooklyn.

"Some of these guys have *no mind*, Rudy. With the mouth you got, you wouldn't last two days."

Kenny had seen a zillion obscure movies in the theaters of New York, and he was a master at recounting their plots. One of his full-blown performances could take half an hour, and I'd feel like I was seeing the film unfold on the ceiling of our room. Sometimes, I'd later learn, Kenny's version might actually be better than the film itself. For years I wanted to see a murder movie called *Peeping Tom* that he'd told me about—and when, forty-five years, later I finally managed to rent it, the experience wasn't nearly as great as hearing Kenny tell it. It's no wonder that he ended up being a lead film-critic for the *Los Angeles Times* and for National Public Radio.

Through Kenny, I met an interesting pair of guys called Barry Feldman and Roger Shatzkin. They were both on the wrestling team, each of them only a little over five feet tall, and they shared a tiny room, squeezed into a bunk bed. They'd known each other in high school on Long Island, which meant that meeting them was like walking in on a couple having a long conversation. Or like meeting two of the Marx brothers.

Roger was somewhat buttoned-down and organized, but with a sneaking love for chaos. He seemed to know every blues or old-timey music record ever made, and he played the harmonica and the guitar. Barry was wild and messy, a natural-born artist, who'd say odd things like, "My name should be Stillborn—to show that, every second of every day, I'm still being born." Or, "Schmuck in Yiddish means your dick, but in German it means jewelry, so your dick is your ornament."

Barry was already an accomplished painter—I once spent an hour watching him busy with a pencil and paper, drawing a bush and capturing every snaky curve of the branches. When he was at work, his lively, sarcastic features would settle into an angelic calm.

Even more nourishing than the male bull-sessions were the conversations with women. They were everywhere—in my classes, in the dining-hall, on the grassy lawns, in the library. Utopia.

One sophomore girl knew my big brother, and she let me hang around with her a bit. She was into lettering words onto big sheets of poster board, coloring in the words to create something like a multidimensional poem— or maybe like a gossip magazine. I was happy when she added my name to her poster, labeling it: "Department Of Missing Persons."

Another girl I hung around with was a big fan of Bob Dylan—who was new to me—and I got hold of his first record. Loner poetry songs, wow! And Dylan was only the same age as Embry! Incredible. Our generation was taking over.

Every night after supper, there'd be a bunch of people on the front porch of the main campus building, some playing guitars and singing, others pitching pennies, still others playing the schoolyard game of "stretch" with table knives lifted from the dining hall. It was like I was finally having a happy childhood. All that I really needed now was a good girlfriend.

I found her on March 21, 1964, the day before my eighteenth birthday. Sylvia. I happened to sit down next to her on a charter bus taking students from Swarthmore to the Washington DC area for spring break—

Sylvia had a friend there, and I was going to see my parents, now in Alexandria, just south of DC.

Sylvia was beautiful, sophisticated and intelligent. I liked her smile and her laugh. We talked about Andy Warhol and Pop Art, about electric eels, and about the game of pretending your finger is a scythe reaching out the bus window to mow the landscape. Sylvia seemed to understand and appreciate me more than anyone I'd ever met in my life.

When I got back to Swarthmore after the spring break, it took me a few days to find her, as I'd gotten her last name wrong. Also she was two years ahead of me at school, so I couldn't find her in the freshman facebook. But then she appeared before me at the condiments table in the dining hall: shy yet confident, tall and eager, curvy-hipped, all smiles.

For our first date we went to all three concerts of the annual Swarthmore Folk Festival together. They had a great lineup of groups: Delta bluesmen, Chicago rockers, New York folkies, and even the fledgling Jefferson Airplane, complete with the first light show that any of us had ever seen—a loop of the cartoon Alice in Wonderland falling endlessly downward, overlaid by the soon-to-be-standard projection of dyed oil globs pulsing in a shallow glass dish.

Swarthmore had a strict curfew for the female students, and if you brought your date back to her dorm late, you had to wait outside with her until eventually the night watchman would show up on his rounds to let her in—and to report her for a demerit.

But the waiting was fun. Sylvia and I sat amid great spreading patches of blooming daffodils on the campus lawn, canopied by the elms and a damp, gently glowing spring sky. We liked to kiss. Not only was Sylvia the smartest woman I'd ever met, she was the best kisser. From the start, we felt just right for each other. A perfect fit, all the way down to the molecular level.

The summer after freshman year, I did some construction work in the developments sprouting up around my parents' new house in northern Virginia—and earned enough money to fly to Geneva, Switzerland, where Sylvia's family lived, and where she spent her summers.

I ended up working this same job several summers in a row, each time to earn money to visit Sylvia. Sometimes my job was running a tamper—an object about the size of an outboard motor-boat engine, with a broad, flat, metal foot on the bottom. After a new basement had been bulldozed out and tidied up with shovels, I'd guide the tamper over the dirt floor for an hour or two, flattening it.

Other times I'd drive a little tanker truck that dribbled water onto the development site's dirt roads, to keep the dust from blowing around and sticking to the fresh-painted houses. And then there were days when I'd just move from spot to spot around the construction site, doing whatever the foremen told me—cutting up metal rebar rods, collecting trash, or stacking lumber.

The interesting thing about the job was the juicy cross-section of blue-collar life that I met. I got to hang out with black men, some older than me, and some my own age. They had great accents, and a different way of seeing the world. Another guy with a memorable accent was a skinny old white hillbilly carpenter called Roller. Roller was always to be found with his partner, a taciturn man who was in some sense Roller's keeper or interpreter. Roller himself was like a high priest of weirdness, to be consulted only with caution. I treasured the pearls that fell from his lips.

"Looks like where the madwoman shits," Roller exclaimed one day, upon stepping into a room where some drunken housepainters had left a welter of empty cans. Another time, finding a room completely filled with stacks of wood trim, the sage observed, "T'ain't enough room to fuck a cat." Pondering his partner's scheme of getting construction work on the new US military bases going up in Vietnam, Roller remarked, "The pay is good, but the snipers are plentiful."

Sylvia's parents, Arpad and Pauline, were Hungarian émigrés. Arpad was a high-ranking diplomat, and Pauline, who'd been an office worker in Washington, was now a slightly reluctant homemaker. I think she missed her job. They lived in a classy high-rise apartment in Geneva, with balconies and yellow awnings on three sides. Soon after the war, Arpad had defected while at a conference in Paris, and Pauline had snuck

Sylvia, her brother, and a nanny across the Austrian border, paying the local guides with jewelry.

Pauline always said the nanny had been more trouble than the children. As soon as they hit Vienna, the nanny took off for Monte Carlo with a plan for winning at roulette—and when that didn't work out, she tried her luck in Hollywood. Meanwhile Sylvia and her family had found their way to Paris.

I'd rarely been around such worldly, charming people. Sylvia's mother was a chatterbox, never at a loss for words, and her father was an inveterate punster—for instance when the maid left a basket of fruit in my room, Arpad told me, "This can be the rudiments of your eating."

Embry, who was still in the army near the East German border, showed up at Sylvia's in a tiny little clown car, a subcompact Fiat. Embry and I followed Sylvia's family Mercedes up to the mountain resort of Zermatt for a week's stay. Embry was surprised to see me walking around the village with Sylvia holding hands. He'd had lots of women friends by now, but maybe he hadn't yet been in love.

Over the next few years, I went to Zermatt with Sylvia's family several times. The place blew my mind. For one thing, I began to realize that, with luck, I might keep on seeing Sylvia forever. And for another—I'd never been around high mountains. Spending a day on the mountain trails with Sylvia was an exact objective correlative for what I wanted to do with my life: climbing towards the peaks, exploring wild terrain, marveling over the wondrous flowers—all this with a sweet-voiced woman at my side.

Of course some days I'd want to push my hiking farther than the others did, and I'd head out alone, scrambling up impossibly steep meadows that would top out at—still more impossibly steep meadows.

I'd remember these climbs in graduate school, when I'd study transfinite set theory, with its notions of higher infinities piled above lower infinities. And when I'd write my SF novel about infinity, *White Light*, Zermatt's Alps would be very much in my mind. But all that came much later.

When I started college in 1963 I'd been planning to major in philosophy or in literature, even though Pop kept urging me to study something more technical. "You can read all those books on your own," he

97

insisted. "Read everything, sure, but learn science too. Be a Renaissance man!"

Although my natural bent was to disagree with Pop, after a couple of semesters, I decided he was right. I wasn't getting much out of the philosophy and literature courses that I was taking. When I asked my philosophy professor about the meaning of life, he deluged me with double-talk. And the English lit professor wanted us to plow through stuff like *Pamela* or *Vanity Fair*.

I found these English books so dull and square that I turned to reading their summaries in our library's treasured resource: *Masterplots*, a twelve volume set with the plot stories of the world's finest literature. Before long, I found it too enervating even to read the plot outlines of the assigned books. But by then it had became a running joke among the other introductory literature students always to check out the *Masterplots* volumes under the name Rudy Rucker.

At least in science you didn't have to read a whole lot of crap. I had a vague notion of majoring in physics and inventing an antigravity machine, but physics turned out not to be my strong suit either. After a grueling semester of Mechanics and Wave Motion—in which I tried unsuccessfully to make a hologram with a laser—I was off the physics track for good.

And so I majored in math. I had some difficulties with my initial calculus course, some basic issues in understanding what we were even talking about. But then I got a fellow student named Arnie Yanoff to help me. He explained the mysterious "chain rule" to me, talking about the infinitesimal quantities dx, dy and dz in a relaxed, cozy tone, as if we were discussing the doings of some little gnomes that lived beneath his floor.

After these first few hurdles, math came quite easily for me. I liked that there were so amazingly few brute facts to memorize. Given that everything followed logically from a few basic assumptions, there really wasn't all that much you had to learn. But you did have to work through some practice problems—which I generally enjoyed.

What else did I learn at college? A little about modern painting and architecture. And I took a German literature class where we read Kafka's *Metamorphosis* in the original German, which allowed me to understand that Kafka had meant for his stories to be in some sense funny. This insight would help me with my own writing. A story can be profound, creepy, lacerating, surreal—without being at all grim or stodgy.

But most of what I learned at college was from my fellow-students: offbeat styles of speech, disruptive behaviors, and real-time wit. I liked talking to my friends, flirting with the girls, walking around the grassy campus, and exploring the nearby Crum woods.

In grade school and high school I'd always been an outsider, but at Swarthmore I was in with the in-crowd. I reveled in that.

With my steady stream of C grades being mailed home semester after semester, Pop sensed how little work I was doing.

"It's like you're sitting at a great banquet, Rudy. And all you're doing is eating a ham sandwich that you brought in your pocket."

Concerned as he was, Pop even paid me a surprise visit one day—appearing in my dorm room in 1966, during the fall of my senior year. It ended up being the best day together that we ever spent. He was accepting and non-judgmental. We walked around the campus talking about the meaning of life. I even took him down to the Crum woods and showed him the impressively high train trestle that crossed the creek.

We boys liked to walk out to the middle of the trestle—it had two tracks so that, in principle, even if a train came by, you could go to the other side, and if, by some horrible fluke, two trains came at once, you could lie down flat between a pair of the rails and hold the ties, not that anyone I knew had ever executed this drastic maneuver, although we talked about it a lot, worrying that the train might have a dangling chain that hung to within millimeters of the ties.

Pop was being such a sport on our big day together that he even walked onto the trestle with me. For those few hours, it was like we were fellow college boys. He really didn't care much about proprieties or appearances. He just wanted me to be okay. He didn't want me to fall off the edge.

During my junior and senior years, Sylvia was off at grad school, so there were many days when I had nothing better to do than get into trouble.

One of my closest Swarthmore friends was a boy named Gregory Gibson. Greg loved drinking and writing as much as I did. He was an English major, and by way of helping to complete my education, on one wonderful rainy morning, he read the whole of *The Miller's Tale* to me in Old English, doing voices and adding glosses comparing the characters to our friends.

In 1966, in our junior year, Greg and I wrote a story called "Confessions of a Stag," using the style of the then-popular black humorist Terry Southern. Our piece was sophomoric, obscene, and very in-your-face. We wanted to transgress, to break free, to alarm the bourgeoisie. We mimeographed the story for a dozen of our friends. They liked it, and they even discussed it with each other.

Due to our heavy drinking, Greg and I became notorious around the campus. We two ended up rooming together senior year. We were known as Dog and Pig or, more affectionately, as Woofie and Oinker. I was Pig.

In part I took on this name in honor of the character Pig Bodine in Thomas Pynchon's novel, *V.*, which I was avidly studying at the time. You could also say that I think of the pig as my totem animal. The pinkness, the grunting, the comfortable curves, the easeful wallow in the mud, the floppy ears, the occasional frantic squeal, the wonderfully curly tail.

Back in grade school, my friend Niles and I used to walk to a nearby pasture with pigs and stare at them, sometimes throwing a stick or a rock to get them to run around. And I'd been delighted when our neighbor Mr. Keith told me that pigs are the most difficult of animals to pen in—as they always tend to find a way out. As I often liked to tell my friends at Swarthmore, "The pig is the most intelligent of animals."

*T*he Sixties juggernaut was cranking up, and we'd begun smoking pot when we could get it. Pot was so new that whenever we smoked it, we worried we might go crazy and never come back. Greg in particular tended to become unhappy when he was high.

"I take to pot like a duck takes to Christmas dinner," he'd say. Nevertheless he tended to glom as much of it off me as he could.

There was one boy named Trevor who was one of the first to be able to score pot regularly—which was still incredibly hard in those days. Trevor would come over to our room and turn on a bunch of us. The downside was that then we'd have to listen to Trevor—and he was nuts.

One time in 1966, after he'd gotten about five of us high, Trevor started pacing around like a ham actor playing Mephistopheles. He leaned down and stuck his face into mine.

"Mr. Rucker! For lease—or altar?" His tones were stern and clipped, like a Grand Inquisitor's.

I had no idea what Trevor meant. In my disoriented state, I thought he was threatening to sacrifice me, or to take possession of my soul. Mutely I shook my head. Trevor posed the question to the next boy. Eventually one of us figured out that Trevor was simply inquiring about our sense of the pot's effects. He was saying, "Release or alter?"

The biggest freak-out of my life was the time I ate some big green hairy buds of peyote cactus. I wouldn't want to undergo such an ordeal again, although the experience was memorable, and, over the years, I've used bits of it in my fiction. My SF mentor Robert Sheckley once remarked, "A writer is someone willing to descend to Hell and suffer the torments of the damned, just so they're assured they can write about it."

I recall being menaced by the leering trees, falling into a Renoir painting, becoming a pinball in a flashing machine, and having a friend's kitchen morph into a lecture hall with me a professor lecturing on relativity—which was, precognitively enough, something I'd actually be doing about ten years later. It's odd how now and then you really do see into the future. The world is strange.

The longer I stayed at Swarthmore, the worse my grades became. I had to suffer through a number of sit-down meetings with the deans. One of them was a spunky old woman with a Southern accent. Dean Cobbs.

"Why don't you go to your classes?" she asked me. "It hurts the professors' feelings when their students don't attend. Isn't there anything we're offering that you want to learn? Tell me, Rudy, what career would you choose if you could?"

"I—I guess I'd like to be a science fiction writer."

"Then do that! Practice your writing. Follow your dream."

I did write a little bit, now and then, using the little portable Olivetti typewriter that my mother had given me. I was still making the beginning author's mistake of writing when I was drinking—depending on the beer to lower my fear of the blank page. But drunk writing very often turns into posing or sentimentality

Greg shared my interest in writing and in the Beats. He and I wrote a couple of things together—first of all that memorable porno pastiche which I mentioned earlier, and, after college, the start of an SF novel. Eventually Greg became a rare book dealer and a fellow author. His works include *Gone Boy*, a memoir revolving around his son's tragic murder by a rampage shooter, and *Hubert's Freaks*, a true account of a bookseller's discovery of rare Diane Arbus photos.

In college, Greg and I liked to quote passages from William Burroughs's *Junky* and *The Yage Letters* to each other, and we spoke of Burroughs as *Der Meister* (The Master), affecting ourselves to be apprentices in some celestial academy of Beatdom.

Part of the appeal of Burroughs was something I'd noticed back in high school: his work was like incredibly cool science fiction. I found that Kerouac himself was interested in SF as well. The Beats regarded the genre as an avant-garde and uniquely American art form, a bit like jazz. For me, that's still how I think of SF when I'm writing it—as mass-market surrealism, as experimental literature, as the fiction of our time.

Although I wasn't actively reading much SF in college, in my senior year, I came upon the paperback novel *Time Out of Joint*, by Philip K. Dick, a writer new to me. It had trippy stuff like a lemonade stand turning into a slip of paper saying "LEMONADE STAND." One time a stoned friend was visiting our room, and he kept picking up the book and grinning and pointing at the word "*Joint*" in the title. In an odd, random way this was actually a good comment about the book, which I found mind-expanding in a new way.

Dick's wonderfully colloquial work struck me as a definite step towards true beatnik science fiction, towards a literature that was ecstatic and countercultural, but with logic and rigor to its weirdness.

Greg and I decorated our room to look like a disco. We found some long cardboard tubes behind a rug-store, and I trimmed them so that they fit between our floor and ceiling like the trunks of trees. Now I was the Magic Pig of the Enchanted Forest.

I painted a watercolor mural on the inside of our room's door, we taped up color comics of such sexy animals as Daisy Duck and Petunia Pig, and we erected a pyramid of bricks surmounted by a glaring Tensor reading lamp. We called this the Temple of the Barely Subhumans. When we were high, we'd turn on the Tensor lamp, and lurch around it, goofing on our caveman shadows on the ceiling.

Such larks.

Some weekends I'd take the bus to visit Sylvia at her grad school, or she would come to visit me. During my junior year she was at Wesleyan University in Connecticut, and in my senior year she was at the University of Pennsylvania, right in Philadelphia.

We were lovers by now, and very tender with each other.

One spring night in 1966, we walked in a campus meadow dotted with blooming plum trees. We stood beneath a tree, kissing, and I shook the trunk. Sweet-smelling pastel petals drifted onto Sylvia's upturned face, the petals like snow, or like confetti for a wedding.

"I love this," said Sylvia, warm and close. There seemed to be no end to the blossoms.

Some nights she'd share my dorm room's chaste single bed with me. She'd push my long, floppy hair off my face and admire me.

"This is my darling Ru's forehead. Nobody sees it but me."

I could hardly believe that a woman was being so tender with me. I wanted to treasure Sylvia and take care of her for the rest of my life.

When I was home for the holidays with my parents at Christmas, 1966, my brother was finally back from the army, and looking to stir up some trouble.

"I guess you'll be needing one of these pretty soon, huh, Rudy?" said Embry, pointing at a full-page ad for diamond rings. Naturally he said this in front of my mother.

Mom started vibrating with joy and approval. She and Pop were crazy about Sylvia. The next thing I knew, I'd gone to the bank to withdraw my leftover construction-work money, and had driven with Mom to Galt Jewelers to pick out an engagement ring.

And while I was at it, I wrote a letter Sylvia's father, asking for permission to marry her. Sylvia told him to say yes. Arpad appreciated this old-school approach. Sylvia says he made a point of using the best possible stationery to write me back.

There was some business about the jeweler having to fabricate the engagement ring and to mail it to me at Swarthmore, so it wasn't till early February, 1967, that I actually presented it to Sylvia. We were standing on a snowy hillside in the Crum woods by the Swarthmore campus, the sun sending flashes off colored light off the ice-crystals, and off our little diamond. A threshold moment.

*I*t was a snowy winter. I took to ice-skating up the Crum creek from my dorm to the campus—a roundabout route, but a rewarding one. And while I skated I thought about my uncertain future.

The Vietnam War was ramping up, and they were drafting more boys my age all the time. I had a self-destructive, adventure-seeking, prove-my-manhood streak that made me want to join the combat. But at a more rational level, I knew full well that—not to mince words—I didn't want to die for nothing in a phony war launched by ruling-class oppressors who despised me, my friends, and everything that we stood for.

Although it was hard to get any iron-clad protection against the draft, being married helped a little, as did being a student. Deep down I'd begun expecting to end up as a professor—by now I wasn't really fit for anything else. I certainly didn't want to take some math-related office job as a statistician, analyst or accountant. And so I began applying to grad schools.

I'd thought I might be able to slide in on the basis of my scores on standardized tests, which I still had the ability to ace. But, unlike when I'd been applying to colleges, I didn't have any good grades or glowing reference letters to back me up. I had a straight C average in college, and my math professors hardly knew me, as I so rarely attended class.

In the end, it was my impending union with Sylvia that got me into a Ph. D. program. She'd been accepted into the French graduate program at Rutgers University in New Jersey with a big scholarship, and the chairman of the French department prevailed upon the chairman of the Mathematics department to admit the bozo that this brilliant woman was about to marry.

Senior week at college was strange. All the other students were gone, and the campus had the feeling of an empty stage set. A shooting war had broken out in the Middle East, and Uncle Sam was stalking our cohort like the Grim Reaper. We partied like mad. There was a lot of good fellow-feeling among my classmates. I realized that in my own oblique way, I'd made a memorable impression on some of them. But then Swarthmore sent us on our way.

The next week I was in Geneva, getting married to Sylvia. The wedding was in June, 1967, at the American Episcopal Church, with none other than Pop officiating. And Embry was the best man. Right before the service, we three were waiting behind the altar, and we very nearly succumbed to a giggling fit. We were elated, excited, and anxious. But then Sylvia appeared, young and vibrant, lovely in her dress, and all was calm.

"The best day's work I ever did," Pop would say in later years, beaming at us. And if Sylvia and I ever had a temporary falling out, my parents always took her side.

After the wedding, Sylvia and I borrowed her parents' car and we took off on a honeymoon trip to Spain. Red poppies bloomed by the roadsides, just like in an Impressionist painting. Children by the roadsides sold bunches of cherries with the stems woven together to make massive braids. Sylvia would hold two skeins of cherries up like earrings, and then she'd eat them all.

At nights we'd stay in clean, inexpensive hotels, marveling that we were married. Sylvia was putting her hair into little pigtails, so she didn't have to worry about fixing it every day. We had fun seeking out new pigtail holders, which were little sets of two glass balls connected by a rubber band. She was wearing silky miniskirts and she had a good tan. She looked wonderful.

When we got back the US, my parents for some reason couldn't pick us up, so Pop sent one his parishioners. When the old guy saw Sylvia in her pigtails and her minidress, he just about lost it.

I'd married a babe.

Summer of Love

I n the fall of 1967, Sylvia and I moved into a top-floor apartment in a brick building in Highland Park, New Jersey, not far from Rutgers University. The rent was a hundred dollars a month. The sunny, white-painted bedroom felt like the inside of an egg. We decorated the place with colored-paper collages and made hanging mobiles of sticks and shells and pieces of glass.

Sometimes in bed, we'd put our mouths next to each other and sing very nearly the same soprano note: "Looooo." The fun thing was that, if we made our voices ever so slightly out of pitch with each other, the overlapping notes would create an auditory moiré pattern, that is, a series of pulsing beats that grew more rapid as we brought our voices ever closer to perfect harmony. Two hearts beating as one.

M y parents phoned us every single day. I'd been pretty much off their radar at college, but now they were really nosing in. If I'd been alone, I probably wouldn't have answered the phone, or if I had, I wouldn't have talked to them much. But Sylvia was always polite to them. They were banking on that. I think they were feeling lonely, or maybe not getting along with each other so well—so it was a nice break for them to talk to us, picking up the vibe of our happiness and our youth.

But after a year or two the daily calls were getting to us. Phones didn't come with jacks back then, or on/off switches, so I bought some parts and fashioned a jack for the single heavy black phone that sat by our dining-table. That way we could at least unplug it during meals.

Every couple of weeks Sylvia and I would take the bus into Manhattan—the bus was a little cheaper than the train. The bus arrived at the memorably seedy Port Authority Bus Terminal. Walking through that lobby was like reading a page out of William Burroughs. And then you got to take the subway! New York was so great.

We often ended up on upper Fifth Avenue, admiring the fancy stores and fashionable people, and we liked checking out the Museum of Modern Art. We saw Salvador Dali in that neighborhood a couple of times, and once we got up the courage to say hello to him in the lobby of the St. Regis hotel. He didn't really want to talk, so he scribbled a signature on a post-card and handed it to me. Sylvia and I were proud of ourselves.

Now and then we'd hit the Village, not that much was happening there in the daytime. And Greg had introduced us to a certain seafood house in Times Square, the McGinnis House of Clams. Sylvia and I would go there for cherrystones and littlenecks, toasting our absent friend. Greg was obsessed with the novel *Moby Dick*, but, unable to face the rigmarole of grad school, he'd enlisted in the Navy. Although they'd promised to make him a frogman, he ended up as a shipfitter, working in a shipboard metal shop, spending the better part of four years anchored in the San Diego Bay.

Greg and I wrote each other frequent letters about our diverging lives, and I wrote my other college friends as well. As I mentioned before, the letter-writing formed my real apprenticeship as a writer. I was learning to write like with natural cadences and a casual vocabulary.

In 1968, Greg and I tried writing a novel together, mailing sections back and forth. I saw the projected book as a science fiction novel called *The Snake People*—about telepathic, wriggling beings that dart through your mind when you're high. Greg saw the book as a wry slice-of-life description of a young guy's experiences in the Navy. The main characters were fictional versions of Greg and me. Parts of the draft made me laugh a lot.

I learned something from our experiment. I'd found that using myself and my friends as characters in a science fiction novel appealed to me very much. Much later on I'd begin calling this technique transrealism, and I'd write, "A Transrealist Manifesto," which appeared in the *Bulletin of the Science Fiction Writers of America* in 1983.

But in 1968 Greg and I didn't push *The Snake People* to a conclusion. We thought we had more important things to do.

M e, I was learning math. For the first time in my life, I was taking courses that I found difficult in an interesting way: abstract algebra, real analysis, topology, and mathematical logic. And, for the first time since high school, I was attending all the class lectures and doing the homework.

Sylvia was finishing her Master's degree in French literature. In the evenings, Sylvia and I would do homework together in our little living room. It was cozy. I liked hearing about the wild books she had to read. I remember her reading aloud to me, in French, from a medieval play about the Garden of Eden, making her voice high and thin for Eve saying, "*Dit moi, Satan,*" or "Tell me, Satan."

She also read me Guillaume Apollinaire's great surreal poem of 1912, "Zone," with its epic opening lines, "*A la fin tu es las de ce monde ancien / Bergère ô tour Eiffel le troupeau des ponts bêle ce matin / Tu en as assez de vivre dans l'antiquité grecque et romaine,*" or "You're finally sick of the ancient world / O shepherdess Eiffel tower the flock of bridges bleats this morning / You've had enough of living in Greek and Roman antiquity."

The Rutgers math department was giving me some financial support as a teaching assistant, and I met twice a week with a section of calculus students to show them how to do their homework problems—they got their lectures from a professor in a big hall. Working through the problems on the board, I finally began to understand calculus myself. It made a lot more sense than I'd realized before.

I was undergoing a constant cascade of mathematical revelations. The mathematical logic course had an especially strong effect on me. Not only was mathematics a map of an unseen real world, it was also a formal system of axioms that we made deductions from. The net of logic bid fair to capture the shiny fish of truth.

I reveled in the hieroglyphic conciseness of symbolic logic, which led me to a deeper level of understanding about even such simple things as the use of zeroes, or the nature of subtraction. I was mastering a new set of mental tools, and everything was coming into focus.

Philosophically, I was beginning to see everything as a mathematical form. But emotionally, everything was love.

Sylvia and I enjoyed the Sixties—we went to the big march on the Pentagon, we had psychedelic posters on our walls, we wore buffalo hide sandals, and we read *Zap Comix*. I smoked pot rolled in paper flavored like strawberries or wheat straw or bananas. Sylvia bought herself a sewing-machine and started making herself brightly patterned dresses.

At the same time, the war in Vietnam was casting its bitter pall. Those who didn't live through those times tend not to understand how strongly the males of my generation were radicalized against the United States government. It grated on me that our so-called leaders wanted to send us off to die, and that they called us cowards if we wouldn't go. It broke my heart to see less-fortunate guys my age being slaughtered. My hair was shoulder-length by now, and occasionally strangers would scream curses at me from cars.

We were friends with a wild math grad student named Jim Carrig, from an Irish family in the Bronx. Jim and his wife, Fran, were huge Rolling Stones fans—they were always talking about the Stones and playing their records. They knew how to sign up early to get a shot at the tickets to the touring Stones shows, and in July, 1972, they took us to see the band play at a wonderful afternoon show at Madison Square Garden.

"Did y'all get off school today?" asked Mick, strutting back and forth. "We did too."

And then they played "Midnight Rambler" and Mick whipped the stage with his belt—a trick that Jim and I took to emulating at home.

The Carrigs threw great Halloween parties. They lived in an apartment on the second floor of a house, and Jim would stand at the head of the stairs like a bouncer, checking up on his guests' attire.

"Get the fuck outta here!" he'd yell if anyone showed up without a costume. "Go on, we don't wanna see you!"

I remember coming to Jim's 1969 Halloween party as a Non-Fascist Pig. That is, I bought some actual pig ears at a store called Fabulous Meat City, punched holes in them, threaded a piece of string through them, and tied them onto my head. I lettered, "Fuck Nixon," onto my T-shirt. I pinned on a five-pointed Lunchmeat Award of Excellence star that I'd cut from a slice of Lebanon bologna. And I carried a pig-trotter in my pocket to hold out if anyone wanted to shake hands with me.

When Sylvia and I went to see the left-wing movie *Joe* in the summer of 1970, the movie theater played "The Star Spangled Banner" before the film, and there was nearly a fight when a guy two rows ahead of us wouldn't stand up. Turned out the guy was a Viet vet himself.

"That's why I went to fight," the vet told the older man harassing him. "To keep this a free country. I don't have to stand up for no goddamn song."

I was very nearly drafted that summer myself, undergoing a physical that classified me 1A—meaning prime choice cannon fodder. I'd thought that my missing spleen would earn me a medical exemption, but no dice. I still remember the medical officer who told me the bad news. Sidney W. Tiesenga. He seemed to have a chip on his shoulder. Maybe he'd been drafted himself.

I bought some time by faking an asthma attack—and then they switched to a lottery system for the draft, and I happened to get a comfortably low-priority number. I wasn't going to Vietnam after all. I was going to keep on learning math, being a newlywed, and having fun.

The tidal wave of underground comix inspired me to get some Rapidograph pens and to start drawing comics on my own. I developed a wacky, left-wing strip called *Wheelie Willie* that occasionally appeared in the Rutgers campus newspaper, the *Targum*, during the years 1970 and 1971. I felt uneasy about my ability to draw arms and legs, so my character Wheelie Willie had a snake-like body that ended in a bicycle wheel.

As I was paranoid about being busted for the politics and the drug humor of *Wheelie Willie*, I published it under a pseudonym, Rubber v. B. Tire. None of the people at the paper knew my real name. Some of the students must have liked the strip, as a fraternity once went so far as to have a *Wheelie Willie* party. But, anonymous as I was, I only found out about that party after it happened.

My fellow math grad student Dave Hungerford had a lively sense of humor, and was very plugged into the burgeoning hippie culture. He was the one who turned me on to underground comix—he showed me how to find them in what he termed "the commie bookstore," an independent shop run by an old leftie couple straight from the 1930s.

Dave was a skinny guy with an odd way of talking, and he looked more like a TV repairman than like a hippie. He liked using words in odd ways, for instance he always said "Rug-ters" instead of "Rutgers," and "pregg-a-nit" instead of "pregnant." His father had been a housepainter, and he liked to talk about color combinations he'd like to try in his apartment.

"Wal, I think I'll paint these living room walls taupe, with the faintest touch of red in it. And then I'll use a pale vegetable green on the moldings."

He was the first of us to turn thirty, and threw a big party at his apartment. None of us could believe that one of our number was turning thirty. It was like sighting the icy walls of the Antarctic continent.

Mild-mannered though he seemed, Dave was a troublemaker. When he arrived for our grad student orientation session at the start of the first year, he told me that he'd demonstrated against all three of the current presidential candidates: Humphrey, Nixon, and Wallace. And he'd been arrested in the Chicago convention riots. He was always going off to marches and demonstrations. Once, in 1968, he even roped Sylvia and me into making a trip to give support to the AWOL soldiers in the brig at Fort Dix. The soldiers gave us the finger.

Distracted by politics, Dave was an indifferent student, given to napping in the comfortable leather chairs of the Rutgers library. He spent a lot of time worrying about the pigs—that is, the FBI, CIA, Secret Service, Republican party operatives, and ordinary police. He thought they might come after him for his radical politics, which wasn't out of the question in those times.

A poster on a wall in Dave's apartment warned, "The Ears Have Walls." At one point he wanted to keep an escape suitcase in the apartment where Sylvia and I lived, a little get-away case with clothes, some money, and—a gun.

"No way are you bringing a gun into our apartment," Sylvia told him.

In honor of the Beatles 1969 *Abbey Road* album, Sylvia and I had gotten a nice KLH stereo. And now Dave Hungerford got me to start listening to Frank Zappa, who came to be my favorite musician for many years. I'd listen endlessly to Zappa on my record player, sometimes using earphones. Sylvia and I went up to the Fillmore East in New York to see Zappa in person few times as well, sometimes with Dave Hungerford along.

Over time, I developed an ability to hear entire Zappa songs in my head, note for note, as if in real time—that is, it would take me just as much time to play a song mentally as it would have taken to hear it on the radio. Remembering an entire song wasn't actually that hard, now that I was continually honing my mind's sharpness by studying insanely complex mathematical proofs.

One special night in 1969, I was home alone, listening to the song, "The Nancy and Mary Music" from Zappa's epochal disk, *Chunga's Revenge*. During the song's rhythmic chanting sequence that bounces between the left and right speaker channels, I had a peak moment of inspiration. I took up my cartoon-drawing pencil and my art-gum eraser and began sketching pictures of the *Flatland* hero A Square.

I'd always related to A Square, partly because my high-school math teacher Brother Emeric used to call me R Squared, and partly because A Square was a visionary who tried to teach his fellows about a higher dimension. I drew A Square with a nice cartoony eyeball-in-profile, and I drew his wife as a wiggly line segment ending with a similar kind of eye.

Beginning to illustrate the adventures of *Flatland*, I thought of further adventures that A Square might have—this was something I'd been meaning to do for several years. And I began writing a simple text to accompany the pictures. Over the next five years, this project of mine would grow into a set of lecture notes, and eventually into my first published book: *Geometry, Relativity and the Fourth Dimension*, 1977.

Sylvia and I also hung out with Eddie Marritz. I'd gone to Swarthmore with Eddie's big brother Don, who was in Vietnam now. Don had enlisted in an intelligence branch of the Army, hoping to get a comfortable deal like my brother Embry, but they had him riding in helicopters to debrief covert operatives who'd been sent into Laos. He doesn't like to talk about it. Don still argues that, on his return from Nam, our grateful government should have given him a lifetime free pass to major league baseball games.

So far as I know, Don was the only one of my classmates who actually ended up in Nam, which was a sad paradox, as he was the gentlest of us all. Fortunately he survived, got a law degree, and became a heroic public defender, capable of making a federal case of a seemingly mundane tenant-landlord dispute. Back in college, Don and I loved doing word puzzles together, and to this day we exchange excited emails whenever there's a cryptic crossword in the Sunday *Times* magazine.

Sylvia and I got to know Don's younger brother Eddie in September, 1968, when he showed up for his freshman year at Rutgers. When I first saw Eddie on campus, he was wearing a pair of Don's old sunglasses. It was like a weird flashback to my own freshman year. I was struck by a realization that carried the force of a blow: my four college years were truly over.

I was practically in tears over how old I was getting—this at the age of twenty-two! There was no going back, I was married now. It occurred to me that I might as well take the next step down the road: having a baby with Sylvia. With a strange mixture of joy and sorrow I laid out these thoughts to her. She liked the idea of having a baby. She said she'd always wanted to have a family, but she hadn't known I'd be ready this soon. So now that was in the cards. But not quite yet. Maybe in a few months.

Eddie was a lovable kid, and we took him under our wing as if he were a younger brother. It turned out that Eddie always knew where to get pot. Later on, in 1971, he and his roommate had a whole Wheaties box full of the stuff, with a thin layer of oat flakes on the top to disguise their stash.

Eventually this madness became too much for Eddie, and he dropped out of Rutgers, moved in with a woman named Hana in New York City, studied film at Hunter College, and became a successful cinematographer. Eddie and Hana have lived in that same New York apartment for going on forty years now, raising two children along the way. Ah, rent control.

Our friend Roger Shatzkin, a classmate from Swarthmore, was studying English literature at Rutgers while Sylvia and I were there. Roger had an erudite demeanor, and a precise, cautious manner of speech.

Back in college, we'd bonded during a series of conversations in which we'd shared every scrap of information that we'd learned about sex during our extensive researches—into books. Roger was the only guy I ever met who'd actually read Richard von Krafft-Ebing's *Psychopathia Sexualis*. His dentist father had a hell of a home library.

Seeing more of Roger at Rutgers I got to know him quite well. We'd talk things over, trying to figure out what was going on around us. The endless war, the collapse of our government's legitimacy, the demonstrations, the riots and the drugs.

"I've been thinking that studying for my classes is a meaningless social hangup," Roger remarked one day. "It's playing the Man's game—being a plastic person, a tool, a cog. And then I started thinking of ways to push that argument—like paying rent is a meaningless hangup too, so, okay, I should be sleeping on your couch. But how far does it go? Like—what about breathing? Is it a meaningless social hangup to play the breathing game?"

Impoverished students that we were, Sylvia and I spent any number of evenings playing Scrabble with Eddie, Roger, and David Hungerford, usually listening to music, often smoking pot, and occasionally watching late night television, perhaps with the sound turned off and a record playing. I learned that essentially any track of music will wittily illuminate and comment upon any segment of video at all. We're quick to see connections.

Now and then I'd even watch TV with the sound on and once, in 1968, I somehow reached the point of drafting a heartfelt letter to the talk-show host Johnny Carson about the concepts of infinity and the fourth dimension, both of which I felt he'd mentioned (albeit indirectly) on his show.

"When Johnny reads this letter, he's gonna think it's from a real nut," I told Sylvia proudly.

"And he'll be right," she said.

*I*n 1968, I took a class on mathematical logic, taught by an interesting but difficult character called Erik Ellentuck. He had a medical condition that made his limbs skeletally thin, and he walked and wrote on the blackboard with considerable difficulty. He sometimes claimed that his condition had resulted from a motorcycle accident, although, in retrospect,

I think it's more likely that he suffered from anorexia. But that didn't occur to me at the time.

Whatever his problems, Ellentuck was an engaging man with a brilliant mind. But he was a little lazy about teaching. Once he gave our class an extremely difficult assignment that we didn't know how to begin. Rather than explaining how we should proceed, he proposed that we form teams of two students each and help each other. And then, for the grading, he'd simply talk to one student from each team to inquire what we'd done.

I ended up paired with a young rabbi named Arthur. Arthur had little understanding of the course material, and no time or inclination to work on our homework, so whatever small progress we made was due to me. But Ellentuck respected Arthur for being a rabbi, so when it was time to grade our joint work, it was Arthur whom he called into his office. We ended up with a fairly low grade.

I had the impression that Ellentuck supposed that I been leeching off Arthur, rather than the other way around. So I visited his office as well, and talked that over with him. We found that we liked discussing math together.

Not too long after this, Ellentuck invited Sylvia, me and another student for a meal at his house. He was married to a Japanese woman whose father was a well-known neo-impressionist artist in Japan. The meal was good, and we got to drink a lot of hot sake from wooden cups. Sylvia was disturbed by the fact that, throughout the dinner, Ellentuck kept a loaded pistol sitting on the table beside his plate. Not that he was actively threatening us—surely the gun was only there to impress us. You had to feel a little sorry for this weird emaciated man.

I was learning that, if I was going to be a mathematician, I needed to recalibrate any preconceived notions I had about not being friends with extremely weird or socially inept people. Of all the outré subcultures that I eventually became involved with, mathematicians take the crown for being strange—and never mind about hippies, science fiction writers, punk rockers, computer programmers, or Berkeley cyberfreaks.

One of our Rutgers math professors, the short, ropy-lipped Harry Gonshor, was so amazingly off the norm that even the other profs were in awe of him. He wore extremely powerful glasses, and he kept his head perpetually tilted back, so that the glasses seemed to be staring up at you like a toad's eyes. At all times he carried a briefcase filled with his scribbled math manuscripts.

Someone told me that Gonshor had been drafted into the army a few years earlier, and that, all through base camp, no matter what the officers said to him, he'd refused to put down his briefcase, not even when he was crawling under barbed wire on the obstacle course. Finally the army gave up and released him as unfit for military service.

Once Sylvia and I sat with Gonshor on the train into New York City, where he was headed for a meeting of the Game Club. As with most odd mathematicians—once you sat down and talked with the guy, he turned out to be fascinating and intelligent.

Another memorably weird guy was my fellow mathematics grad student David Slater. Slater had extremely long hair and a tangled beard. He had black lines of dirt under his long fingernails. He often wore an opera cape. He had trouble remembering other people's names, and would regularly greet me by holding up a wizardly finger and declaiming my middle name—which had somehow found a home in his densely packed brain.

"Ah! Von Bitter!"

Slater was the only one of us who bothered to learn anything about computers in those early years. The rest of us assumed we'd never have to deal with those lowly, infernal machines.

By the spring of 1969, Sylvia had finished the course work for our Master's degrees. Sylvia now had to take an oral exam to get her Master's degree. Although she was one of the best students in the program, she was very anxious about the orals—in fact she postponed taking them by a semester. When the big day came, I waited for Sylvia outside the building where she was taking her exam. With nothing else to do besides worry, I focused on the beauty of the physical world. The sun was setting, illuminating the ivy on an old brick wall. And then Sylvia emerged, looking wrung out, but triumphant. When they asked her the first question, her mind had gone utterly blank. But the teachers knew her and liked her. They'd coaxed her along until suddenly she'd remembered everything. She'd passed.

I was going for a Ph. D., but before starting my thesis, I too had to pass a set of oral exams—these were in the summer of 1969. The math orals were only given once a year, so there were a bunch of us sweating out the preparations. This one guy, call him Roper, had found some weird book of trick problems in higher math, and every time I saw him, he'd zing me with one of them. He was convinced the orals would be all trick questions. I wondered if I'd be able to pass.

The morning of the orals, I saw Roper in the hall, white as a sheet, with his wife next to him, propping him up. He was vomiting every fifteen minutes. He didn't pass the exams.

The way the test was set up, we went from room to room, fielding questions about mathematical subspecialties by different little groups of professors. When I saw Harry Gonshor sitting in with the first group to grill me, I realized this was going to be okay. It was just a matter of talking with some crazy mathematicians. And by now I knew how to do that. I passed the exam.

Despite all the warning flags surrounding his prickly personality, I asked Erik Ellentuck to be my thesis advisor. In some ways, I liked how unusual the man was. And I found his specialty, mathematical logic, to be the most interesting of the available areas of higher mathematics. I was particularly interested in the area of mathematical logic known as set theory. Set theory teases out facts about different levels of higher infinity.

To me, set theory felt like mathematical theology—which was a perfect fit for those late Sixties times. And there were certain big problems in set theory that remained stubbornly unsolved. Now that I'd really started studying, I had dreams of becoming a famous mathematician.

Perhaps, at the gambling tables of set theory, I could break the bank of the infinite.

White Light

Late in 1968, Sylvia got pregnant and her belly began to grow. It was amazing. Somewhat recklessly, in June of 1969, when Sylvia was in her seventh month, she and I flew down to visit Embry at his new home on the tiny island of South Caicos, near the end of the long chain of West Indies islands angling out into the Atlantic from the tip of Florida.

After Embry had been released from the army, he'd gotten a pilot's license. He was working for Caicos Airways, flying small planes among the islands. He'd met an Irish woman named Noreen who'd been visiting her sister down there. Noreen was wearing a bikini, and Embry proposed to her on the spot. Love at first sight.

They were married in Ireland by a Catholic priest in 1968. Perversely, my father didn't attend the wedding, and Sylvia and I couldn't afford to go either. Loyal Mom was the only one at the wedding to back Embry up. I still feel bad about this.

It was fascinating to visit Embry and Noreen on South Caicos—everything was slow-paced, and things often happened hours or even days after they were scheduled. Embry called it "island time." Wild donkeys roamed around, eating people's gardens. One of the neighbors owned a skinny, mean pig whom he'd named Embry.

Near the end of our visit in the summer of 1969, we all went to stay with Noreen's sister, who lived on the slightly more cosmopolitan island of Grand Turk. One of Embry's friends there took us SCUBA diving—a spacy, otherworldly experience that I would come to love for the rest of my life. Diving is as close to magical flight or to drifting in outer space as we can get.

I'm fascinated by undersea creatures—the sponges and corals seem like cross-sections of hyperdimensional beings. Often as not, when I need to describe some science fictional beings or settings, I fall back on images I've gleaned from snorkeling and diving.

After our visit to the Turks and Caicos Islands, it was back to New Jersey. Sylvia's pregnancy was coming to term. By now she was uncomfortable no matter what position she was in. The last night before the birth, I made us a little picnic, and we ate with Dave Hungerford in the park across the street from our apartment building. Sylvia was walking around in an A-shaped blue dress, peering at flowers, lovely in the gathering dusk.

"She looks like Alice in Wonderland," said Dave.

None of our friends had babies yet, and natural childbirth was relatively unheard of—so when Sylvia went into labor on the night of August 22, 1969, we went to the hospital with no idea what to expect.

It felt strange to be living out so basic and traditional a human scenario, Sylvia huge and in pain, me staring unseeing at magazines in the waiting room. And then a nurse wheeled out a bed with Sylvia—she was still alive! And a second nurse was holding our baby, a little girl, her skin a little waxy looking. Yes, she had ten fingers. One of her bright little eyes was open, and I felt she could see me. One of her pinkies waved. We named her Georgia.

Sylvia was breast-feeding Georgia, but after we got home, to make things a little easier, every night at three a.m. I'd feed the baby a tiny bottle no bigger than a bottle of ink. That first night at home, it was wonderful to see baby Georgia resting on my forearm, the size of a small loaf of bread, slurping at the bottle in a disorganized newborn way. The moonlight came in through the window behind me, spilling silver over my shoulder and onto the white ink-bottle and the earnest round brow. This was our baby. Our lives had changed forever.

As a grad student, I had plenty of free time, and I took care of Georgia quite a bit. Sylvia and I were a little unsure of ourselves—I wished the hospital had have given us a book of instructions. Before the nurses sent us on our way, all they did was show us how to change a diaper and how to wrap the baby in a blanket.

But we had our baby care book by Dr. Spock. We were always thumbing through the index, looking up "crying: redness in, blueness in, shrillness of . . ." For some reason, Dr. Spock was on the Presidential ballot that year, running under the aegis of the People's Party. Given how often I was consulting his book, I went ahead and voted for him.

Georgia was indeed a big crier for her first few months. Mom and Pop said I'd been the same way too.

"But was I cute?" I asked Mom.

"Of course," put in Pop. "But mostly you cried."

I liked caring for Georgia—wheeling her around in her carriage, holding her up in the air, feeding her mushy cereal, bathing her, singing to her in her crib. Every day she seemed a little different. The child care was exhausting, but deeply rewarding. Often as not, as soon as we'd gotten Georgia to sleep, we'd sit down and start looking at pictures of her.

There weren't all that many other young fathers around with kids. Sometimes, when I was out wheeling Georgia, a Jersey mother would look at me suspiciously.

"I don't know if you have a job, or what?"

Our parents were thrilled to have a granddaughter, and we all visited each other a zillion times, even flying Georgia over to Geneva in 1969 for her first Christmas. Sylvia and I went out to play in the snow while her parents watched the baby.

"But you are still children, too!" exclaimed her father when we came in from the snow. "How can you have children?" I was twenty-three.

With Georgia on the way, we'd moved to a slightly larger apartment in Highland Park. Hungerford, Roger and Eddie helped us with the move. The apartment was basically a retrofitted attic, but the price was right. Georgia's room was about the size of a VW van, and very dingy. "Looks like the room Dostoevsky grew up in," I remarked to Hungerford. To cheer it up, I painted the floor blue, and the walls red and white.

We liked dressing up Georgia in her baby clothes. One particular outfit amused us; it was a pair of pale blue hand-knit overalls that we'd pull over a long-sleeved T-shirt. We'd call her Elmer when she was wearing these particular pants. We liked to bathe her, dress her in her Elmer overalls and lay her on our bed, cooing over her as she looked up at us, wide-eyed and pink-cheeked.

120

Sylvia was always pointing things out to Georgia, so much so that her first word was "See!" Before long, Georgia was walking and talking, although not always in familiar words. Once, when she found a nasty-looking root in the sandbox, she told me it was *eggpop*. I liked that word. For some reason she took to saying the name Malcolm, and just for the sound of it, I'd sometimes call her Malcolm X. She utterly silenced the man behind the deli counter when she told him that was her name.

Sylvia was wonderful with Georgia, reading to her and teaching her things. She liked showing me the baby's latest tricks when I'd come home from working on my thesis.

"Find *Quack-Quack!*" Sylvia might say to the baby, referring to a particular worn cloth book that Georgia loved. And Georgia would toddle around the room, chattering and smiling, and eventually she'd find the book where Sylvia had hidden it amid a sheaf of newspapers.

And I remember a magical day in 1970 when we drove Georgia out to the Jersey shore and watched her riding on a tiny little kiddie ride, a toy fire-engine, sitting there ringing the bell. Our hearts nearly burst.

My mathematical study of higher infinities dovetailed nicely with my growing fascination with mysticism as expressed both in the Western tradition starting with Plato, and in the Eastern teachings of Zen Buddhism. I was fascinated by the concept that I might somehow be able to meet directly with the One Mind.

I got my meeting on Memorial Day in 1970, when Greg Gibson appeared at our doorstep, on leave from the Navy. He'd brought a dose of the new drug LSD for me. He himself had taken the drug the day before, and hadn't enjoyed it very much, even though he'd seen the *Zap Comix* characters Flakey Foont and Mr. Natural, not to mention the Great White Whale. Greg was depressed in any case because he'd just gotten a Dear John letter from his college girlfriend—written in dark purple ink on pale purple paper. But despite Greg's caveats about the acid, I took my medicine.

My mind blew like an over-amped light-bulb. There was no evading the ego-death. I was immersed in white light. God. The One. All of a sudden, my theoretical high school notion of merging with the life-force pool had become literally true.

"I'm always here, Rudy," the voice told me. "I'll always love you."

I never really recovered from that experience—and I mean this in a good way. Even now, forty years later, I still feel more comfortable about the world, more confident that there is indeed a divine presence that glows in every particle of being. I see the One as sunlight shining through a huge stained glass window, or like a cosmic giant whose body cells we temporarily are. The One is everywhere.

Although I profited spiritually from my acid trip, I didn't see much point in taking psychedelics again. It was a one-time door that I'd passed through. I didn't want to risk ruining my brain. I needed to keep it together to be a husband and a father. And I was hoping to become a big-time mathematician, or maybe even a science fiction novelist. I was becoming ambitious.

I recall a solitary hike that I took while visiting with Sylvia's parents in Zermatt that summer. I was an extremely exalted state from the intense exercise in the thin air. I'd been thinking about time and the fourth dimension—a topic that had become dear to me from my repeated readings of *Flatland* and of the columns of mathematics-writer Martin Gardner. I was beginning to dream of writing about higher dimensions. I felt on the verge of a new approach that nobody had quite nailed down before. I was going to clarify the ways in which time both is and is not like the fourth dimension of space that we talk about in science fiction. And I was going to explain my ideas with new stories about *Flatland*'s A Square.

As I walked and thought, alpine beauty ringed me on every side. Coming upon a raging stream, the water gray with the dust of ground-up stones, I realized that, by flicking my eyes from side to side, I could speed up my perception to the point where I could see the instantaneous shapes of the water's curled, forking claws.

Just then a quiver of birds darted past, only a few feet from my head. To my ears, they seemed to be squawking a divinatory message from the gods.

"Genius! Genius!"

My destiny? I sat by the stream, filled with the promise, happy to be living my life.

Rutgers was only about twenty miles from Princeton University. Sylvia and I occasionally went over to Princeton to look at the chic stores, bringing Georgia in a stroller. It was always a treat to look at things through her baby eyes.

Sometimes we'd leave Georgia with a sitter and go to see a show of some kind at Princeton. The Princeton concerts were in a beautiful little wooden theater. Compared to pimply Rutgers, the place was unbelievably posh. I recall an epic performance by the Firesign Theater—this was a group of four or five crazy guys whose comedy act took the format of a radio show, complete with ads and sound effects, liberally sprinkled with left-wing politics and drug references.

I liked the Firesign Theater more than Sylvia did—in fact I'd listen to their albums with my stereo earphones, absorbing the details as intently as if I were auditing a reading of the Dead Sea Scrolls. Their 1971 master-piece, *We're All Bozos On This Bus*, was essentially a science fiction novella, composed very much in the style that I wanted to use—loaded with street-humor jokes and with what I'd begun to call SF power chords.

With this term, I was thinking of a literary equivalent of heavy musical riffs that people instantly respond to. A more formal word would be "tropes". Literature at large has its own tropes or power chords: the unwed mother, the cruel father, the buried treasure, the midnight phone call, the stranger in town and so forth.

I was beginning to amass a mental list of SF power chords that I loved. Eventually I'd use many of them in my novels and stories. Blaster guns, spaceships, time machines, aliens, telepathy, flying saucers, warped space, faster-than-light travel, immersive virtual reality, robots, teleportation, endless shrinking, levitation, the destruction of Earth, pleasure-center zappers, mind viruses, the attack of the giant ants, and—always, always—infinity and the fourth dimension.

The inner heart of Princeton's intellectual Vatican was the Institute for Advanced Study, where the mighty Einstein had spent his later years, and where the great mathematician Kurt Gödel was now housed. Professors could obtain grants to spend a year or two studying at the Insti-tute, and while I was working on my thesis, my adviser Ellentuck was there. He'd published exceedingly many papers, quite a few of them first-rate.

In 1970, Ellentuck got me into a set theory seminar at the Institute being run by the visiting mathematician Gaisi Takeuti. I liked Takeuti at first sight, he seemed sly and devil-may-care. Seeker that I was, I asked him a question about Zen.

"Oh, for us, Zen is very boring," said Takeuti. "It's like you feel about going to church." He wagged his finger, imitating a lecturing priest. But he had a teasing, insolent glint in his eyes that made me wonder if his remark was in fact a deep teaching.

"Zen is very boring." Yes!

There were a couple of Princeton mathematics grad students in the set theory seminar with Takeuti and me, but eventually they dropped out. One of them was such a know-it-all that I imagined his abilities to be far ahead of mine. But he was all talk. When it was this boy's turn to present a paper to our seminar he botched it—and he didn't come back.

"He has lost his face," said Takeuti.

A high point of my visits to the Institute was having lunch with Takeuti in the cafeteria. The food was great—you could order up a steak if you wanted—and it was free. Takeuti always ate a lot. He could be bitingly sarcastic about other mathematicians. Once a respected older mathematician joined us for lunch, and eloquently told me that intellectual discourse needed the *farfelu*—a French word meaning eccentric, weird, or far out. I heartily approved of that.

But after the older man left, Takeuti remarked, "He did some work thirty years ago that nobody cares about anymore. Now he should be quiet."

Takeuti had his own *farfelu* way of looking at set theory, and I think I may have been one of the very few people in the world who ever understood what he was talking about. The issue he was dealing with had to do with a problem in talking about the class of all sets.

What is a set? You might call it the form of a possible thought—as long as you assume that thoughts can be infinitely large. Or you might say that a set is the abstract form of any conceivable entity. The class of all sets—sometimes called V for short—is viewed as not being a set itself. The reason is that if V were a set, then, as the class of all sets, it would have to be a member of itself, and this would eventually lead to a contradiction. But if V isn't a set, then V isn't conceivable, as, once again, a set is the form of any conceivable entity. Okay, fine, but if V isn't conceivable, then how can it be that set theorists are always talking about it?

Takeuti's answer to this problem was something that he called Nodal Transfinite Type Theory. He argued that whenever we think we're talking about the full set-theoretic universe V, we're really just talking about an approximation to it. In Takeuti's theory, saying something is true for V really means that it's true for most of the approximations to V. But, of course, his theory gets a lot more complicated than this—as math always does. Eventually, in 1977, I'd publish a paper about Takeuti's work called "The One/Many Problem in the Foundations of Set Theory."

At one of our seminar meetings I told Takeuti that I'd proved an important result about Nodal Transfinite Type Theory that he'd been inching towards. I'd worked the proof out in my mind during the drive from Highland Park to Princeton. I tended to see these complex set theory proofs not in terms of symbols but in terms of patterns—things like radiating fins or Gothic flying buttresses or cascades of collapsing concentric shells. But when I tried to explain my new proof to Takeuti, I realized that it had a hole in it.

"I always like to quit for the day after I prove a very big theorem," said Takeuti kindly. "Then at least I am happy for a little while."

He meant that, in the morning, you'd usually find a mistake in yesterday's proof. Math was very harsh that way. Often there was no way to fix a broken proof. You'd find an unbridgeable gap and be left with nothing.

*I*nitially I'd been writing my thesis on a particular problem that Erik Ellentuck proposed in the subject of model theory. It had to do with enumerating how many different models a given mathematical theory might have. I'd gotten stuck on a proof I was trying to find, and then, in the kitchen with me at another math professor's party, Ellentuck had offered a suggestion about a new approach I could use. I finished the proof, and I thought maybe I had enough for a thesis.

In the summer of 1970, Sylvia and I left baby Georgia with my parents for a week, and went to a big mathematical logic conference at the University of California at Berkeley, in honor of Alfred Tarski. All the most famous logicians were there. I gave a short talk about the new result that I'd proved for my thesis, and it was well received. Before the talk, I was more nervous than I'd ever been in my life. Although I did mention that Ellentuck was my advisor, I didn't say anything about the fact that he'd helped me with my proof. I was eager to take as much credit as I could for this, my first theorem.

Sylvia and I were excited to be in California. There were a couple of Hungarian mathematicians that she thought were cute, Erdös and Rado, always talking together. Like real old-school Hungarians, they wore their white shirts with the big collars smoothed down on the outsides of their suit jacket lapels.

We took a day off from the conference, and went to a free concert by hippies in Golden Gate Park. People were smoking pot and painting their faces, just the way they were supposed to. Walking around Berkeley, we could see clear out past the San Francisco Bay, and the fresh clean ocean air carried a whiff of menthol from the eucalyptus trees.

We celebrated our third wedding anniversary in Berkeley, and went out to a fish restaurant recommended by our perennial seafood maven, Greg Gibson. Sylvia wore a beautiful red dress that night, with a frilly bib pattern on it. After all our baby care, it was a thrill for us be out on our own together again, seeing a bit more of the world.

When I got back to Rutgers, I found that Ellentuck was envious about my talk, and angry with me. Someone had told him that I hadn't emphasized his role in my proof. And now he said that, in order for him to get his fair share of the credit, I had drop the proof from my thesis and write it up as a joint paper to be published in a mathematics journal under our two names. I'd have to find something else for my thesis—and it was up to me to figure that part out on my own. He wasn't going to help me any further.

He was in an extremely agitated state. He kept looking out his living room window and asking me if his mother was hiding inside my car. He thought he could see her out there. He was nuts.

What to do? I wrote up most of our paper, and he added a final section on his own. It was a nice little article, "Martin's Axiom and Saturated Models," and in 1972 we'd publish it in a journal called the *Proceedings of the American Mathematical Society*. As for my thesis—well, I was just as happy to proceed on my own and pursue some ideas that I had. I wasn't really very interested in saturated models.

For a little while in 1970, I hoped to unearth some kind of logical contradiction in the foundations of mathematics—briefly Ellentuck became concerned that I might succeed, and said my efforts were "immensely destructive," which was music to my ears.

But in the end no contradictions were to be found. Mathematics is like some tough old goddess, powerful enough to withstand the onslaughts of generation after generation of young ruffians.

For my first few years at Rutgers, the math department was housed in a historic-landmark-type Victorian house right beside the main library. But in 1971, the department moved into a huge, brand-new concrete building that also housed those lower forms of life known as computer scientists.

The movers cleaned all the furniture and boxes out of the old math building, the janitors removed all the grime and dust, and the building stood completely empty for about a year. I still had the key to the building, and I took to doing my thesis work in there, working on some ideas about definability and set theory that stemmed from the great logician Kurt Gödel's celebrated Incompleteness Theorem of 1931.

In mathematical logic, it's possible to define a coding system whereby each possible statement about mathematics corresponds to its own code number. It would be convenient if there were some simple and mechanistic procedure that we could apply to any candidate code number so as to decide whether this number represents a true sentence or not. But—and this is the interesting thing—there can never be such a formula. In other words, no mathematically precise formula can define mathematical truth.

Why not? Well, if you *could* precisely define mathematical truth, then you could craft a mathematical Liar Sentence that in effect says, "This sentence isn't true." But the Liar Sentence is true if and only it's not true—which is a contradiction. Therefore you shouldn't have been able to construct the Liar Sentence. And therefore truth must not have been definable after all. Mathematical logicians love thinking along these lines—it's what we call a proof by contradiction, or a *reductio ad absurdum*.

The logician Alfred Tarski gets some credit for the undefinability of truth result, as he wrote about it in 1936. But the bulk of the credit lies with Kurt Gödel and his Incompleteness Theorem of 1931, whose proof develops the machinery for constructing paradoxical mathematical expressions like the Liar Sentence.

So okay, fine, truth is undefinable. Could I prove that undefinability is truth?

That was to be the main topic of my thesis. I wanted to show that the undefinability of truth might be the only reason why any other sets were undefinable. To be more precise, I thought in terms of a set called Truth that holds the code numbers of all the true sentences. We knew that Truth was undefinable. I was wondering if, given any undefinable set X at all, I could always find a way to define the Truth set in terms of X. In these cases, I could say that X was undefinable *because* truth is undefinable. And if all undefinable sets X have this quality, then it would indeed make sense to say that undefinability is truth.

On a typical morning in 1971, I'd let myself into the empty old math building and go upstairs, lying on a pleasantly soft parquet floor, writing with a pencil on sheets of paper that I was assembling into a three-ring binder. I erased and revised a lot. I loved those days alone with mathematics.

I'd bring along a kalimba, or African thumb piano. It was like a miniature cigar box with curved strips of metal. I'd gotten it in a toy store. When I wanted a break, I'd play little songs, enjoying the echoes. Or maybe I'd just lie on my wood floor, pondering the beautifully three-dimensional shape of the room, thinking about the spacetime trails everything was leaving as we moved forward in time.

Before too long, I was able to prove my result about undefinability and truth, although only for the somewhat limited universe of the so-called constructible sets. But it was a nice theorem in any case, and in 1974 I'd be able to publish it under the title "Undefinable Sets," in the *Annals of Mathematical Logic*. But in 1972, I still hoped to find some bigger and better theorems for my thesis, and I worked on into the spring.

Takeuti gave me some help, as he was still visiting at the Institute for Advanced Study. And eventually Ellentuck started helping me again too. He didn't act crazy all the time—on a good day, he could be perceptive, helpful, and even genial. But I don't think he actually read much of what I wrote.

As I mentioned earlier, an exciting thing about the Institute for Advanced Study was that the reclusive genius logician Kurt Gödel was still in residence there. As a student of mathematical logic, I thought of Gödel as a supreme guru.

Not only had he proved the fabulous Incompleteness Theorem, he'd formulated the notion of constructible sets as a way to prove something about the legendary Cantor's Continuum Problem.

This problem—which would loom large in my life for many years—goes back to 1874 when the German mathematician Georg Cantor proved a startling fact: there are different levels of infinity. In particular, there are more points in continuous space than there are integers. This theorem leads to a very interesting problem, the Continuum Problem, where "continuum" is a scholarly word for a continuous stretch of space. Which level of infinity best characterizes the continuum, that is, how many points are there in continuous space?

Cantor coined some esoteric-sounding names for the first few levels of infinity: alef-null, alef-one, alef-two, and so on. The set of integers has the size alef-null, but we don't know which alef matches the size of the continuum. Is it alef-one, alef-two . . . or something else? Cantor thought the continuum's size might be alef-one, and this guess is known as Cantor's Continuum Hypothesis.

In 1940 Gödel proved that the Continuum Hypothesis is indeed consistent with the known facts about set theory. But in 1963, the mathematician Paul Cohen proved that the negation of the Continuum Hypothesis is consistent with set theory as well! In other words, on the basis of what we currently know about sets, the Continuum Hypothesis is undecidable. You can't prove it and you can't disprove it on the basis of any currently accepted axioms for set theory. But Gödel had remarked several times that, by pondering the nature of infinity, he hoped to unearth some new axioms that would solve the Continuum Problem for once and for all.

One day in 1970, a Xerox of a hand-written manuscript appeared in my mailbox in the Rutgers math department office. It was four or five pages covered with spidery writing, replete with corrections and footnotes, entitled, "Some considerations leading to the probable conclusion that the true power of the continuum is alef-two." The author was Kurt Gödel.

I never did find out who put that paper in my mailbox—probably it was Ellentuck, who liked being secretive. In any case, I flipped out with joy. I dropped everything and spent the next week poring over the little manuscript, struggling to decipher it.

I recall that I scoured the depths of the Rutgers library, emerging with an obscure tome in French that elucidated some of the turn-of-the-century concepts that Gödel had used. He'd unearthed an arcane way of drawing pictures of higher infinities in terms of slanting curves, where a first curve is viewed as "bigger-by-end-pieces" than a second curve if, as you move out towards the right, the first curve eventually crosses the second, and remains above it. Gödel used the word "scales" for his sequences of steeper and steeper curves. I thought about them a lot, and eventually, I'd put pictures of them into my popular book on the philosophy of mathematics, *Infinity and the Mind*, 1982.

Everyone at Rutgers was curious about Gödel's new sketch of a proof. I gave a seminar talk on it, and discussed it with Takeuti. Gödel's new argument was intriguing, but it seemed to have some—logical gaps.

Takeuti knew Gödel fairly well, and perhaps due to Takeuti's influence, the great man invited me to come to his office for a conversation early in 1972. It's hard to express just how big a deal this was for me. It was as if I'd been at art school learning to paint—and suddenly Picasso had asked me to come to his studio. As I wrote in *Infinity and the Mind*:

> I didn't know where his real office door was, so I went around to knock on the outside door instead. This was a glass patio door, looking out on a little pond and the peaceful woods beyond the Institute for Advanced Study. It was a sunny March day, but the office was quite dark. I couldn't see in. Did Kurt Gödel really want to see me?
>
> Suddenly he was there, floating up before the long glass door like some fantastic deep-sea fish in a pressurized aquarium. He let me in, and I took a seat by his desk.

I felt comfortable with Gödel right away. For some reason he reminded me my German grandmother—partly it was his accent, and partly it was his kindly, inquisitive demeanor.

Gödel had a way of instantly understanding anything that I said. When I described my thesis work to him, it took him about ten seconds to figure out my proof that undefinability is truth.

We spent an hour talking together—about set theory, about the nature of time, and about the teachings of mysticism. He laughed a lot, and even the laughter seemed like speech. It was wonderful to be in contact with so powerful a mind. It wasn't at all like being with a regular person. Compared to Gödel, the rest of us are like talking dogs.

I managed to visit Gödel two more times over the next couple of years. Perhaps he had some hope that I might be the one to fix up the logic of his manuscript on the continuum problem. And in any case, he seemed to enjoy my enthusiasm and my odd way of looking at things.

I remember, for instance, a discussion about time travel paradoxes. If you can travel to the past, then you might conceivably kill your father as a boy, so you wouldn't be born, but then you wouldn't have traveled to the past . . . and so on. One escape route used by science fiction writers is to suppose that you don't actually travel to your own past, but rather to the past timeline of some parallel world. I thought about this for awhile and drew up some intricate spacetime diagram, referring to the dimension between the parallel timelines as "eternity."

Gödel got a kick out of my drawing. "This is a *very* strange idea," he said. "A *bizarre* idea." I was proud.

Years later I'd meet the famous mathematician Paul Cohen, and he expressed his own sense of wonder and good fortune at having met Gödel. "I was walking across the lawn to Gödel's office," said Cohen. "And I'm thinking, how does a kid from New Jersey end up sitting down with the world's greatest mathematician?"

When I met Gödel, I felt the same way. Just a few years ago, I'd been a feckless college boy, and now I was discussing philosophy and logic with the smartest man I'd ever meet. It was as if I'd broken out of a chrysalis at Rutgers, or as if I'd emerged from a long series of dreams.

I'd been hoping that I might get a post-doctorate position at the Institute for the fall of 1972, but that didn't pan out. My paper with Ellentuck and my thesis work, although publishable, weren't compelling enough to land me a position as a high-powered logician. I began to sense that the highest echelons of mathematical achievement would remain inaccessible to me. I'd had my chance with this thesis—and I hadn't scored.

I tried to tell myself that I was okay with being, as it were, a low-level stone carver among the artisans working to perfect the great cathedral of set theory. But honestly I wasn't content with this. I wanted to be a star at something—and if I wasn't going to win at technical academic mathematics, I was going to have to find another game to play.

Even finding a "low-level stone carver" type of job turned out to be hard. During the spring of 1972, I mailed out an exceedingly large number of job application letters, and I attended a couple of dreary math-job fairs. Finally I got a tip from the Rutgers math chairman. There was a position open at a state college in Geneseo, New York, up near the Great Lakes. And another Rutgers graduate was on the recruitment committee there. I phoned him up, and he helped me get the job.

My friends and I loaded all our crap into a U-Haul truck, and in August, 1972, a math pal named Nort Fowler helped me drive the stuff to Geneseo and unload it. Nort and I drove the truck back to Highland Park, and then I ferried my little family to Geneseo.

A few month later, in January, 1973, I had to return to Rutgers one last time for my formal thesis defense. Anyone at all can show up for these seminar-like events, possibly to pose challenges to the work that the candidate has done. A Princeton mathematician turned up and asked me a series of juicy questions, suggesting some interesting further work that I might do. Fearing a rewrite request, Ellentuck intervened and shut down the discussion. Enough said. I'd passed. I had my Ph. D.

Nort and I went to a bar, and he phoned his wife. "They found a big hole in Rudy's thesis," he told her, grinning at me. "Poor guy didn't take it very well. He broke down in front of everyone."

Life with Kids

I n May, 1972, shortly before our move to Geneseo, Sylvia and I had our second child, a son, Rudy Jr. This time we'd gone to natural childbirth classes, and I was in on the delivery.

Rudy's umbilical cord was an impressive connection cable—glistening, semi-transparent, with a vein and an artery inside. It was a helical coil, reminiscent of an old-time telephone cord. I had a flash of Rudy's cord leading back through Sylvia's spacetime body to her own umbilical cord, and thus back to Sylvia's mother, to *her* mother, and so on, all the way to Eve in the Garden of Eden.

But mainly I was looking at the baby. He was bluish for that second or two before he took his first breath, and then he was pink—although his boy-parts were bright from the start. Ornaments.

"La!" he yelled. "Waaaah!"

Later Sylvia would say that the gentle ambient music in the hospital hall sounded like the beautiful soundtrack of a Fellini film. We were movie stars that day, we three. When I left the hospital to see Georgia and my Mom, I shook hands with a young cop in the parking lot, me with my ratty bell-bottoms and my long hair.

"My wife just had a son!"

"Right on."

Up in Geneseo, New York, we rented a tiny little house, practically a dwarves' cottage, with teensy doors and windows. In the afternoons I'd take my son for a ride in his carriage, a nice plush model that Sylvia's brother, Henry, had gotten us for Georgia. This was really some carriage, covered in bright blue velour, with luxurious springs and chrome fenders. In later years it would pass on to family after family in Geneseo.

Rudy was a very alert baby, prone to thinking things over. Inside the house, he'd often watch the tree shadows that angled in through the windows to dance on the floors and walls. And when I wheeled him around town, he'd stare up at the maples, oaks and elms arching overhead, his bright, interested eyes studying the branches and, above them, the clouds.

Looking at him, I'd think of the Bible verse: "Behold! This is my son, with whom I am well-pleased!"

Once Georgia got over her initial shock at having to share her parents, she was nice to little Rudy. Sometimes she'd lug him around like a cheerful doll. He liked watching her too. Sometimes we'd get him all cleaned up and call him Mr. Tidy. When we took Rudy to visit Sylvia's parents in Geneva, she got a passport picture of him, and she claimed the picture looked like Cark Gable. She kept a large blow-up of this picture on her dressing table.

On Rudy's first birthday, in 1973, Georgia and one of her friends ate all the lemony icing off Rudy's layer-cake, scooping the icing off bit by bit with their tiny fingers, standing on chairs to reach the cake where it was sitting on top of the china closet. We grown-ups didn't notice the missing icing till serving time. Oh well. We stuck in a candle, sliced it up, and it tasted fine.

I loved eating that particular kind of layer-cake; I'd had it for all my birthdays as a boy. Sylvia had learned the recipe from Mom, it was a von Bitter family recipe. The layers were like thin hard pancakes, individually baked, and the cook would pile them with alternating smears of red currant jelly and orange marmalade between the layers.

In the summer of 1973, we managed, with our parents' help, to buy a three-bedroom house in Geneseo. It was a great not to have a landlord. I painted nearly all of the rooms, and I replaced some twenty missing panes of glass. The family before us had featured distracted parents and rambunctious boys.

It was said that in the past, our house had stood empty for a few years—some of the locals even said it was haunted. I got a little paranoid about this, and I went so far as to have my father read the exorcism service from the Book of Common Prayer. But eventually I figured out that the noises I'd been hearing in the attic were squirrels, not Lovecraftian four-dimensional monsters. I found some squirrel-gnawed holes in the eaves and covered them over with flattened tin cans.

Before long we were expecting a baby again. Isabel would be born in Warsaw, New York, the nearest town to Geneseo with a hospital. It was a thirty or forty minute drive from out house.

Sylvia and I made a number of practice runs to Warsaw before the birth; we were taking a natural childbirth class there. The road was a beautiful little two-lane highway through rolling cow pastures, set here and there with silos. Sylvia got interested in the patterns of these fields, and she began making large paintings of them, increasingly abstract. Eventually she reached the point of using masking tape to get sharp edges on her harmonious pastel triangles.

It was the era of women's lib, and a couple of women drove Sylvia wild with resentment by putting her down for having a third child instead of getting a job. But she stuck by her plan. Having this child was something that she and I both wanted to do. One factor was that, with both Sylvia and I coming from two-child families, we wanted to experience a different dynamic in our own family. A bigger factor was that Georgia and Rudy had turned out to be so wonderful that we couldn't resist having one more.

Isabel's birth was scary. It started with that drive to Warsaw, but in the middle of the night. Near dawn, a thunderstorm began, and we moved into the delivery room. Surprisingly there was a window beside the delivery table. I could look out at the misty green pastures and plowed fields, with cars hissing past in the early morning rain. Lightning flickered in the low, dark clouds.

Sylvia began pushing. There was something great, monumental, and noble in her masks of pain. Later she told me that each time she pushed, she saw a skull that came closer. Isabel was having trouble getting out.

The doctor sent me out to the waiting room, and got to work helping with the birth. I was worried that Sylvia might die. In my fear and despair I had a Zen flash, remembering an obscure koan: "Once you're born, the worst has already happened."

Grasping at straws, I took the koan to mean that, even if some horrible tragedy were about to occur, the sorrow would be, after all, a natural and

135

inevitable part of the human life that I myself had been born into years before. Like it or not, I was inescapably immersed in whatever was going to come down.

And quite soon, despite all worries, everything was fine. Little Isabel was like a yellow-pink rosebud—by far the largest and the most aware of our three newborns. Although she seemed a little discomfited by the difficult delivery, within half an hour, she was looking us over, sizing us up. Sylvia was joyful, relieved, exhausted.

Sylvia's mother, Pauline, was staying with us for the birth. When Sylvia and I brought Isabel home, Pauline had dressed the kids up in their best clothes, as if they were meeting a dignitary—and I'm sure Isabel would say that they *were*.

It was a great occasion. First we set Isabel on a pillow in a straw basket on the living-room couch, and then we put her in a wicker bassinet in our bedroom. Little Rudy pulled up a chair next to the bassinet, and sat there watching the new baby.

The costs of living were low enough that we could live off my meager teaching salary. Sylvia spent most of her time with the kids, and I put in a certain amount of time too. To some extent, it was exciting and fulfilling to be raising our two, and then three, children. But the reality was more grueling, as anyone who's had children knows.

The weather was often gray and rainy in Geneseo, and in the winters we were cooped up inside. Sylvia said there were times when she thought she'd go crazy. It got to me as well. At the same time, I was worried about keeping my job, about doing some publishable research, and about whether I'd ever find a way to something more personally meaningful than trying to prove difficult theorems in mathematics.

Sylvia and I had a saying that we liked to intone when things got tough. "The filth. The stench. The din."

I'd always say this in a sepulchral, tragic tone, with long pauses between the sentences, like the narrator of a documentary film about the lower depths of society. It would cheer us up.

Sylvia would make it clear when she'd reached the point where I had to stay home with the kids for a day so she could go out. We'd argue if I didn't give her enough free time. Sometimes she went up to Rochester to take art classes, and sometimes she'd shop or hang around with friends.

Of course, if I relaxed into it, the children were wonderful to be with—cuddly and fun to watch. I always felt very comfortable talking with them. I would joke about everything, and be frank about the world—more so than when I talk to adults. My parents—and particularly my mother—had that same way of being direct and frank with me.

By way of keeping our sanity intact, Sylvia and I became quite creative in Geneseo. I started getting into writing. Sylvia sewed many outfits for the kids, often inventing the patterns. She took further art classes at the college and became ever more involved in painting, developing a special sharp-edged, cartoony style, colored in warm tones. She sold some pictures and had a show.

But always there was the child care. The days started early, and ran full bore. Once when I was taking care of the kids alone, I picked out Isabel's outfit on the basis of having everything be red: red shoes, socks, pants, turtleneck and sweater. Of course the reds didn't match. Even though I, as a man, was unable to perceive this, Isabel already could, and she was frowning about it.

"Red," she complained, sitting on our front steps.

Just then another mother from the neighborhood came by and burst out laughing. "Did your father dress you, honey?"

Feeding the children wasn't too hard, as they all liked to eat. Often we'd give them slices of salami with cream cheese on bagels. They liked biting out the middles of the salami slices and looking through the remains as if they were glasses.

Frequently Rudy would forget what time of day it was. "Did I eat supper yet?" he might ask in mid-morning.

In the evenings we'd bathe the three kids, read them books and then they'd call for their evening snack.

"Full warm milk!"

Around this time my brother Embry and his family left the islands and moved to a farm in Kentucky. He and Noreen had two children of their own by then.

"Here comes Rudy and his traveling circus," Embry would say when we'd show up for a holiday visit.

Once our three kids and Embry's two caught lice on his farm. Embry's wife Noreen argued that the lice had not come from her barn, but rather from an elephant that the children had touched at a menagerie. Another time our kids had an infestation of pinworms. These plagues were exciting, providing a lot to talk and think about for days on end.

The kids' birthday parties were big events, with balloons and party hats and games. I'd flash back to the birthday parties of my own childhood— and to Mom's layer-cakes. At one of my parties, Pop had filled a galvanized washing-tub with water, set a little cup under the water, and let us kids try and drop pennies so that they'd fall through the water into the cup. If your penny went in, you'd get a piece of bubble gum, and if it missed, you'd get a piece, too. Good old Pop.

For Georgia's fourth birthday party, I set up the same game, with the same rules. Georgia wore eager pigtails and a yellow dress with an exclamation point on it—a perfect outfit for her.

Over the years, Isabel became known in our family for always taking the biggest possible first bite out of her slices of birthday cake—often I'd manage to photograph her in the act. She liked sweets a lot. Later, when we lived in Lynchburg, Virginia, one of the first sentences Isabel wrote out on her own was, "Say! I'm having candy!"

By way of expressing how small a town Geneseo was, I used to lay three fingers of one hand across three fingers on the other hand and say, "That's our street map."

It was like a factory town, with the college down the hill towards the flat bottomland along the Genesee River, and the little residential streets up top. The village-like quality meant that we had a full social life, with most of our new friends living only one or two blocks away. Lots of the professors and administrators had young children, and it was easy to find playmates for the kids.

We hung out a lot with a film-oriented English professor called Lee Poague and his wife Susie. Susie was a warm, humorous woman with a cozy voice. Lee and I could while away hours in discussing our meager odds at getting tenure—but then we'd forget about all that and immerse ourselves in rock and roll.

A nice elementary school abutted the college, and Georgia went there. She often talked about one of the workers at the school, a stout lady that she called Miss Ims. Georgia was impressed that Miss Ims would take two full trays of lunch every day.

We had a hamster, and our little book about hamsters said that you could determine a hamster's sex by finding the genitals, which were "located a quarter inch from the vent." This euphemism reliably sent Georgia into paroxysms of laughter, and at school she made a point of asking her teacher if she could open the vent.

Rudy Jr. was eager to start school—the yellow bus stopped right in front of our house, and he was impressed to see Georgia riding off to kindergarten every day. When Rudy's turn finally rolled around in 1977, he'd be out at the bus stop a few minutes early every day, ready to go. He was a little absent-minded, a dreamer like me, and one time he forgot to get off the homebound bus, and rode it all the way to the bus barn. They brought him to our house in a car—naturally by then we were frantic.

For a little while, Georgia liked to pretend she was a teacher, enlisting her brother and sister to be her pupils. She'd set up a blackboard under our chestnut tree, write D-O-G, and then rap her chalk against the board, making a show of being piqued by her class's slowness to read what she'd written. Of course Rudy bridled at any discipline from his older sister. In retaliation, she'd call him an upstart barbarian.

This particular chestnut tree that they played under was extremely fecund, and in the autumns, the kids would gather hundreds of lustrous brown buckeyes. They'd load their red wagon with the chestnuts and haul them around, they'd fill buckets, they'd arrange the chestnuts in patterns on the sidewalk, they'd throw them onto our roof, they'd barter them with the neighbor kids. I loved the gnarly variegated whorls of browns on the buckeyes' gleaming skins.

Halloweens were great in Geneseo. We'd have a children's parade down Main Street, with the wet sidewalks papered by orange leaves. And then the children in their costumes would flit along the cozy streets—skeletons, cats, angels, devils. Sylvia and I enjoyed carving pumpkins, each year we'd try to outdo each other. I'd make mine scarier than the year before, and she'd make hers yet more stylized and elegant.

As I've mentioned, the winters were brutally long. Taking the kids outside would become quite a production, as they needed some eight pieces of clothing apiece—hat, scarf, gloves, snow pants, coat, boots—and if you neglected so much as one item, they'd catch an earache or a cold. It was like gearing up for SCUBA diving or a trip into space. And of course as soon as the children were outside, one of them would want to come back inside to go to the bathroom.

Around 1975, Sylvia and I took up cross-country skiing, and that made it easier to get through the winter. If you could ski right out of our door, the endless snow could be a source of entertainment. I myself liked skiing down the hill to the farmlands by the winding Genesee River. Unobserved in a flat, wintry field, I'd feel like a jellyfish in an endless sea, my legs beating in a mindless rhythm, finding my way towards infinity.

We took the kids out into the woods in the winter as well. The streams would be frozen over, with scary ice-rimmed black holes at the bases of the waterfalls, silently beckoning, like doors to the underworld. The hills would be drifted deep in snow, and good for sledding.

In the summers, eager for sun, we'd pile into our car and drive to the Outer Banks in North Carolina, renting a ratty, inexpensive cottage by the beach. Sylvia and the children would turn as brown as coffee beans. When I waded into the water, I'd sometimes step onto the flesh mound of a dozing sea skate. It would twitch in a sudden spasm, I'd let out a juicy scream, and the children would squeal with joy.

"Made a mistake, touched a skate!"

Rudy liked making drip castles and gathering the busy, digging sand-crabs. Isabel ate as much sand as she could. I'd take Georgia for long walks along the water, and she'd cheerfully sing songs about the objects we'd find.

"Dead bone of crab!"

*P*op had bought us a basic white Ford. One summer afternoon in 1973, I got the idea of painting flames onto it. I used regular paint brushes and a couple of quarts of enamel paint. I was rebelling against my fated career as a family-man and professor.

I knew a little about car-flaming from brother Embry's hot-rod maga-zines. I painted yellow background flame shapes first, with the flames billowing back along the car from the front wheel wells. I added sinuous black outlines around the edges of the yellow flames, and filled the flames with colored cores—red on the left side of the car, and a blue flame-core on the right. I made the flames funky with forks and curling tips.

"This must be a real test for your marriage," said a neighbor to Sylvia.

"Oh, I've always wanted a car with flames," said my insouciant wife. In high-school in DC, she'd dated some guys who were always customizing their cars.

Generally we got respect for our flames—although they also meant that everyone in the little town always knew exactly where we were, and what we were up to, simply by tracking the location of our easily recognizable car. One time Sylvia was pulled over for speeding, and she was expecting to charm her way out of a fine, but the cop was staring at the flames on the side of the car. Wordlessly, he wrote out a ticket.

*I*nitially I was very nervous about meeting my classes—for the very first one, in September, 1972, I ended up walking past the open door two or three times before mustering the courage to go in. But I got the hang of it pretty quickly, and the students liked me—after all, I was only about ten years older than them. From the start, I avoided collecting homework, and I tried not to give too many tests. I never liked grading.

As a break from the calculus courses that were the department's bread and butter, I was allowed to teach a few higher-level courses. One that I loved was on the history of mathematics, a topic that truly boggled my mind.

I discovered that the seemingly seamless edifice of mathematical knowledge has in fact grown up as organically and unpredictably as a coral reef. Things as simple as inventing the equals sign were huge, intense deals. Throughout history, mathematicians have been irritable coots, often feuding with each other—just like the mathematicians I knew. Things in math have never been fully rational or congenial.

I bought a set of the thirteen books of Euclid's *Elements* in an inexpensive Dover paperback edition, edited by the wonderful British scholar, Thomas Little Heath, who'd died before I was born. I took to drawing intricate figures of circles and lines, and even found a large wooden compass for drawing these constructions on the blackboard. I also studied Heath's *History of Greek Mathematics*, and marveled at Archytas's construction of the cube root of two, which uses the intersection point of a cylinder, a cone and a torus.

My investigations gave me the courage to take charge of our departmental course on the foundations of geometry. Most of the suggested textbooks seemed utterly absurd to me—for they contained no pictures! Some benighted authors believe in teaching geometry as if it were a language game, an arbitrary formal system. Fools. As a logician, I well knew the limits of a methodology based only upon axioms and proofs. If you're doing *geometry*, you should be *looking at shapes*, for crying out loud!

It occurred to me that I might fashion a text from my notes about A Square and the higher dimensions. That way I could talk about the topics that interested me. I was still wondering, for instance, about how best to reconcile the notion of the fourth dimension as an unknown spatial direction with the notion of the fourth dimension as time. And I wanted to find a user-friendly way to elucidate Einstein's notions about curved space.

I dug out my binder with pictures of A Square—the one I'd started while listening to Frank Zappa at Rutgers. I copied my drawings onto mimeograph masters, and typed in my explanations, bulking the thing up with material drawn from T. L. Heath and from Euclid's *Elements*. I stayed just a little bit ahead of the students, handing out some ten mimeographed pages a week. By the end of the semester, I'd produced something like a book.

The students loved the class, and I taught it perhaps five times during the years 1973 to 1978, with ever-increasing enrollments. Over and over I'd rework and retype the notes, larding them with fresh information about hyperspheres, the illusion of the passage of time, the many-worlds interpretation of quantum mechanics, the special theory of relativity, and the shape of spacetime. I was a professor lecturing about relativity, just I'd hallucinated during that peyote trip at Swarthmore ten years before.

Starting in the fall of 1973, I began having the campus book store photo-offset the latest version of my notes, and each year we'd sell copies to the students under the title, *Geometry and Reality*. I showed my volume to some of the textbook salesmen who haunted my office, and they passed it on to their editors. But the big companies thought my book too quirky and untextbook-like.

Finally I hit upon the idea of sending *Geometry and Reality* to the publisher that was keeping in print so many of the esoteric mathematical and philosophical books that I enjoyed: Dover Books. Back in Louisville, Mom had regularly ordered Dover books for me on obscure topics like infinity, cryptography, mazes, hieroglyphs, and wave mechanics. And all of T. L. Heath's books were Dover books as well.

With surprising alacrity, Dover agreed in 1976 to publish me, suggesting only that I give my book a title more indicative of the contents. So it became *Geometry, Relativity and the Fourth Dimension*. Wanting to veil how young and shaggy I was, I identified myself to the unseen editors as "Professor Rudolf v. B. Rucker." They offered me a thousand dollars for perpetual rights to publish my book. I wondered about any lack of ongoing royalties, but Dover said that, since they were largely a reprint house, they weren't set up for issuing royalties. So what the heck, I took the thousand bucks. It was real money for a real book. *Geometry, Relativity and the Fourth Dimension* appeared as a nice, glossy paperback early in 1977. I imagine they've sold quite a few copies over the years, but I don't regret the deal. It pointed my way to my real career.

Although I was also getting a couple of my set theory papers into journals, academic publishing was slow and painful, with no sense of there being an actual readership, and with no checks in the mail. And, even though I could write publishable mathematics papers, I still wasn't managing to prove any really big theorems. My academic math career wasn't going anywhere. I started thinking more about writing popular science books or maybe even science fiction.

In the fall of 1977, the year that *Geometry, Relativity and the Fourth Dimension* was published, a woman editor from Dover turned up at our house. She was in Geneseo to deliver one of her children to the college. She was surprised how young I was—the "Rudolf v. B. Rucker" ruse really had convinced my publishers that I was a distinguished old scholar. We had a good laugh, and the editor remarked that mine was one of the few non-public-domain books that they'd published.

"We have a saying at Dover," she said. "The only good author is a dead author."

*I*n March, 1976, with my Dover advance in hand, I threw a big thirtieth birthday party for myself, with a keg of beer and a country ham.

Grandly I bought plane tickets so that my college friends Greg Gibson and Barry Feldman could come. I half expected the world to dissolve when I turned thirty, so I didn't much care what I did with the money. The house was so full that Feldman slept under one of our rugs.

I got very drunk at the party—Rudy Jr. says it was the first time he ever noticed me being that way. I was in fact tanking up on beer a couple of times a week in those days, and I usually got drunk at parties. There was a nice bar in the middle of Geneseo that I liked, it was called the Idle Hour, sometimes I'd stop in there for a beer on a Friday afternoon. But at this point alcohol still seemed like as much of a friend as an enemy.

As for pot, that was still hard to get, although once a friend mailed me some with the return address "Slim's Dude Ranch, Stone Arabia, NY." Another occasional source of pot was Dennis Poague. He was the fascinating and screwy younger brother of my professor friend Lee, who lived across the street. By now, Lee and I often got high together on Friday nights.

Dennis would orbit through Geneseo once or twice a year. Once Dennis showed up with a whole suitcase of green weed that he'd bought at Mardi Gras in New Orleans. The stuff was of such an inferior grade that Dennis ended up boiling it down in water to try and obtain a reasonably potent extract—a procedure that failed to work. While he was doing the boiling, Dennis gave Sylvia and Lee's wife Susie an impromptu kitchen-lecture on his techniques for unusual sex. The wives dissolved in ribald hilarity..

Dennis always had wild ideas, and he never stopped talking. Sometimes I'd want to clobber him to shut him up—but sometimes I'd get onto his wavelength and I'd have a great time hanging out with him. One of the things I always enjoyed about getting high was that the lifestyle brought me close to strange people with surreal ways of expressing themselves.

Dennis was a nice contrast to the somewhat goody-goody professors I usually hung with. And as a younger brother myself, I felt a certain bond with him. At another level, I was also mindful of the mileage that Jack Kerouac had gotten out of his association with his wildman pal Neal Cassady. With his hyperactive, unreflective nihilism, Dennis seemed like a character in an underground novel. And so, as his speech patterns and conversational tics sank into my mind, I started thinking that I might eventually model a fictional character on him.

Around 1975, I began team-teaching some experimental courses on the philosophy of mathematics with Bill Edgar, a charismatic Geneseo philosophy professor. One of our courses was called The Inconceivable. Edgar was an intense and brilliant debater. Often he'd put me on the spot in class, driving to debunk my feeling that our physical world is infinite in some very literal sense of the world. I wrote up and distributed sets of notes for my lectures—entitling them *Mystic Fuzz*, just to get a rise out of Bill.

The thing was, Bill claimed to be a hard-boiled materialist, and I claimed to be a spaced-out mystic—but my special twist was that I was trying to buttress my gut feelings with rigorously logical arguments drawn from higher mathematics. Thus I supported the slogan, "All is one," by saying that anything can be viewed as a mathematical form, and all the mathematical forms live together in the universe of all possible sets. And to argue that mere logical thinking isn't enough, I described Gödel's proof that no logical system can deduce all the things that are true.

So, in a sense, I was really much more hard-boiled than Bill—which is why I enjoyed putting a twist on things by giving my notes a hippy-dippy title like *Mystic Fuzz*. In your face, materialist-man!

Just as my notes for my lectures on geometry led to a book, my lecture notes for the philosophy of math courses would lead to a book as well. But this was going to take me a few more years.

The summers were nice in Geneseo, with the Genesee River snaking through the valley's flat bottomland. Some of the valley was plowed into fields, but large tracts had been left wild—the largest local landowners were into fox-hunting, and they liked having woodsy areas to ride in. Most of the time these woods were deserted, and I liked to walk around down there, looking things over.

One time I found three brass links of a heavy chain in a stream, and brought it home. The three-link chain's mass and luster made it seem like a power object. That night I dreamed that the frogs who lived in that stream were begging me to return their treasure, so I brought it back. It seemed best to be on good terms with the resident spirits of the place.

On our tenth wedding anniversary, in June, 1977, Sylvia and I went down into those woods with crystal glasses and had a picnic with champagne and roast chicken. The setting sun was fat and slow on the horizon, bathing us in honeyed light. Life was beautiful. We were in love.

By now our children were approaching the ages of eight, five and three. We were emerging from the difficult early stages—from the filth, the stench and the din. The kids were more fun all the time. Sylvia was still painting a lot, and feeling good about herself. She longed to start a paying career of her own, but for now she was content to let it slide for a few more years.

We often took the kids to a huge public swimming-pool in Letchworth State Park or, which was more exciting, to a swimming hole at Triphammer Creek. The pastures around Triphammer Creek were private land, but the owners were mellow, and quite a few people would hike in along the creek to the swimming spot—which lay at the base of a waterfall that was the height of a man.

The swimming hole was deep enough that, if you were reckless, you could jump into it from the rocks at the edge of the falls. Another fun thing to do was to worm into the rocky space behind the waterfall itself, squeezing into that damp ringing cavity where, in fairytales, the nymphs keep a magic harp or a pot of gold.

We went to Triphammer Creek often enough that eventually I thought to bring along a diving mask. I saw dozens of sizable fish in the water, enjoying the bubbles from the falls. One Lord of the Trout was two feet long. These fish were so adept at dodging us that I'd never known they were there. It occurred to me that maybe some elusive beings live in the air around us as well, elemental sprites visible only as an occasional twitch glimpsed from the corner of one's eye.

Bicycling became popular around then, and I got myself a ten-speed. I had a lot of fun riding out on the deserted country roads in the baking summer sun. One time, out into the middle of nowhere, I found my way down to a creek where enormous butterflies flitted about. The air was so still that, just like when I was a boy, I could hear the world turning. I imagined that I was on another planet, an explorer observing, like, the legendary stinging butterflies of the Genesee Rift.

Ignition

Deep down I was still dreaming of being a literary author like the Beats. I was reading and rereading Thomas Pynchon's masterpiece, *Gravity's Rainbow*, trying to winkle out the secrets of his florid yet colloquial style. I was also studying the essays and short stories of Jorge Luis Borges, admiring his skill at creating high literature on the border of science fiction. I found Borges's essays to be among the most informative and profound things I'd ever read—I'm thinking here of his writings on infinity, the passage of time, and the nature of language.

My way of finally wading into literary writing was to write poems. With all due respect to serious poets, it's pretty easy to write something that *resembles* a poem. All you need is a typewriter and a single sheet of paper! And maybe a few drinks.

I happened to have a very nice typewriter, a rose-red IBM Selectric that I'd bought because it had an interchangeable type head. When I wrote math papers, I'd switch out the heads so as to type in Greek letters and mathematical symbols.

Off and on during the years 1975 through 1978 at Geneseo, I'd write poems on my red Selectric at night. Not that I bothered sending the poems out to magazines—submitting my math papers was heartbreak enough. A published poet friend on the English faculty, Dave Kelly, encouraged me to join in the periodic faculty poetry readings, where I'd hand out my works in mimeographed form. I enjoyed performing for a literary crowd. Like the professional poets I'd seen reading before, I'd preface each poem with an anecdote about how I came to write it.

Eventually I put my poems into a little Xeroxed chapbook called *Light Fuse and Get Away*—I made fifty copies in 1983 and gave them away. The title was taken from the instructions on the packs of firecrackers that Niles and I used to get. I thought my poems might act as a fuse to light an explosive career as a writer. Years later I saw a copy being offered for a couple of hundred dollars on eBay. The starving artist's dream!

In 2007, I ran into Thom Metzger in Rochester, New York. Thom had been a student of mine at Geneseo, and has since become a successful writer. He still remembered a poem that didn't make it into my chapbook, and he even had what may be the sole surviving copy of a mimeographed handout that I distributed at a Geneseo faculty reading in 1976. Here's the poem.

Dick Tracy with Crutches in a Bucket

Imagine
A national restaurant chain with
"crutches" of french-fries and
"chicken" of Tracy
a pot of honey with each meal
and French ticklers in the men's room.

I remember exactly what I had in mind while writing this. When I was a country kid in Louisville, my favorite restaurant was called Pryor's. They had a big sign showing a tousled rooster playing golf. Their specialty was a dish called "Chicken in the Rough"—a huge mound of French fries, with pieces of fried chicken nestled into it. The meal came with soft dinner rolls and a tub of honey. And, as I've mentioned, my favorite newspaper comic strip as a boy was Chester Gould's surreal *Dick Tracy*, with its peculiar insistence on grotesque criminals and the details of physical objects, often with lettered labels.

In my poem, I imagined a large bucket filled with dismembered and deep-fried limbs of Tracy, packed in among soft limp crutches of the kind you'd see in a painting by Salvador Dali. I liked mixing together the images of a pleasant and inexpensive restaurant meal, a pop culture reference to

Dick Tracy, a countercultural suggestion of eating the police, and the sexual frisson of "pot of honey" conjoined with "French ticklers." I like that the poem is worded so flatly, which has the effect of making the odd imagery that much more of an affront—and in the context of a poem, an affront can be a good thing, in that it means you're waking up the reader. Making their blood boil, one hopes, as opposed to boring them stiff.

In other words, for me, this poem still feels like a successful work of art. But I fully realize that the references are so personal that my lines could well leave many people cold or indifferent.

In writing, there's a balancing act between making your piece specific enough to come alive, and making it general enough to have a wide appeal. Stylistically I've always tended towards the lively and the specific. But I try to counterbalance this by casting my stories' plots into fairly archetypal forms—such as a love triangle or an initiation into adulthood.

The real start of my writing career happened in 1976, after Sylvia and I went to see the Rolling Stones play once more. The concert was outdoors at a football stadium in Buffalo, New York. Back then the Stones seemed radical and of-the-moment. We drove to the concert with Brooks, a young friend of ours who was an apprentice printer—old-school metal and ink printing.

I was once again awed to see Mick and Keith on stage, right there, in person—two leaders I felt willing to follow in that overhyped year of the United States Bicentennial, two public figures in whom I could believe. The day after the concert I sat down at my red Selectric and started writing my first beatnik science fiction novel: *Spacetime Donuts*.

I composed the book in the style of my father telling a story after a meal, that is, I made it up as I went along. The early sections of *Spacetime Donuts* were loosely based on my experiences in graduate school, and the hero's love interest was modeled on Sylvia.

My story was guided by a particular science speculation I wanted to present: If you keep shrinking long enough, you'll eventually end up back where you started—in the same place and the same size.

The notion of finding planets within our atoms is of course something of a cliché—it's the kind of thing that screenwriters have characters talk about in order to indicate that the characters are stoned. But I was talking about finding our *own* planet down there. This is a notion that I dubbed "circular scale."

Over the years, I've found that every possible idea can be found in some pre-existing piece of science fiction—the corpus of SF is our own home-grown Library of Babel. But at the time I imagined I was the first to think of circular scale.

In one of her journal notes, Susan Sontag says that, in order to be a writer, you need to be a nut and a moron. A nut to be obsessed enough with an idea to spend months writing a book about it, and a moron to think other people will want to read the book! I had these personality traits in place from the start.

Spacetime Donuts included another element: a cadre of characters able to plug their minds directly into their society's Big Computer. In some ways this prefigures William Gibson's epochal cyberpunk novel *Neuromancer*, where console cowboys jack their brains into the planetary computer net that Gibson dubbed cyberspace. In proto-cyberpunk fashion, my characters in *Spacetime Donuts* take drugs, have sex, listen to rock and roll, and are enemies of the establishment.

I was initially unable to sell *Spacetime Donuts*. I had no real idea of where to begin, but I noticed that Bantam Books was publishing a series of SF novels labeled as "Fredrik Pohl Selections." I'd always loved Pohl's writing—most especially the novels *Wolfbane* and *The Space Merchants* that he'd co-authored with Cyril Kornbluth. So I sent him my manuscript in care of Bantam Books. He actually looked at the book and sent back a friendly rejection letter saying something like, "This is a fun read, but it's not science fiction."

I wasn't entirely discouraged. My hope was that older writers like Pohl simply didn't realize how drastically SF was about to change.

A young guy named Barry Caplan ran a bookstore called Sundance Books on the main street of Geneseo. Barry was a rabid fan of the Grateful Dead, he had long blonde hair down to his ass, and he encouraged people to call him Sundance. Even so, he was every inch a businessman, and very competent at running his store. He had a good collection of countercultural literature and science fiction. One day I found a new SF magazine called *Unearth* for sale on his shelves.

It turned out that *Unearth* was printing only stories by previously unpublished SF authors, which seemed like a perfect opportunity for me. At first I was going to sell them a short story called "Enlightenment Rabies," but then, after some correspondence, it turned out they would be willing to run my novel *Spacetime Donuts* in three installments, the first of which appeared in the summer of 1978. I think they even paid me a couple of hundred bucks. It was an incredible rush to see my name on the lurid cover of a digest-sized pulp magazine. I imagined I was off and running as a real science fiction writer.

But *Unearth* went out of business after only publishing two of the three installments. And I still couldn't sell the novel as a book.

I was beginning to grasp how long a row a writer has to hoe.

My parents had bought a cabin near Boothbay Harbor, Maine, and all through the years 1970 through 1985, we went up there for a couple of weeks in the summer, sometimes with brother Embry turning up with his wife and two children. Pop was still an Episcopal minister in northern Virginia, where he'd taken over his own church in a town called Reston. He still owned his old Champion Wood company near Louisville, Kentucky, and in the early 1970s, the business was doing fine. Pop was prospering. As well as the cabin, we had an old-style varnished wooden motorboat.

We'd tool along the fractal coast, with its coves within coves and islands beyond islands. A little beach lay near our cabin, and we'd often spend the day there with the kids. The water was unspeakably cold and pellucid. If I dove deep, I'd find striped, snaky brittle sea-stars. Half-inch long baby lobsters scuttled at the water's edge, little gray fellows, nearly transparent. Their full-grown aunts and uncles were collected by the Maine lobstermen, puttering around in their little boats. At night the water would glow with phosphorescent sea life.

At our Maine cabin, there was a long flight of slippery wooden stairs leading up from the dock where we tied up our boat. In 1974, I noticed that my father was having trouble on these stairs, he said they made his chest hurt. And then, back in Virginia, at age sixty, he had a heart attack. In order to replace his clogged coronary arteries, his surgeon did bypass surgery on him.

151

This operation was still quite new. They opened up his whole chest, leaving a vertical scar at least a foot long. The drugs and the trauma had a bad effect on Pop. He became disoriented—once on the phone he told me that he could see American troops burning Vietnamese huts from his hospital room window, although, near the end of this conversation he said he knew it was a hallucination. When he got back home he had tortuous, freaky dreams that set him to crying out in his sleep.

He had to return to the hospital a couple of times until his heart condition stabilized. During the Christmas season of 1974, we were visiting my parents with the three kids, and I snuck newborn Isabel into the hospital under my coat to cheer Pop. A half hour later, the night nurse came upon Pop happily cradling the baby.

She smiled and said, "Congratulations."

The brush with death seemed to change Pop. He grew a white beard. He'd show me his scar and run his finger along it like a zipper. "This is where they opened me up," he'd say in a tight voice.

His sense that he was living on borrowed time made him unhappy with his lot, and less patient with my mother. He began casting around for some kind of vindication for his career, some dramatic achievement to mark his passage.

"All my life I've had the feeling that something really *big* was going to happen to me," Pop told me. "I feel like I have to give it a chance." I sympathized with this—I knew a little about career struggle from all my job and grant applications over the years, and from my ongoing attempts to get my math papers and my literary writings published.

In 1976, Pop ran for the bishop of Virginia, and when that didn't work out, he unexpectedly resigned from the ministry and ran for the Virginia state legislature. We were rooting for him, wanting him to be happy, but that election didn't work out either. I was sad to see world so incompliant with my aging father's dreams.

My brother Embry and his family had moved back to Louisville in 1976. He'd taken over the running of Pop's Champion Wood Products, which had unexpectedly fallen upon hard times. Embry did a good job at turning the business around. I myself was completely out of the picture as far as the business went—I'd never taken any interest in it.

At loose ends after his sudden retirement, Pop began putting some of his energy back into his old wood business—not that Embry really wanted

Pop to be breathing down his neck. And then in 1977, completely out of the blue, Pop decreed that he and Mom should abandon Virginia and move back to Louisville too.

Perhaps Mom suspected the real reason, but it would take another year until Embry and I figured it out. Pop was planning to leave Mom, and he wanted to get her situated near my brother so she'd have someone to take care of her. At some level this might have been a price that my father figured my brother owed him in exchange for the family company.

Mom, Pop and Sylvia's parents were all at our house in 1977, for what was to be our last Christmas in Geneseo.

It was a classic holiday—Georgia got a Barbie Townhouse that she'd been longing for, Rudy got a Lionel electric train on a loop of track, and Isabel had a nice red fire-engine that she could pedal. Sylvia's father bought us a new TV, and when I shorted it out by spilling a scotch and soda through the vent on top, I took it back to the giant discount store it had come from, and they gave me a new one. Sylvia was in a sewing group with the manager's wife, which must have helped.

Mom and Pop seemed edgy with each other—no matter what one of them said, the other would bitterly disagree. I was worried about them. I wanted them to be happy. Pop kept joking about wanting to drink Arpad's hair tonic. Pop was in fact drinking pretty heavily. Given that I liked to drink, it was convenient to have my father bringing wine and whiskey into the house, but it was also depressing. At some level, we both felt it was wrong to drink together, but we did it anyway.

Sylvia and I took the grandparents out to go sledding with the kiddies one afternoon, but that wasn't a big success, as the temperature was fifteen below zero. The breeze coming up from the valley felt like the air from a freezer, or like the fumes from dry ice.

But in spite of my parents' tensions, that Christmas was generally cozy. I loved the pleasant physicality of lying on the rug like a dogfather in his den, with the kids crawling on me, poking and wrestling. Little Rudy and I liked to squeeze under the tree, staring up at the wooden figurines and the colored lights. Sylvia was great at assembling presents for us all, wrapping them up like works of art, writing cute labels, arranging them under the tree. By now a number of ornaments had migrated from our parents' houses to ours.

Mom was endlessly considerate with the children. She'd relax in their presence, forgetting her worries, reading books to them, handing them toys, smiling and nodding.

In the spring of 1978, Pop left Mom for Priscilla Ames, the woman who'd managed his campaign for the Virginia State Legislature. We all knew her—she was a pleasant, well-meaning person who'd faced a terrible tragedy. Her teenage daughter had been murdered right outside her house, and the killer had never been caught. Her own marriage had broken up in the wake. Priscilla was a parishioner of Pop's. He'd counseled her, and they'd grown close. She thought he was a hero, and of course he appreciated that.

It was now that my brother Embry and I understood the motivation for Pop's move to Louisville.

It was a terrible time, with lots of drama. Mom was heartbroken, devastated. She said she'd been thrown out like an old dish. I couldn't help but hold this against my father and his new woman. Loyal to my mother as I was, I considered Priscilla to be stiff and plastic.

Meanwhile, Pop and Priscilla were lying low on a prolonged road trip in the Cadillac that Pop had bought himself. He had an eight-track tape system in the car with a bunch of Kenny Rogers tapes. He liked to say that his white beard made him look like Hemingway—or like Kenny.

The math department at Geneseo was quite dysfunctional, with two power groups sniping at each other during our unbelievably boring departmental meetings, held in the asphalt-tiled basement once a week. Professors can be so petty and vindictive—and the sad thing is how tiny are the stakes that they're fighting over.

In 1978, the economy was in a recession, and the Geneseo administrators were talking about eliminating faculty positions. I was coming up for a tenure decision—either they'd have to fire me or they'd have to let me stay forever. It wasn't looking that good for me, even though I'd published a book and several papers and the students liked me.

I had the longest hair of any professor on campus. I hung around with the English and philosophy professors. A few of the senior math faculty disliked me. One of them, a guy named Don Trasher, took me to task for

154

Age two, with my puppy Muffin in Louisville, 1948.

Visiting our grandparents Rudolf and Lily in Hannover, Germany, around 1953.

Age thirteen, just back from my year in Germany, 1959.

With my mother and brother at my parents' house in Alexandria, Virginia, 1966, during my junior year at college. Embry was just back from the Army.

On a honeymoon visit with our parents near Boothbay Harbor, Maine, 1967.

With daughter Georgia in 1970. The storm door had no glass.

With Gregory Gibson at my thirtieth birthday party in 1976.

My office at the Mathematics Institute at the University of Heidelberg, Germany. The formula on the blackboard took me a year to prove, and was published in the *Proceedings of the American Mathematical Society,* 1978.

My brief stint as lead singer of the punk-rock Dead Pigs in Lynchburg, Virginia, 1982.

Sylvia gets a classic Buick for her birthday, 1983.

With Dennis "Sta-Hi" Poague on our way to see the Beastie Boys, Los Gatos, California, 1987.

With R. U. Sirius, Queen Mu, and Bart Nagel in 1992.

Photo by Bart Nagel. Used with permission.

With my super-hacker friend Bill Gosper with some of his puzzles
in an Indian restaurant, 2006.

With Sylvia at my show in the Live Worms Gallery
in North Beach, 2007.

With Sylvia, our children, their spouses, and the four grandchildren in Santa Cruz, 2009. Left to right: Gus, Isabel, Rudy, Zimry, Sylvia, me, Desmond, Courtney, Georgia, Jasper, Althea, Penny.

using my favorably-reviewed book, *Geometry, Relativity and the Fourth Dimension,* in my geometry class—for which my students were giving me top ratings. No good deed goes unpunished!

"This one particular problem at the end of Chapter Three, it has a calculus symbol in it," Trasher said reprovingly. "And calculus isn't a prerequisite for our geometry course."

Later he became chairman of the math department—and they went back to teaching the geometry course out of books with no pictures. *Feh!*

In the end, I was denied tenure at Geneseo. At age thirty-two, I was out of my first job—although I did have the option of staying on for one final year as a lame duck. But then, miraculously, one of my endless job and grant applications bore fruit.

Sylvia found out about it one afternoon in June, 1978, when she came back with the kids from the swimming-pool at Letchworth Park. I was on a ladder, painting our weather-peeled white clapboards.

"We're selling the house?" she cried. "You got a new job?"

Yes! On the strength of my math papers about infinity, the Alexander von Humboldt Foundation of Germany had invited me for a year as a visiting scholar at the Mathematics Institute of the University of Heidelberg.

Sylvia was happy about the impending change. Although cozy and rustic, Geneseo was also somewhat dull and small. The climate was brutal. There weren't a wide range of possibilities there, in terms of her finding a career. And she didn't want to see me zombie-march through a final lame duck year of work at SUCAS Geneseo. We'd seen other professors suffer through this, and it was a demoralizing sight, like seeing someone being pilloried in the stocks.

Instead we'd be swanning off to Europe. Sylvia had grown up there, and her parents still lived in Geneva. So, fine! The children weren't as enthused. At this point, all they knew of the world was Geneseo, so it was hard for them to contemplate such a great change. But they, too, felt some excitement and curiosity about the great adventure.

Everything began happening very fast—and in the space of two months, we'd done the big move.

We sold our house to some neighbors who'd always had their eye on it.

A local kid bought our car with the flames. He said he planned to leave my paint-job intact. As he put it, "Someone told me it's, uh, Pop art?"

We had a yard sale, and packed our remaining goods into a rented van. Meanwhile, down in Louisville, Embry walled off part of the Champion Wood warehouse for me to store our stuff.

Sylvia and the kids flew to her parents in Geneva, and I drove the van alone to Louisville before going to join them. Driving that ungainly van away from our emptied house, I burst into tears.

"I love you," I said to the old home. "I love you."

But then I was free, and out on the road.

Transrealism

We felt uprooted in Heidelberg in the fall of 1978, like dust in the wind. Our nine-year-old Georgia was especially sad about leaving her friends and the comfortable world that she'd just begun to figure out. She'd talk about it at night when I tucked her in. Her voice was small, high, anxious, brave.

"It's okay," I'd say, hugging her. "It's going to be okay."

At the start, Germany felt like a maze. I had to make numerous trips to the immigration office to get our visas in order—I'd hang around there for most of a day, waiting for a final orgiastic flurry of paper-stamping. *Thock, thock, thump*—how good it felt.

We had some trouble finding our apartment—there was a guy who was counseling arriving scholars from overseas, but my boyhood knowledge of German wasn't fully restarted yet. I only understood about half of what the advisor said, or less than that.

If I'd actually understood what the advisor was saying, I would have grasped that the cheapest and best place for us to live would be in the so-called University Guest House, an apartment complex that the university ran for its visiting foreign scholars.

But somehow we ended up renting the top floor of an ancient stone house on a steep slope overlooking the Nekar river near Heidelberg—and we had to pay some realtor a whole month's extra rent as commission for having told us the address. In any case, it was an awesome old building with a great view.

The landlord and his family lived downstairs. He pretended to be nice, but he was stingy. It was tough getting him to turn our radiators on. His wife was an imposing woman named Jutta, with an operatic voice that always seemed ready to break into a scream of fury. I was glad I wasn't married to her.

Sometimes we'd find hedgehogs in the garden—cute little beasts who could roll themselves up into something like a spiky croquet ball.

Trying to find out way into the culture, we tried going to a service at the Lutheran church across the street, but it was as depressing as a Bergmann movie. When it was time for the sermon, the minister stared stonily down at the congregation for quite a long time. And then, still in silence, he began reprovingly wagging his finger.

There was an English language church at the U.S. Army base, but that was worse. The preacher there was an evangelical type, and he interspersed the service with renditions of country-music-style gospel songs, complete with acoustic guitar.

One song in particular nearly sent our whole family into convulsions of laughter. "Jaaaaysus," brayed the singer. "Maaaster. Saaavior. There's just somethin' about that name." To keep a straight face, I had to think about hospitals and funerals, not any funerals in particular, as I hadn't really been to any—just generalized funerals.

We abandoned that Army version of our home culture and tried to act like Germans. We made frequent trips into downtown Heidelberg via one of the buses that ran along the river—or by driving the rather horrible little used car that we'd bought. The unctuous car salesman had called Sylvia, "Frau Professor Doktor von Bitter Rucker."

"Where am *I* in that list?" she asked me.

As usual, so far as the outer world was concerned, the main person was the husband with the official job. It was unjust, yes, and Sylvia was indeed as important as me. And she worked just as hard.

An especially difficult thing for Sylvia was that the German school days only lasted till noon. And then the three kids were home for lunch, with big homework assignments that we had to help them with in the afternoons and evenings. By now I'd remembered the German I'd learned during my year in the Black Forest, but even I found the homework hard.

Oh well—we were only guest-workers, low-ranking immigrants, and so what if our children didn't do all their homework. Really, we didn't worry all that much about the school, or even about my job. It was just a grant, and there were no worries about tenure.

In the winter, our car's battery tended to die. If I parked it on a hill, I could start it by putting it in second gear, pressing down the clutch, letting it roll, and then popping out the clutch. But if I was parked somewhere flat, I'd have to beg strangers to push the car up to speed—not always easy. If I couldn't find anyone to help, I'd lose my temper and kick the car in the side, making dents in its fenders.

Given that the streets were flat in the vicinity of the Mathematics Institute, I generally used a combination of bus and trolley to get there in the winter. It was okay that it took me a little while. It's not like there was any big rush. I could think about infinity or science fiction on the street as well as in an office. And it was fun looking at all the Germans, most of them fit and well-dressed. I'd brought my bicycle along from America, and on warm, clear days, I might ride that instead of taking the bus.

The kids attended a German school near our apartment. They picked up the language quite fast. Georgia did well—she was in third grade and soon she was at the head of her class. Isabel was having fun in the kindergarten, but it was hard for Rudy, as he was starting first grade, and they were learning to read, but with the spoken names of the alphabet letters different all of a sudden. It was so frustrating for him that he'd run around the classroom roaring like a lion. The other kids admired him for this, and before long he'd befriended a number of the other boys.

Isabel's kindergarten was like an Eden before the rigors of the strict German elementary school years. Her teachers were cheerful hippie women, always singing, dancing, and playing music. On a warm day, the children would play in the sand in their underwear. In the mornings, I'd give Isabel a ride down the hill sitting on the crossbar of my bike. None of us wore helmets back then.

One weekend, Rudy's new friends set up a tent in our landlord's front yard and they slept out together. The landlord had given permission, but when he saw the tent, he didn't like it. To add to his outrage, one of the boys broke a branch off a tree for tent stakes. Instantly a hand-lettered warning sign appeared on the tree. At dawn, seized by a fit of impishness, Rudy capered across the dewy grass, hooting the landlord's name at the top of his lungs. Georgia ran outside and nearly choked him.

Frustrated at her inability to talk to people or even to do the children's homework, Sylvia signed up for a beginning German class at the Univer-

159

sity, and she made friends with some other foreigners there. She usually drove to class with a visiting Israeli woman who felt very conflicted about being in Germany at all. One night the German police stopped Sylvia—they were always looking for terrorists. These were the days of the Baader-Meinhof gang. One of the cops aimed a machine-gun at Sylvia and her friend, while the others looked through our battered little car. You didn't want to mess with the German cops.

Georgia's particular burden at school was an American boy named Chad, whose father was also visiting at the University. Chad arrived about six months after us, and the teacher asked Georgia to be his interpreter. Chad wasn't a particularly likeable kid. Georgia was just starting to blend into her class but now, to her dismay, she was put into a two-person desk with Chad. As Chad had very poor vision, the desk had to be placed in front of the classroom, only a foot or two away from the blackboard.

Chad's parents, who were from Kansas, wanted Ronald Reagan to be president, which seemed very strange to Sylvia and me. We thought they were joking—at that time, in the late Seventies, Reagan's image was more that of a right-wing clown than of a Great Communicator. We didn't realize how rapidly the U.S. was changing while we were gone. I was still imagining that the glorious 1960s would return. Little did I realize what the United States was in for.

*T*he head of the Mathematics Institute didn't particularly care what I did, which was great. He'd helped me line up the grant, and his group was being reimbursed, and there was nothing more to worry about. In a way, I could do no wrong. He gave me a nice quiet office in the institute's modern building, with no teaching duties at all.

I thought about Cantor's Continuum Problem for a few months, reading most of Cantor's philosophical writings in German. It made me feel like a real scholar to be studying these obscure essays, which weren't available in English. Cantor was interested in three kinds of infinity: the mathematical, the physical and the theological.

Given that mathematical set theory has developed such a precise system for talking about infinities, I had already been thinking it would be nice if set theory had some physical applications. It very often takes decades or even centuries till a mathematical theory finds a use in physics—for instance it was sixty years before Riemann's 1852 theory of curved space appeared in Einstein's 1916 General Theory of Relativity.

It was intriguing that Cantor had talked about physical infinities from the very start, way back in the 1880s. I also found it interesting that Cantor didn't shy away from discussing the relationship between infinity and God. For the non-mathematician, this seems natural, but academics are—not without reason—squeamish about dragging religion into scientific discussions. Nevertheless, it is reasonable to look for connections between theology and set theory.

For instance, a theologian might say, "God is greater than anything that we can conceive." Rather than dismissing this as sheer bombast, a mathematician of a certain stripe might reformulate the claim as, "The class of all sets is bigger than any set we can define." Each viewpoint sheds light upon the other. In both cases, we're trying to think about philosophically ultimate concepts. This was just the kind of topic I'd been discussing with Gaisi Takeuti at the Institute for Advanced Study in Princeton, so it was great to read Cantor's thoughts about it.

I set up a seminar at the Mathematics Institute, and gave some lectures along these lines. The mathematical logic faculty enjoyed my discussions, even though their real interests lay in more technical work. I began combining my notes for these talks with the notes for the lectures on the philosophy of mathematics that I'd given at Geneseo when I'd been team-teaching with Bill Edgar. I was beginning to see the outlines for the popular nonfiction book about infinity which I would ultimately write—*Infinity and the Mind.*

As the fall of 1978 wore on, I finally came to accept that I was never going to make any big technical breakthrough in extending Gödel's work to solve Cantor's questions about the different levels of infinity. By the start of 1979, I'd decided to make better use of my time in Heidelberg—and write more science fiction.

I started by writing science fiction stories, some of them inspired by paradoxical notions from the philosophy of science. I began having some luck selling my stories to SF magazines. Not all of my tales were hard SF—one was about Franz Kafka being reborn in a new body every year. I was reading Kafka's journals at the time, loving him for being such a desperately romantic fanatic.

I wrote seven short stories—and then I wrote *White Light*, a science fiction novel about infinity. *Spacetime Donuts* had been a fun book, but really it was a work of apprenticeship. With *White Light* I got serious about being a novelist.

I began writing the book in longhand one weekend in January, 1979, while I was alone with the kids. Sylvia was visiting her dying grandmother in Budapest. I called my novel *White Light*, in memory of my memorable acid trip back at Rutgers. And I gave it a subtitle lifted from a paper by Kurt Gödel: *What is Cantor's Continuum Problem?*

I'd been corresponding with my college friend Greg Gibson about a new approach to writing science fiction. He'd crystallized the basic idea very clearly: "The cool thing to do would be to write a science fiction novel, but write it about your actual life."

The main character of *White Light* was a math professor, closely modeled on me, and the setting was very much like Geneseo. As I mentioned earlier, the practice of writing science fiction about real life is what I began calling *transrealism* in the early 1980s.

In *White Light*, my life in Geneseo was the *real* part, and the *trans* part was that my character in the novel leaves his body and journeys to a land where Cantor's infinities are as common as rocks and plants.

White Light was also influenced by the *Donald Duck* and *Zap* comics that I loved so well. One chapter features Donald and his nephews, and in another chapter, objects start talking, as they sometimes do in R. Crumb comic strips. I also used the papers by Cantor that I'd been reading—and I included the man himself as a character.

Over the years, I've often worked by alternating between writing science fiction and writing popular science. So it was fitting that I began working on an early draft of *Infinity and the Mind*, my nonfiction book about infinity, at the same time that I was writing *White Light*. Each endeavor was feeding the other.

I got into a very pleasant and exalted mental state during this period of time. I remember having a magical dream in which I was scrambling up the ridge of a mountain. The stone underfoot was slippery pieces of shale, and among the stones I was finding wonderful polyhedral crystals the size of chestnuts or hedgehogs. Even within the dream, I knew that these treasures represented my wonderful new ideas.

I finished the manuscript for *White Light* in the summer of 1979, when I was thirty-three. It would take me a few more years to finish the tome, *Infinity and the Mind*. I tried sending *White Light* to the Scott Meredith literary agency. They charged me a couple of hundred bucks to have someone read my manuscript. The anonymous reader disliked the book, and Scott Meredith refused to submit it to any publishers. So then I decided trying to sell the manuscript by myself.

I sent it off to Ace Books, getting their address from the title page of Ian Watson's *Miracle Visitors*, a wonderful book written on the same wavelength as *White Light*. While I was waiting for my book to work its way through the Ace slush pile, I went to my first world science fiction convention, in Brighton, England, August, 1979—taking the train and ferry from Heidelberg.

The atmosphere at mathematics conferences had always been rather frosty. There weren't enough jobs to go around, and newcomers weren't particularly welcome. But the science fiction folks were, like, "the more the merrier." I loved the vibe.

Some well-dressed hippies from London got me high on hashish and introduced me to a hipster named Maxim Jakubowski. Maxim was editing a new line of books for the Virgin record company. His first book was going to be about the punk band The Sex Pistols, but he was looking for radical SF novels as well.

I'd brought along a single Xerox of the *White Light* manuscript, and I handed it to Maxim on the spot. And a few weeks later he made an offer to buy the British rights for the book. A month after that, in the fall of 1979, the editor Jim Baen at Ace made an offer for the US rights. I felt like a plant pushing out from the soil into the sun and air.

The word "transreal" that I came to apply to my novels was inspired by a blurb on the back of my copy of *A Scanner Darkly*, saying that Philip K. Dick had written "a transcendental autobiography."

A Scanner Darkly is a hilarious, sorrowful, transreal masterpiece. I got my copy at that SF convention in Brighton—the book was just out, and my new stoner friends had been talking about it, complaining that it was "too anti-drug." They didn't seem to understand that the book was funny.

After that convention, waiting for my train back to London, and thus back to Germany, I was reading *Scanner*, and I was laughing so hard that I left my suitcase on the platform—which I suddenly realized as the train started to move. I jumped back out in the nick of time. Up until *Scanner*, I hadn't fully grasped how close Phil Dick's novels were to the kinds of books that I wanted to write. I particularly liked the language-with-a-flat tire way that his characters talked in *Scanner*, and over the years I'd begin to emulate his peculiarly Californian tone. And even more, I liked the sense that Phil was writing about real people.

I, too, felt that the characters of my novels should be based on actual people. The characters should do more than woodenly move the plot along. They should be sarcastic, miss the point, change the subject, break the set, and do surprising things.

I find it dull when novels have characters who are supposed to be normal people. My sense has always been that there actually *aren't* any normal people. Everyone I've ever met is weird at some level. It's liberating to have quirky, unpredictable characters—instead of the impossibly good and bad paper dolls of mass-culture. As I mentioned above while talking about *White Light*, lifelike characters are the "real" part of transreal.

As for the "trans" part—it seemed to me that I could use the special effects and power chords of SF as a way to thicken and intensify the material. The tools of science fiction can be a way, if you will, to directly manipulate the subtext, that is, a way to add a more artistic shape to the suppressed fears and desires that you inevitably incorporate into your fiction.

Time travel, levitation, alternate worlds, aliens, telepathy—they're all symbols of archetypal modes of experience. Time travel is memory, levitation is enlightenment, alternate worlds are travel, aliens are other people, and telepathy is the fleeting hope of finally being fully understood.

I saw transrealism as a way to describe not only immediate reality, but also the higher reality in which life is embedded. And I saw transrealism as way to smash the oppressive lie of consensus reality.

---

*I*n the summer 1979, my von Humboldt grant was about to run out. Rather than restarting the dreary charade of looking for another teaching job in the US, I managed to get the grant renewed for a second year, which would carry us into 1980. We changed apartments, finally moving into the University Guest House that we'd missed out on before.

The Guest House was a lively, congenial place, filled with foreign scholars and their families. We found plenty of friends for us and the kids. The only problem was the house manager, with whom Chad's Reagan-fan Kansas parents had started a feud. His name was Herr Böhm, although the Kansans insisted on calling him Herr Boom.

Georgia got caught up in a guerilla campaign against Herr Böhm, planting insulting drawings of him around the premises where he or his wife would find them. That Georgia! Eventually the man turned up at our door to yell at us, but nothing more really happened.

Well, there was one more thing. Herr Böhm's son had an extra car that he liked to park in my assigned slot in basement lot. So—like any logical mathematician would do—I took my pen-knife and punctured one of his tires. I told my German-Hungarian friend Imre Molnar about about my exploit. He approved.

"Irgendwie muss der Mensch sich die Freude nehmen," said Imre, meaning, "A man's got to grab his joy somehow."

The next evening I found that the house manager's son had punctured one of *my* car's tires. Without any discussion, each of us patched our tire—and after that his car stayed out of my slot.

We liked it in the Guest House. Thanks to Sylvia's parents, we'd acquired a magnificent stash of Lego blocks—a full bushel basket of them. The kids and I worked with the Legos nearly every day, making castles, spaceships, dolls, playhouses, and cows. Eventually Rudy and I got hold of a battery-operated Lego engine, and we built a foot-long car that we could send tooling through the felt-covered hallways.

The down side of the Guest House was that there was so much demand for space in this complex that our family could only get a one-bedroom apartment. None of us could sleep very soundly in such close quarters, so after a few months we managed to get an extra room for the kids to sleep in. It was three or four doors down. At night I'd go in there with the kids and tell them stories or read to them before they fell asleep.

For security, you'd roll down steel window covers at night, just like you'd see on shops in a big city. So after you turned out the light in the kids' room, it was really pitch dark. Once in awhile—and the kids still talk about this—I'd pretend to leave their room, but in fact shut myself inside with them. There was a slight hallway into the room that kept them from being able to see the door from their beds.

And then, in the dark, moving ever so slowly and quietly, I'd creep across the floor and—all of a sudden—grab one the children by the shoulders, yelling "Kidnapper!" They'd scream like crazy. And then they'd ask me to do it again—or beg me not to. They could never quite decide. Probably I shouldn't have scared them that way. But it gave us something else to talk about.

In the winters we'd take plastic sleds to the park at very top of the hill—beyond the woods above the Guest House. One time we were there, climbing back up for another ride, and some boys started yelling at Georgia in German.

"Get out of the way, girl!"

She'd mastered the language by now, and she unleashed an impressive tirade against them, calling them silly dumb-heads. I was proud of her. She wasn't going to let men push her around.

Mom and Pop completed their divorce in the spring of 1979—and they never spoke to each other again. Mom even had her wedding ring melted into a puddle of gold that she occasionally wore as a pendant. It was awful.

Pop and his woman friend Priscilla came to visit us in Heidelberg in the fall of 1979. It was a mournful, uncomfortable encounter. Pop was a mess—he was consumed with guilt about leaving Mom, and he was drinking more heavily than ever before. Priscilla was stiff and brittle with us. She disapproved of me, as if I were unworthy of being Pop's son.

After a few long days, I put them on a train for Paris. They were planning to stay in a good hotel and live it up. Poor Pop. He'd done his duty all his life. Now Death was stalking him and he was trying to have fun. Seeing his train pull away, I stood there feeling as if my heart would break.

166

I wanted Pop to be happy, but just now he seemed totally screwed up. And my poor mother was alone in Louisville, instead of having an exciting time in Europe. Each of them was, in one way or another, difficult to live with—but how I wished they'd found a way to work things out.

What to do? I started work on another science fiction novel. When faced with life's intolerable realities, I tend to transmute them into literary art. In this case, I planned to write a transreal novel as before—but without using myself as a character. I sensed that not having any specific Rudy-inspired character would give the other characters more space to develop and to open up.

One character, called Cobb Anderson, would be an old man modeled on my father in his current state. To some extent I could project myself into this character too. For all our disagreements over the years, Pop and I never were all that different. Another factor in my writing about Pop was that I was in some sense trying to inoculate myself against ending up like him—besotted, afraid of death, and on the run from the family.

The other character in my novel was a young guy called Sta-Hi Mooney. After all these years, I wanted finally to develop a character based on my wild and wacky friend Dennis Poague—the guy who used to turn up in Geneseo to visit his big brother Lee who was teaching there. What I liked about Dennis was that he seemed to have no internal censor. He always said exactly what he was thinking. He was relatively uneducated, but he had a fanciful mind, and a hipster, motor-mouth style of speech.

In the opening scene, Cobb is sitting on a beach in Florida, drinking sherry, and he's approached by his double. At first I thought I was writing a time-travel novel, but then I hit on the notion that Cobb's double should in fact be a robot copy of him.

To make this work, I developed the idea that it will become possible to extract a person's personality from their brain, and that it will then be possible to run the extracted human software on some fresh hardware—and why not have the hardware be a robot resembling the person's former body!

Software. In 1979, this was a technical and little-known word—I'd picked it up from an article in the *Scientific American*. I decided to use it

167

for the title of my book. I finished *Software* near the end of our stay in Heidelberg, in the summer of 1980, and I had no trouble selling it to Susan Allison, the pleasant and intelligent woman who'd taken over from Jim Baen as the science fiction editor at Ace Books.

My idea of copying a person onto a robot was a fresh concept in those days, and my book gained power from the intensity of its father/son themes and from the colorful anarchism of my robot characters, whom I called "boppers." Also I had some over-the-top scenes of which I was proud. At one point, some sleazy biker types are about to cut off the top of Sta-Hi's skull and eat his brain while he's still alive. They wanted to extract the software, you understand.

I do recall that Susan Allison got me to take out a scene in which the stoned Sta-Hi takes a shit in the ocean while he's swimming. "Excise the turd," was the way she put it. Why would I even write a scene like that? I guess I thought it was funny—and a fresh way to outrage any straitlaced readers. But there were plenty of other outrageous things in the book.

Regarding the computer-science theme of the book, although I knew all about the theory of computation from my studies of mathematical logic, I didn't know jack about real-world computers—we SF writers very often don't know the technical details of what we're talking about. In terms of my teaching career, I could see the wave of computer science starting to build, but I didn't quite know how to get onto it. The only way to access a machine was to use a text terminal with its nasty, inscrutable protocols—or to feed a deck of punched programming cards to a giant machine in a basement.

An oddly anachronistic thing about *Software* is that, in those years, I couldn't imagine there being a really small computing device with the power of a human brain. So, instead of giving my Cobb-emulating robot a supercomputer that could fit inside this bopper's skull, I had the Cobb-robot's brain be a big supercooled clunker that follows the robot around in the back of a refrigerated van that's disguised as a Mr. Frostee truck. But that's okay. It makes the book more fun. And, at a deeper level, the brain in the truck is nice concrete symbol for an organization which maintains complete control over its agents.

Near the end of our stay in Heidelberg, I did take a programming course involving an old-school language called PL/I. I managed to punch a deck of cards that would emulate a Universal Turing Machine. This meant that my deck could emulate any possible computation, provided you added a supplemental deck of punch cards to describe the computation you wanted to emulate. I was amused by the self-referential aspect of my project. And now I could tell my job interviewers that I knew a little computer science.

There was no way to stretch out my grant any further than 1980. I made some attempts to find a teaching job in Germany, but that didn't work. I had to face the music and once again look for a math professor job in the US.

I flew back for a series of job interviews and, in the end, I received but one job offer, from a place called Randolph-Macon Woman's College in Lynchburg, Virginia, known as R-MWC for short. They had a three-person math department.

The R-MWC math department chairman was a plump, uptight guy a couple of years younger than me. From the very start we felt zero empathy towards each other. My first thought upon seeing him at the Lynchburg airport was, "This is a terrible mistake."

But I made a good impression on the Dean and the President, and I gave a very well-received demonstration lecture, a highly polished, low-level presentation of Gödel's Incompleteness Theorem—which I'd been thinking about for years. The professors other than the math chairman loved my lecture, and it could be that they pressured him into hiring me.

And so my family and I moved back to the U.S. In the summer of 1980, with a job in hand, Sylvia and I bought a car and a house in about a week. It was exhilarating to find America's bigness still in place. And, ah, the supermarkets! Outside a Winn-Dixie in Louisville, we two had a moment of ecstasy, hearing the Beatles "Back in the USSR" on the radio.

We'd enjoyed our time in Germany, but were glad to be back in our native culture where we more or less knew what was going on. The children were gung-ho for diving back into American life. And moving to Virginia sounded like fun.

Lynchburg?

ynchburg, Virginia, was the home town of the infamous TV evangelist Jerry Falwell. His supporters mostly lived in a different part of town from our part, which was near the college. People seemed to dress very strangely in our neighborhood. You'd see women in lime-green skirts and hot-pink blouses patterned with little white whales.

We couldn't decide if it was a time-warp or a space-warp, that is, whether people looked like this everywhere in America in 1980, or whether they'd always looked this way in Lynchburg.

"It's the preppy look," Georgia told us.

This use of the word was new to me. "Preppy means tweedy," I protested. "Like button-down shirts."

"You're old and out of it," she scolded. "You're *groovy!*" In her new circle of friends, *groovy* was a word of extreme opprobrium.

Many of the students at Randolph-Macon wore Add-A-Bead necklaces, with a few more gold beads added to the chain after each holiday with their parents. Of course, given that I was teaching math classes, there were a few bright and enthusiastic faces. But overall I couldn't relate to my students very well.

I'd been listening to the Blondie song, "I'm Not Living in the Real World," and I quoted the title line to my calculus class. A stern young woman impatiently asked, "Then where *are* you living?" There was no way to explain.

I'd only been teaching there about three months when the chairman told me that he wanted to fire me.

"You can't do that," I implored. "I just moved my whole family here. We bought a house. Why do you want to fire me?"

"You haven't been collecting homework. Some of the students told me."

"I'll collect homework, I will, I promise."

"It's not enough just to *do* it, Rudy. You have to *want* to do it."

I buckled down and started collecting homework, and the chairman backed off—for a time.

Early in 1981, I finally finished putting together my popular book about logic and set theory. By now I'd accumulated a great mass of material, both in the form of course notes and in the form of academic papers I'd been publishing in various offbeat journals. My final insight about how to structure my book came to me while I was at, of all things, a religious retreat.

Jerry Falwell's Thomas Roads Baptist Church cast a shadow across all of Lynchburg. One of the first things people would ask when they met you was where you went to church. There were stories that on Sunday mornings Jerry's people would send vans into the residential neighborhoods, luring children with promises of cake and fun, so as to ferry them to Jerry's church for a session of his Sunday school.

We warned our children never to get into one of Jerry's vans. And to be really safe, we began attending the local Episcopal church—which was only a block or two from our house. They had a young minister there named Rich Jones who was a good guy—he and his wife had two kids the ages of Georgia and Rudy, and we often hung out together. Rich talked me into attending this religious retreat to be held at a lodge in the Blue Ridge Mountains, some forty miles away. Sylvia was stuck staying home with the kids.

I was in a state of mental crisis, trying to switch over from being a free-living expatriate science fiction writer to being a plodding pedagogue in a conservative Southern town. The dinkiness and smarminess of Randolph-Macon was oppressive—the tiny campus felt like a stage set, a dollhouse, a heap of pink faces and wriggling arms. The students paid a hefty tuition, and there was an unspoken understanding that we faculty were to think of ourselves as servants. One night they even made us act as croupiers at a Casino Night for the girls and their dates. Ugh.

171

It was a horrible job, but I couldn't find a better one. My only hope for escape lay in my writing, not that the advances I'd gotten for my first two novels were anywhere near being enough to support a family. But maybe, if I could just twist my mind around into the right configuration, I could write a best-seller.

At the Blue Ridge retreat, I quickly tired of the break-out groups and the uplifting chalk-talks. I skeeved off and went walking in the mountains, part of me looking into myself, part of me reaching outward in search of the White Light. When you get down to it, Nature's always been the real church for me. Yes, there's something soothing about praying or singing with a group of people. But I always feel closer to the Absolute when I'm outdoors.

The practical pay-off from the retreat was that I came up with a chapter outline for my nonfiction book and, come to think of it, the title, *Infinity and the Mind*. This would in fact turn out to be my best-selling book.

As I write this memoir, there's over half a million copies of *Infinity and the Mind* in print, in nine different languages, with a new English edition out from Princeton University Press—who published monographs by Einstein and Gödel. But somehow the success of the book came at such a slow and gradual pace that I never did get any large amount of money at any one time.

*I*n the summer of 1981 my little family and I took a road trip from Lynchburg to the Naropa Institute in Boulder, Colorado. Naropa was the brain-child of a Tibetan guru called the Rimpoche, who'd brought his followers there. The Rimpoche was close to Allen Ginsberg. Along with the poet Anne Waldman, Allen had started up a heavily beatnik literary program at Naropa, including lectures and workshops. In memory of the deceased king of the Beats, they called it "The Jack Kerouac Disembodied School of Poetics."

I had a mathematician friend, Newcomb Greenleaf, who happened to be a follower of the Rimpoche, and he got me invited out there to give some lectures Rather than being there in my role as an SF writer, I was to talk about the philosophical One/Many Problem, as filtered through the concepts of set theory and mathematical logic. We'd get a free apartment and a little money.

It was our family's first drive out West, and we loved it. We five squeezed into our station wagon, making a special cushioned area in the way-back that we called the Pig's Nest. The big thrill for me was, of course, to meet my beatnik heroes, Allen Ginsberg and William Burroughs, who were on the summer program as well.

It was amazing to see Burroughs giving his talk, dressed in his invariable suit and tie, reading his lecture in a bone-dry voice. Allen Ginsberg was in the background, saintly and helpful, adjusting the windows, the mike, and the chairs. There were only about twenty people in the audience, and they'd allotted quite a bit of time for questions, so I posed the Master a few.

"You seem so serious today," I said. "Do you laugh when you're writing?"

He gave a thin, sly smile. "I might. If it's funny."

"Do you have any good SF ideas on how to send yourself into outer space without using rockets?" I asked.

"Go as a virus," answered Burroughs.. "Code your information into a bug that others catch,"

"You used to say the word is a virus," I pressed. "Would you say that a writer reproduces personality-software in a virus-like fashion so that, later on, readers embody the writer's mind?"

"That's why they call us the immortals."

This was great stuff. And I even got to press a paperback copy of *White Light* into Bill's hands. "Far out," he said.

Later I'd use Burroughs's notion of making your personality into a communicable virus in at least three of my novels: *Freeware*, *Saucer Wisdom*, and *Hylozoic*. And for that matter, the idea lies at the heart of my non-fiction tome, *The Lifebox, the Seashell, and the Soul*. I kept the trope new by implementing it in a different way each time.

Sylvia and I made friends with a pair of Naropa tai-chi teachers and grant-writers—Bataan and his wife Jane. Bataan seemed always to be high, armed with a pint of brandy and a pipe of weed. I remember him telling Sylvia and me his vision of reality: "Life is a river. A long and winding river."

One night my family and I went for dinner at Bataan and Jane's. We were deep into loud African pop music, laughing it up.

"Let's do a hot-tub," proposed Jane.

I was happy at the prospect of getting into a hot-tub—I don't think I'd ever even seen one before. But no way were our three kids about to undress with drunk grown-ups. And the modest Sylvia wasn't into the concept either. They left me alone at Bataan and Jane's and went back to our temporary apartment. Meanwhile I started bragging to my hosts about what a great novelist I was going to be—a beatnik SF writer.

So Jane said, "Well, we'll tell Allen to come over." And the next thing I knew, Ginsberg was there.

Allen and shared a joint. I was babbling about having read "Howl" aloud with Niles with Louisville, and how much it had meant to me—but of course he'd heard that routine a zillion times. He perked up when I starting talking about beatnik science fiction.

Emboldened, I burst out, "What I want from you, Allen, after being hung-up on the Beats all these years, what I want is your blessing."

And real fast Allen whapped his hand down on my head like a skull-cap or an electric-chair metal cap that goes *zzt zzt.*

"BLESS YOU!" he yelled.

We rapped a little more. "How did the beatniks get so much ink?" I asked, trying to plan a career.

"Fine writing."

And then I was into the hot-tub with Bataan, Jane, Allen, and Allen's young boyfriend, passing around Bataan's brandy. Allen and I started quoting Kerouac haikus to each other. I told him my favorite:

"Useless, useless, Heavy rain falling into the sea."

"Neal liked that one too."

A few days later, Sylvia and I went to see Allen recite poetry with a new-wave band, the Gluons, at a club in Boulder. Bataan drifted in, sat with us, and broke out his trusty corn-cob pot-pipe. And now the Beat poet Gregory Corso appeared, sitting with us as well, looking like a criminal saint.

Meanwhile Allen was reading his latest poem, "Birdbrain," snaking back and forth, his bald head twitching like a Hindi dancer's, holding up a sheaf of papers.

"I am Birdbrain!" he declaimed. "I declare Birdbrain to be victor in the Poetry Contest!"

There was a break, and in the quiet, I tapped Gregory on the shoulder, hoping to talk to him. He whirled around.

"Do you so love me?" He pushed his face an inch away from mine, "Do you so love me?"

"Uh, yeah, sure."

"Why?"

"Well, I always really dug Jack and he was your friend . . . "

"Okay. We're all here. We're all here but something's wrong. What?"

"Jack's dead."

"You got it. Lissen to this. Blukka. Whats'at mean? Blukka."

"I don't know."

"Here and now. Like right there, trying to understand that, you got a blukka."

"Yeah, sure. Satori." I twitched in excitement and our heads banged hard into each other.

"Here and now," said Gregory. "Like you can't hold onto it. Let it go past. A knot on your head."

On the stage, Allen was back. "This poem is for Gregory Corso," he announced.

Gregory, reacting to that, locked his head against my shoulder to continue talking, mouth to ear like prisoners in the pen. "I knew a guy who died," intoned Gregory. "I knew a guy who died."

"You mean Jack?"

"I knew him, you know. And he died. I didn't meet him after he was dead. I knew a guy who died."

"Yeah." I kind of felt like we should be listening to Ginsberg's poem.

Gregory chuckled and leaned back, picking up on my tension. "Look at him," he said, admiring Allen onstage. "Look at Ginsey go." Ginsey was flickering like a flame, spouting total anarchist propaganda, it was just so Beat. "He's the master," added Gregory. "We're like two guys at a ball-game. On the mound, the master."

When the poem was over Allen walked back to us. "Did you listen to your poem, Gregory?"

Sylvia started talking to Gregory then, and he rolled up his sleeve to show her his special tattoo. It was a little oval with a red dot and a green dot inside the oval, and coming off the top of the oval was a line that branched at its end.

"What is it?" he asked Sylvia.

"It's a stop-light," she shot back.

"No no, it's the first thing man ever drew. What you got is the brush and the bag to keep—what they paint with, the stuff. The place to dip different colors. It's a painting of itself."

A big time.

And then it was back to Lynchburg. Despite my job troubles there, the town proved to be a comfortable nest where Sylvia and I would spend six years raising our kids.

In the fall of 1981, for Isabel's seventh birthday we looked in the classified ads and found an ad for *Free Puppies*. The place was out in the sticks, it was a farm with lots of bare red dirt. The farmer's dog had borne a litter of six. Five of the puppies were black and short-haired, one was orange and white with long hair.

This pup liked to lie on his back when you petted him. The farm-wife liked him best; she said she always brought him inside to play with while she watched TV. We all practiced petting him, and he eagerly rolled over to offer us his stomach. On the drive home we agreed to name our new dog Arf, with the nickname Arfie. That's what my first real math teacher, Gigi Taylor, had called her dog in Louisville, or rather, that's the name that her two-year-old son had given the dog. I'd always admired that name's simplicity.

We had a big enough house that Arf spent a lot of time inside, and never mind my talk about my hay fever. There was a wide pie-slice-shaped step where the carpeted staircase turned: that was Arf's special spot. He could sit there and hear whatever was going on upstairs or down. The children loved to spend time petting Arf, confiding with him when the world seemed against them.

"If you're ever sitting on the ground," observed Isabel, "Arf comes up and sticks his nose in your face to see what you're doing. The nerve!"

Sylvia liked taking him for walks, she was proud of what a cute puppy he was, and of how everyone would comment on him. She particularly

176

admired his high-held feathery tail—sometimes she called him "Plume."

In the summer, Arf hung out under our front porch. This was a four-foot-high space about forty feet wide, with that bare red Virginia dirt on the ground. It was cool and shady there, and Arf could dig as much as he liked without getting scolded.

The children liked it under that porch too. Arf had made several large crater-like depressions to lie in, and Rudy would fill these pits with water from the hose so that there'd be a really good supply of mud for building walls on our driveway. Later we had a discarded mattress that made its way under the porch in real hillbilly fashion, and Isabel once tried to camp out down there with a friend—although eventually the mosquitoes drove them to the bunk-bed in Isabel's room.

One problem with Arf being outside a lot was that he would roam all over the neighborhood, and into neighborhoods further and further beyond. He was looking for female dogs in heat. If we waited a few hours, or at most a day, he'd always come home, sometimes looking a bit exhausted and wrung-out.

We didn't want to chain Arf or pen him up, so it was more or less impossible to keep him from roaming. Especially in the springtime, he'd sniff the air in a certain way, and you'd know he was going to make a break for it. Now and then the city dogcatcher would pick him up, and I'd have to pay to get Arf out of the kennel and maybe even go to court to pay a ticket.

For some reason I had the idea that Arf was highly intelligent. So I spent some time trying to teach him that he should always run away from the dogcatcher. Arf and I sat down together in the driveway, and I moved two little rocks around on the ground to stand for Arf and the dogcatcher.

"Dog-catcher come. Arf run away! Dog-catcher bad. Arf run away!"

Arf almost looked like he understood, but then he started sniffing at my hands to see if there was food in them.

Rudy and Isabel were attending a nice old public school called Garland-Rhodes, about three blocks from our house. They'd walk all the way—it was great to see them marching down the street, tidy and eager. If Rudy and I saw each other a block away, we'd take off our hats and wave them at each other. One problem was that Arf wanted to follow them every day. I'd try and keep him in the house, but sometimes he'd get out the back door and take off after Rudy and Isabel.

They'd die of embarrassment when, now and then, Arf would manage to get inside the school and go tearing down the halls looking for them, with his nails clicking on the floor, kids running after him, and teachers yelling. Rudy and Isabel would sit stiffly at their desks, pretending they didn't know Arf at all.

Our kids joined the choir in our Episcopal church, and it turned out that one of the hymns they sang was that very song that had seemed so comical to us when we'd tried attending the U.S. Army church in Heidelberg, "There's Just Something About That Name." Georgia had a very sweet and musical voice, and she adapted this hymn for praising our pet at home.

"Arfie. Master. Savior. There's just something about that name."

Georgia went to a private girls' school called Seven Hills School, which was a couple of blocks further away. We usually drove her there. Seven Hills had a list of novels that they recommended for the students to read and Georgia read practically every book on the list before classes began. She was determined to do well—and she enjoyed reading.

I once gave away the ending of *Jane Eyre* to Georgia by asking, "Did you get to the part where she finds the guy's crazy wife in the attic?" She scolded me about this for years.

Huge numbers of daffodils came out in the springtime, particularly in the woods down at the bottom of the hill our house was on. Georgia and Isabel liked going to pick bouquets. There were some friendly kids living right next door to us, but one of them wasn't too bright. When she saw our girls picking daffodils, she took a wagon down there, and picked every single flower in the woods, hauling them up to wither in a heap in her back yard.

The father of these girls was a Southern guy called R. G. He worked as an estimator for an electrical contractor. He was actually quite sharp, but he liked playing the redneck, if only to tease me. When we'd been living next door to him for about a month, R. G. asked me if I wanted to go to a KKK rally. It took me a few anxious days to realize he'd been kidding me.

R. G. liked mowing his lawn and trimming his hedges, but he didn't have a hedge-trimmer. One day he convinced me to help him tidy up the top of his hedges by helping him to hold his lawnmower up in the air and lower it onto the sprouts. We were each holding two wheels, standing on either side of the hedge. After a couple of minutes, it became quite evident to me that this was a terrible idea, and we quit.

For as long as we lived there, R.G.'s wife never could learn how to spell my first name. Every year her Christmas card was addressed to "Rundy Rucker," which delighted the kids.

Another Lynchburg Christmas story. Some carolers came by our house one year, and I called the kids to come see. They crawled to the door on all fours, barking, making faces, and peering out at the carolers as if they had no idea what was going on. The more I scolded them, the harder they barked and laughed.

Sometimes they liked to give me a taste of my own rebelliousness.

With the kids all in school, Sylvia finally had the chance to start working. Her first job in Lynchburg was the fulfillment of a long-standing fantasy of hers—being a sign painter. She'd always been good at painting sharp, clear lines, and in 1981 she found work hand-lettering billboards. "BABCOCK AUTO REPAIR" was one of her strongest works, over fifty feet long. I greatly admired the skill of the lettering. It was, like, Pop art.

She hoped to start using the airbrush and maybe even bending neon tubes, but the others in the shop wouldn't let her share these tasks. She was the only woman working there—a matter of some comment in Lynchburg, Virginia. One of the clients, a woman realtor, actually complained to the owner about seeing Sylvia in the shop. For some reason it bothered this nitwit realtor that Sylvia was wearing jeans.

The sign-painting business took a down-turn before long, but Sylvia managed to switch to a new job. Thanks to her graduate work, she was able to get a Virginia teaching credential, and she had a shot at high-school teaching. Her first teaching job was at a public school in Naruna, Virginia, a long drive out into the boonies, a place with a deep-South feel.

She taught a couple of English classes, and one day she had me come guest-teach for an hour. I was going to read a science fiction story about higher dimensions, and to introduce it, I talked a little about the concept of a two-dimensional world. I asked if anyone had ever heard of *Flatland*.

"That's where you grow peanuts at," volunteered one of the pupils in all seriousness. It was indeed true that gooberiferous zones of Virginia were the sandy flats inland from the shore.

179

Before long, Sylvia tired of the long drive to Naruna, and of the place's backwater vibe. She found a better job teaching Latin and French at the private Seven Hills School in Lynchburg where Georgia was going.

*I*n the fall of my second year at Randolph Macon—this would be 1981, soon after we got Arf—I found out that I was fired for real, but for no explicitly stated reason. I never was quite sure what the specific problem was. I never missed a class, most of the students liked me, I was publishing some papers—but admittedly, I never really did *want* to grade homework.

This time around, time the math chairman didn't try to fire me face to face. He had the Dean write me a letter while he was on a trip to Randolph-Macon's sister school in England. I was resentful, downcast, and anxious about the future. I couldn't face trying to find another teaching job just then, so I decided to put more energy into my writing. Maybe, just maybe, I could break through to commercial success.

I wanted to write the best possible books I could, and I knew that, given the kind of person that I am, these were not going to be in the conventional bestseller mode. But I was hoping that I could hit it big with my own style of avant-garde SF.

By now I'd also come to understand that I didn't really have the option of writing in a more conventional mode. My sense was that if I were to try to water down my style and write something that felt weak to me, then, first of all, it wouldn't be fun to do, and secondly, it wouldn't be very readable. What gives bestsellers their zing is that their authors are going all out, and they believe in what they're doing.

I'd been confirmed in this belief the summer before, when I'd been invited to a workshop at the Naropa Institute for Further Studies in Boulder, Colorado. I got to meet William Burroughs there, and to attend one of his talks. Somebody asked William Burroughs why he didn't just write a bestseller to make some money. He said that something like the following, which appears in one of his printed interviews.

> "It's not possible. People may think they can sit down
> and write a bestseller, but you can't do it. A bestseller is

written up to the level of a man's ability. You can't write
down to the reading public."

Far from starting a bestseller in 1981, I began working on *The Sex Sphere*, a transreal SF novel loosely based on our experiences in Europe, starring a married couple with three children. The "trans" part is that they're menaced by giant ass from the fourth dimension, an alien being named Babs. While I was at it, I included detailed instructions about how build a contraband atomic bomb.

I'm not sure I'd have the gall to write a book like that anymore. I think it was in part a reaction to the namby-pamby environment of R-MWC.

With regards to Babs, I might blandly insist that, as I'm interested in the fourth dimension, I wanted to echo the *Flatland* theme of a sphere that lifts a lower-dimensional being into higher space. And I could say that I thought of Babs as embodying the archetypal notion of a love goddess. But it's also true that I was looking to shock people. It was kind of a punk, underground comix thing.

But at the same time, *The Sex Sphere* was an attempt to depict the give and take of a loving marriage. To this end, I wrote half the chapters are from the husband's point of view, and half from the wife's. Sylvia liked the book a lot.

When I finished *The Sex Sphere* early in 1982, Susan Allison at Ace agreed to publish it. I still have a wonderful letter from her about this book in my files, with one sentence in particular that warms my heart.

> "You've created a marriage here that for all its looniness
> is rounded and wonderful, and you may not even be
> aware how rare it is for a writer to be able to do that at
> all—to say nothing of doing it with one hand while
> playing the most unlikely arpeggios with the other."

E very four years, the R-MWC faculty were dragooned into presenting a winter talent show to entertain the students. As fate would have it, a show was coming up just a few months after I found out I was losing my job. Some other terminated faculty and I decided to perform as a punk band, which I named The Dead Pigs.

My reason for the name was, first of all, that it sounded punk, what with "Dead" in it. And, as I mentioned earlier, I've always had a warm feeling towards pigs. Being in this band, I got more pig-like all the time.

We practiced all through that fall and winter of 1981, and into the start of 1982. I was the singer, even though I can't really sing—but I can't play any instruments either. It was exciting to be playing the part of a punk rocker, to be screaming my resentments into a microphone. And I liked rehearsing with the others. Other than my ninth-grade year of football, I'd never been on any kind of team. It was refreshing to be part of a group. I also liked that making music was so visceral and non-digital.

Our performance at the faculty show in February, 1982, was in the band's estimation, a triumph. We played punked-out versions of "Louie, Louie" and "Duke of Earl," complete with a roasted pig's head onstage, and a guy running a chain-saw. I wore shades and tight leather pants. The students screamed like we were the Beatles, and the authorities were shocked. They rang down the curtain on us before we were done.

I wanted to get us some more gigs, but, as per usual with punk bands, the group fell apart. We played a few parties and one more concert at R-MWC, and that was all. It felt like driving a car off a cliff at a hundred miles an hour. For several days, I was obsessively replaying the final concert in my mind.

My fifteen minutes of rockstar fame had come and gone. I went back to teaching my calculus classes, knowing I'd be out on the street in a couple of months.

One of my best friends at Randolph Macon was Mike Gambone, an economics professor my age and an admirer of Thorsten Veblen's *Theory of the Leisure Class*. It irked him to run conventional economics courses at RMW-C.

"I feel like I'm teaching my students Bible stories," he'd say. "Or Soviet propaganda."

I was always running into Mike around the campus, and he played the bass saxophone in the Dead Pigs. Mike had lived all over, but he sometimes called himself a Texan—although he was a Texan more like the guys in Z Z Top or like Lighting Hopkins than like George W. Bush.

Mike was a fellow traveler, another secret agent from the world of ideas. He'd often come party with Sylvia and me on the weekends, and sometimes I'd go over to his house. Sometimes we go back and forth, from house to house, getting higher and higher.

I remember him telling me about attending a tent revival meeting, and there being a dissolute guy in the middle of the tent, draped around the pole, and crying out, "Lord oh Lord, I've been a mizzuble sinner!"

Mike had a knack for acquiring white elephants at bargain rates—pool tables, pianos, factory tools, furniture—eventually he rented a warehouse by the river just to store his booty. He owned a maximum-sized white Cadillac convertible, and near the end of the year, he drove me and another guy east through Richmond, Virginia—where we paid respects to Edgar Allen Poe's house—and onward to Williamsburg, where we saw an epic concert by the mighty punk band, the Clash. For this expedition I wore my Dead Pigs outfit—leather pants, leather coat and shades. Sylvia stayed in Lynchburg with her brother, Henry, who was visiting us right then.

"Nice knowing you," said Henry, watching me get into the cackling Gambone's pimpmobile.

At times Mike was married, at other times not—he'd gone through maybe five wives, and he always seemed to be on the prowl. He had an easy, charming manner that was enhanced by his smooth accent. According to what he told me, he had a very high success rate.

One spring day in 1982, near the very end of my teaching stint, Mike and I found our way down to the James River and climbed up high into two poplar trees immediately adjacent to each other. The river was running high, and was pocked with whirlpools. The branches were bedecked with the tender greens of spring leaves. We hung out there for quite some time, chatting and imagining we were on another planet.

Mike and I talked about science a lot. He knew a lot about technical things and was an inveterate tinkerer, with myriads of offbeat army surplus devices in his basement, such as a powerful gyroscope in a greenish box that you plugged into the wall. This thing was designed to be used for navigational purposes on a bomber plane. I was fascinated by it, and Mike generously gave it to me. Eventually this super-gyro turned up in my 1983 short story, "Inertia," featuring a pair of mad scientists called Fletcher and

Harry. Fletcher was loosely modeled on Mike, and Harry was a blend of me and that memorably weird Rutgers math professor, Harry Gonshor.

So, fine, I was unemployed now, and this was my chance to be a free-lance writer. For lack of a better plan, we decided to stay on in Lynchburg. Stubbornly staying on would be, in a small way, a thumb in the eye of those who wanted me to disappear. And it seemed practical to stay, given that our mortgage payments weren't very high, and given that Sylvia had her job teaching high-school.

In the spring of 1982, as if descending from Olympus, no less a figure than my boyhood hero, Robert Sheckley, arrived to bless my writing endeavors. Along with Philip K. Dick, Sheckley is one of the original transreal SF writers. For me, Sheckley's stories were a model for how to write SF that is funny, hip, sad and exciting—all without seeming to try very hard. And later, when I started trying to write SF on my own, his style served as a beacon and a guide.

Sheckley was touring the country in a camper van with his then-wife Jay Rothbel Sheckley. He knew where I lived because I'd recently sent a story, "The Last Einstein-Rosen Bridge," to the slick magazine *Omni*, where he'd been the fiction editor. Although Sheckley had bought my story, his editor in chief, Ben Bova, wouldn't print it. Bova said my story was too traditional—and then in the next issue of *Omni*, Bova published a story of his own that began with a countdown for a rocket ship blast-off! We writers never forget a slight.

In any case the near-miss hadn't been a complete loss for me. I'd gotten paid something, I'd refashioned the rejected story into a chapter of *The Sex Sphere*, and, most importantly, a connection with the Sheck-man had been made.

Sheckley parked his van in our driveway for several days, plugging into our electricity and water. He said I should call him Bob. My mother was visiting as well, and it was fun to see the two of them together, almost flirting with each other. They were about the same age. But of course Bob's young wife, Jay, was along.

Jay was quite a character in her own right, very dramatic and volatile. She kept talking about an ant-farm that she wanted to mail to her son. In the end, she left the ant-farm at our house—really it was just a plastic box. If you wanted ants for the farm, you were supposed to send off to get them. And we already had plenty of ants to look at in our yard. So we threw the plastic box away.

I took Bob on some walks around the town, showing him things that I'd looked at and that I wanted to write about. Sheckley was immensely cultured and cosmopolitan, with a slight stutter that made him all the more charming. He'd read *White Light*, and he said he liked it . . . *exceedingly*. How that word of praise thrilled me!

It was great to discuss writing with him. I was trying to write a post-WW-III novel named *Twinks*, featuring ghosts that could see the past, the present, and the future. In order to give my ghosts—I called them "bolgies"—a suitably weird style of speech, I was using the cut-up technique that William Burroughs adopted in his later years. My idea was to write out some scenes that would appear later in the book, and then to use scissors to cut up these scenes into scraps of a few words each, and to shuffle these paper scraps together with similar scraps obtained from some earlier scenes, along with some scraps made up from a speech that the given bolgie-ghost was actually supposed to deliver.

I had a wooden drawing board on the floor behind my office armchair with a reservoir of typed scraps lying on it, and when I needed a bolgie speech, I'd draw out some scraps at random, rearrange them till they made some kind of poetic sense, and then fasten them to a page with rubber cement, typing the results into my book.

Bob loved this idea, he peered over the back of my armchair as happily as if he were looking at a basket of cheeping baby chicks. "I should try this," he enthused. "I'm always looking for ways to give my prose a new texture."

As it happened, *Twinks* turned out to be the only novel of mine that I never finished. The problem was that I was so resentful about getting fired from Randolph-Macon that I lost control of the story. That's a definite risk with transrealism—you can get onto a fantasy power-trip that's overly self-serving. My *Twinks* villains were too bad, and the heroes were too good. I soon realized that I needed to move on. And so my use of the cut-up technique never really got a fair try.

Be that as it may, I loved discussing the textures of prose with Sheckley. When you're writing about aliens and talking robots, you need to find interesting ways to make their dialog sound different. The default (and brain-dead) technique for rendering the speech of extraterrestrials and supercomputers is to expand all the contractions, that is, to replace, for instance, "don't" and "I'm" by "do not" and "I am."

But of course Sheckley was way past doing something that predictable and dumb. I'd say that I learned how to write robot and alien characters from him. Bob's trick was to have the robots and aliens speak just as colloquially as humans, but to have them be working from odd-ball assumptions about how the world works.

An interesting corollary to Sheckley's approach is that you can turn it around. Aliens are like people, yes—but people are like aliens. It's a useful way to think of the people you encounter every day. They're aliens from other worlds.

A few months before Sheckley visited us in Lynchburg, Sylvia and I got together with him and Jay in Manhattan. We smoked a joint and went out to dinner together. Crossing the street, deep in conversation, Bob and I were nearly run down by a cab—clearly piloted by an ornery Sheckley alien.

And when we went into the restaurant that night, our waiter behaved like an AAA Ace Glaxxon Model robot with a malfunctioning super-heterodyne unit. The waiter flirted shamelessly with Jay, allowing her to feed him bits of her food—and then spilled half a pitcher of ice-water across our table.

Being with Sheckley was like transrealism in reverse. Regular life took on the aura of a satirical SF adventure.

Freelance Writer

School's out for summer—school's out forever. Or so I thought. I was ready to be a freelance writer.

In the fall of 1982, Sylvia and I began making new friends around Lynchburg, quickly meeting a bunch of local entrepreneurs our age. It was nice to get away from the professors.

Our entree to a broader social life came through Wendy Watson, an arty, waifish woman whom we met at our church. This didn't necessarily mean that any of us was particularly pious. It was almost like meeting someone at a restaurant or a museum. In Lynchburg, church was just a place that a lot of people went to band together for an hour or two on Sundays. If you stayed home alone, Jerry Falwell's vans might get you!

Wendy was a partner in a local graphics business called the Design Group. She was divorced, with a handsome and rebellious son, Tyler, who was Georgia's age. We had them over for cookouts a couple of times. Georgia developed a crush on Tyler, and later that year, Tyler would in fact take Georgia to a Christmas dance.

"Tyler said my dress was soft," Georgia told us after the date. She was thrilled and almost unbelieving that this uncouth boy had managed to say something nice to her.

One evening after a few drinks at our house, Wendy got Sylvia and I to walk over to the house of some other friends of hers, Henry and Diana Vaughan. We left our kids on their own.

The Vaughans lived a block away from us, on a street running along the crest of a ridge. Lynchburg was a hilly city—the richer neighborhoods were on the tops of the hills and the less affluent ones in the valleys between. The Vaughans' big house even had fluted Ionic columns on the inside, separating one living-room from the other.

As soon as we walked in there, it was a party. Henry and Diana were playing Neil Young and drinking quality wine. I spilled my second glass onto a silk-covered couch—fortunately for me the wine was white and not red.

Diana was a savage gossip and a pitch-perfect mimic, a party girl, a fashion-plate, a jaded flapper. Henry was a tall, willful guy, never tense, frequently stoned. His favorite words were *uh* and *damn*, as in, "Uh, uh, where's the damn key, Diana?"

They ran two women's clothing stores, one in Roanoke, and one in Lynchburg. Henry handled the business end of things, while Diana picked out the clothes, charmed or insulted the customers, and dominated her sales staff. Sylvia and I saw a lot of them over the next few years, often going out together.

The Design Group—that is, the graphic design business Wendy was involved in—owned two whipped old houses next to each other on a hill in downtown Lynchburg. First they'd had their offices in the uphill house, and then, for some reason that I never grasped, they'd moved everything into the downhill house. The uphill house was standing more or less empty, cluttered with graphics debris like color chips, obsolete computer hardware, patterned stickers, stencils, rulers, and mounds of sample print runs.

I was looking for an office outside our home where I could write—so I suggested to Wendy that I rent a room in the Design Group's uphill building. It seemed like a perfect spot for clandestine creative activity—a rundown, abandoned building in a sleepy Southern town.

We talked over the rental with Wendy's business partner Nancy Blackwell Marion, and Nancy said it was fine. Nancy was a small, friendly woman with curly hair. She looked much primmer than she really was. She and Wendy thought it would be cool to rent space to a writer. I agreed to pay them fifty dollars a month.

I spent four years in that office, from 1982 to 1986, and I'd end up writing quite a few short stories and science articles, as well as six books—that is, three novels, a memoir, and two nonfiction books. These were among the most intensely creative years of my life, the blazing forge within which I mastered my craft.

It was an exhilarating time, but stressful. Sometimes I'd feel like a piano with its wires tightened to the point where the surrounding frame is about to snap. Exquisitely overwrought. Bursting with beautiful music.

With no monthly paycheck coming in, I had to sell a lot of my writing. I started with *The Fourth Dimension*—for me, nonfiction tends to pay more than novels. Even though I'd written about the fourth dimension in my very first book, I'd accumulated a lot more ideas and information. I was eager to engage with hyperspace again.

I still didn't have a literary agent—I couldn't quite figure out how to get one, and I wasn't sure that I really needed one. I wrote letters of inquiry to a number of publishers on my own, proposing a popular book on higher dimensions. Houghton Mifflin went for it. They offered me a decent advance, the equivalent of half a year's teaching salary. So that was cool.

At the same time, I was selling some articles to a popular science magazine that was then called *Science 82*—they had this silly thing of repeatedly changing their name to match the year.

The beloved popular mathematics writer Martin Gardner had just retired from his post at *Scientific American*. I'd worshipped Martin's columns as a boy, and over the years I'd corresponded with him a little bit—he was great about answering his fan letters. So in the summer of 1982 I got *Science 82* to send me to interview him at his house in North Carolina.

This was the first truly journalistic outing of mine, and I enjoyed it a lot. Martin was a kindly old guy, very sharp, and a wizard at sleight of hand. He showed me a trick where he made a coin move right through a sheet of latex rubber that he stretched tight over a shot-glass. He claimed he'd made the coin move through the fourth dimension.

"Please tell me the secret!" I cried. "I'll give you half the money I'm being paid for this interview!" I've always been a sucker for the fourth dimension.

Martin waved off my foolish offer. Not only did he show me how to work the trick, but he gave the requisite supplies so that I could mystify my family and friends. They appreciated the trick, not that any of them ever offered to pay *me* for the secret!

Rather than using a tape recorder, I just jotted down notes on Martin's answers to my questions, and that was enough to help me later on when I had to write out the full answers on my typewriter. I have a good memory.

Something that impressed me about Martin was that he'd been a free-lance writer his whole life. He'd even sold some mathematics-based science fiction stories when he'd been starting out. Up near the ceiling of his base-ment office, he had a very long bookshelf with all the books he'd published, each title in numerous editions and translations. I dreamed that someday my books could fill a shelf like that.

Before dinner Martin made martinis for his wife, himself and me, using a special eyedropper to measure out the vermouth. I went to my motel and smoked a joint, then met Martin and his wife at a local restaurant for dinner. At the table, I excitedly rattled on about infinite dimensional space and parallel worlds. Martin and his wife gave each other a look. They had sons. They knew exactly where I was at.

The next morning, before I left, Martin lent me a box of rare books on the fourth dimension. And eventually he even wrote a preface for my book, *The Fourth Dimension*, even though he had a philosophical disagreement with my mystical notion of an overarching One Mind. Martin was a pluralist, believing that there are many higher forces at work, rather than just one. He loved pondering arcane metaphysics, indeed he wrote a little-known novel about theology called *The Flight of Peter Fromm*. A fascinating and warm-hearted man.

Another benefit from working with *Science 82* was that I made contact with an artist, David Povilaitis, who illustrated one of my articles for them. I arranged with Povilaitis to redraw the illustrations I was creating for *The Fourth Dimension*—my feeling was that under Povilaitis's ministrations, my pictures would take on a more fanciful and professional look. I didn't have enough money to pay him at his usual level, at least not in advance. So we made an unusual arrangement: I'd give him an ongoing cut of the royal-ties for my book as the checks came in.

The Fourth Dimension got good reviews and sold pretty well. I was in the writing business for real.

During the summer and fall of 1982, Sylvia and I were arguing a lot and I was drinking too much. Partly it was the stress of me losing my job, partly it was a midlife crisis. We were in our mid-thirties, and wondering if we really wanted to spend the rest of our lives together.

That fall was when Sylvia switched over to teaching at Seven Hills School in Lynchburg, not so far from our house. She ended up teaching French and Latin, which was a challenge, as she didn't actually know Latin. But, with her facility at languages, she didn't have a problem staying a few lessons ahead. Georgia was still going to Seven Hills as a student, and she was in Sylvia's Latin class, chattering and passing notes to her friends the whole time.

As my relationship with Sylvia see-sawed up and down, we'd sometimes reach the point of conversing with each other by writing letters back and forth between my office and her workplace. We were trying hard to piece things together. If we talked face to face about our problems, we tended to start fighting. The letters were a more chilled-out communication channel. In her letters, Sylvia was level-headed, loving and sensible—I could tell she was doing her best to hang onto me. And I wrote back as charmingly as I could. I didn't want to lose her either.

But sometimes our passions would flare. We reached a low point after a Halloween party in 1982, a huge party in the house of an aging libertine who lived near the R-MWC campus. The Dead Pigs regrouped for the party—this would be our last gig ever. We improvised a version of Jerry Lee Lewis's "Whole Lot of Shakin' Goin' On," that lasted about an hour. It got crazy, with broken bottles. When Sylvia and I got home, we had a terrible argument about my increasingly erratic behavior. She wanted me to move out, at least for a few days.

The next morning I got on a plane to stay with my old friend Greg Gibson in Gloucester, Massachusetts. I was in terrible state, I barely knew what I was doing. I packed my suitcase with vinyl Clash records and with my faithful red Selectric typewriter.

Greg talked sense to me. "You think you have an idiosyncrasy credit," he said. "Since you're a writer, you think you can do anything you like. But you're not a character in a story. You're a suffering human being."

I realized that all my books, all my great ideas and my valued contacts—they didn't mean anything if I couldn't live my life. I didn't have to rip my guts out to be a writer. Nobody wanted me to. It wasn't going to make my work any hipper or any better if I destroyed myself like Kerouac or Poe. I'd just be dead.

"We're young men in search of answers," mused Greg on the last evening of my visit. "Except we're not young anymore . . . and there aren't any answers."

When I got back home, I pulled myself together and things settled down. I reawakened to the knowledge that Sylvia was a warm fellow human who needed affection, a person with her own dreams and disappointments, the smartest woman I'd ever met—and the love of my life.

We had more friends in Lynchburg all the time. I was getting to like the Southerners—their accents, and the casual way they behaved.

The manager of the local movie theater turned out to be a science fiction fan, and he gave me a full family pass so we could see as many movies as we liked for free. As chance would have it, the kid selling popcorn at that theater had in fact been the lead guitarist for the Dead Pigs. Even though he was only a high-schooler, we'd brought him in as a ringer because he could play so well.

"Those were the best times of my life," he told me.

He was talking about the camaraderie of our rehearsal sessions, the satisfaction at hearing our songs come together, the intoxication of hearing the cheers of a crowd, and the cachet of being in a disreputable band. I missed all that too—but for me it had come at too stiff a cost to my personal life. I didn't want to go back. I was happy to be moving forward with my writing and my family.

While I was working on *The Fourth Dimension* in the fall of 1982, Ace Books bought my old novel *Spacetime Donuts*, also *The Sex Sphere* and a story anthology called *The 57th Franz Kafka*, thus bringing my published SF output to five books. I was getting paid very little for these books—I think the advances were five thousand dollars or less—and the books weren't selling well enough to earn further royalties.

My Ace editor, Susan Allison, remarked, "Your books seem to be disappearing into the fourth dimension." But she continued supporting my work. By way of building up my reputation, she mailed copies of *The 57th*

Franz Kafka to all the influential writers she knew. The SF editor/writer/gadfly Charles Platt helped her with this.

I'd see Charles off and on every few years for the rest of my life. In the early years, he was a favorite drinking companion of mine at SF cons. Charles had an low tolerance for alcohol and would very quickly begin saying outrageous things—which suited me very well. And when sober—as he more commonly was—he was also fun to be around. He knew a lot of gossip, and had an unkind word for everyone. And he was interested in computer graphics. Most endearingly, he liked my work, although he also enjoyed scolding me about what he regarded as bad habits of mine that were preventing me from living up to my potential. I appreciated that he cared.

Early in 1983, I had a little extra money from my advance for *The Fourth Dimension* and from the books I'd sold to Ace. I wanted to get Sylvia a new car for her birthday, and I hit on the idea of getting her some vintage wheels, like the cars she'd admired in high-school. Nosing around Lynchburg, I found a black and white 1956 Buick at a very reasonable price—something like $300. It was a car very much like the Buick that Barbara Tucker had driven me to kindergarten in.

On the morning of Sylvia's birthday in February, 1983, I gave her the crufty old car keys—and she didn't understand what this meant. But in the night I'd parked the car in front of our house—I'd been hiding it up at the Vaughans for the previous few days. The kids thought it looked like a saddle shoe. Sylvia loved it.

"Can I drive it? Right now?"

So we did a tour around the neighborhood in our bathrobes. As part of the gift, I'd reserved us a room at the Mayflower Hotel in Washington, DC. We had a great time, and then we got to stay away from home for an extra night up because of an unexpected blizzard—we spent that second night with Pop and his woman friend Priscilla, in their apartment in Reston, Virginia, that planned community just south of DC, the same town where he'd had his congregation before he quite the ministry.

Pop had it fairly together again. He wasn't drinking as heavily as before—in fact he'd taken to chiding *me* about my drinking. Not that I took his advice on the subject very seriously.

By now I'd to some extent gotten used to Priscilla. She and Pop had opened a tiny food store in the Reston square plaza, picking up the slack from the supermarket, which tended to close early. To me it seemed like a really odd job for him—and they didn't keep the store going for all that long—but while it lasted, Pop liked sitting in there and talking to people. He'd been working on his self-acceptance techniques, and he was into quoting the Popeye line from the old cartoons: "I yam what I yam." I almost had to admire the way he kept reinventing his life.

The day after the blizzard it was brilliantly sunny. Sylvia and I motored south on soft white highways. We passed through Ruckersville, Virginia, a town founded by my earliest U.S. ancestors, in the 1700s, a dead place now, little more than a traffic light and a discount shoe store.

As we waited at the light, Sylvia drew our copy of Allen Ginsberg's *Howl* from of our black and white Buick's glove compartment and began reading some lines from it aloud.

> angelheaded hipsters burning for the ancient
> > heavenly connection to the starry dynamo
> > in the machinery of night,
> who poverty and tatters and hollow-eyed and high
> > sat up smoking in the supernatural darkness
> > of cold-water flats floating across
> > the tops of cities contemplating jazz,
> who bared their brains to Heaven under the El and
> > saw Mohammedan angels staggering
> > on tenement roofs illuminated

All was well with us two.

My office in the abandoned Design Group building was on the second floor, and, as I mentioned, the rest of the building held random art-junk. Some of the other rooms leaked in the rain, but not mine. I had a nice big desk with a soft black top, a creaky office chair, and a built-in bookcase where I kept a few select volumes—Einstein, Borges, the poet Anselm Hollo, Kerouac, the *Encyclopedia of Science Fiction*, and a collection of William Burroughs's letters from Tangier.

Every weekday I'd go into that office to write. Nonfiction, stories, essays, novels—I loved it all. At any given time, my current project would be like an immense sliding-blocks puzzle in my head. I'd carry it around inside me all day and all night, fiddling with it, moving things around, working to improve the patterns.

Even when I'd spend time doing other things, the steady river would still be flowing. In my subconscious mind, I'd continue trying things out, thinking ahead, feeling for the best idea. And when I'd focus back in on the work, I'd find that the river had changed a little.

The characters in my fiction would get to be like imaginary friends—I'd laugh to myself about things they'd said or done, puzzle over what they might do to improve their situations, and interrogate them to learn more about their pasts.

The best was when the world around me would begin to merge with my writing. I'd see or hear things that were just what I needed for the next chapter of my book. Conversely, I'd write something and the next day something very similar would actually happen. I came to think of this as the world dancing with me. The intense mental discipline of writing was putting me into such a sensitive state that I was touching the soul of the world, hanging out with the Muse. With the Muse at my elbow, it wasn't like I had to sit at my desk alone all the time.

Sometimes, if one of our three kids had a cold and couldn't go to school, I'd take them to my downtown office with me. I remember Rudy coming along one day. He brought some plastic toy soldiers that he liked—the green kind that come two hundred to a bag—and his battery-operated Japanese robot. He put the soldiers in a circle around the robot and turned on the robot, and it was like seeing an SF flick right there. Later we walked down to a fast-food restaurant for lunch—Hardee's—I liked their fried chicken sandwich, although Rudy preferred their barbecue.

This particular Hardee's was entertaining because there'd often be an odd man there wearing an orange knit cap—he'd be with his aged mother, and she'd always be trying to calm him down. The day that Rudy came with me, the guy in the orange hat was excited about his hot drink, and yelling about it.

"Cup of tea! Cup of tea! Cup of tea! Cup of tea!"

We loved it.

The city Armory was right near the Hardee's and they had wrestling there on the weekends. Rudy and I went in there and inspected the wrestling ring. We discovered that the floor of the ring was constructed in a special way so that it would make a really loud noise whenever anyone was thrown to the ground—or even sat down hard. The floor was of two parallel sheets of plywood, you see, held apart by fairly weak springs, and if you struck the upper sheet abruptly, it would clap against the lower sheet—*wham*! Rudy jumped up and down on it, filling the Armory with echoes. Nobody stopped us. Lynchburg wasn't all that well organized.

My new friend Rick Carrington had his framing shop and art gallery in a crumbling old building near my office. He was a real Southern rake, with a deep-fried accent and a taste for wild parties. He'd started out as an artist, and had drifted into the business end. The last work of art he'd made was a wall-mounted pinball device. You'd pull back a plunger and release it. A steel ball would race around a spiral under the glass and emerge from the mouth of a Joker, rolling out along his carved wooden tongue. And written on the tongue was, "You Lose."

"That sums it up," Rick told me. "My art career."

Rick's artist friend Bucky rented some space up there, too. Bucky was a far-out head who liked to stare at trees until they turned into halos or spirals. And then he'd paint what he was seeing, producing a beautiful *Field and Stream* type rendition of a landscape—but the trees would be mandalas and shooting stars. There was more to Lynchburg than met the eye.

Henry Vaughan had an office downtown, too, and many afternoons he'd come by my workplace. He'd lounge on a comfortable white plastic couch that I'd found. His voice was a comforting buzz, like the sound of a cricket.

"I thought I'd feel grown-up or something," he complained on his fortieth birthday, in the early spring of 1983. "But it's just another day."

"My father always says that he still doesn't feel grown-up," I told him.

"Some people were already grown-up in high-school," said Henry. "Assholes."

"That's not us," I said.

That night Diana threw Henry a surprise party, for which all the guests had been told to dress up as if they were even older than forty. One woman

196

was frighteningly good at it, she was hanging out on the porch in a bathrobe and fuzzy slippers, plucking at the loose skin on the backs of her hands, and querulously asking, "Does blue go with purple?"

Now that I'm in my sixties, of course, it's hard to imagine that I thought forty was old.

On days when I was alone and I'd written enough for the day, I'd go out walking. As I mentioned before, Lynchburg was a strange patchwork of neighborhoods. In the downtown area, the white people lived on the tops of the hills and ridges, and the black people inhabited the vales and flat spots in between. It was interesting to wander past the faded gingerbread of the aging Victorian mansions, then slip down a flight of concrete stairs to a street with bars selling chitlins.

There was a 7-11 store down there, where I saw a black guy counting out change to pay for a candy-bar. The coins were mostly pennies. He turned to me and said, "Look at that, my money turned brown."

There was a whole page of Ruckers in the Lynchburg phonebook, but so far as I could tell, all of them except for us were black. My Ruckersville ancestors had been farmers, and some of their slaves had taken on the family name. With this fact in my face, I thought about race quite a bit in Lynchburg. It was odd to me that so many white people would go out of their way to say nasty things about the blacks, given that the blacks in town were economically so much worse off.

Once Georgia and I were riding our bikes through out-of-the-way neighborhoods, and as we walked our bikes up a steep little hill, we heard a young man's drifting out from—where? We couldn't tell. Maybe the voice was coming through the lattice work under a porch.

"Black people's neighborhood," intoned the youth, speaking as softly as if he were talking to himself. "No whites allowed."

Georgia and I quoted that line to each other for weeks, pondering the meanings and the ramifications.

In the late spring of 1983, I got to see Dennis Poague, my model for the hero Sta-Hi of my novel *Software*. This was in the context of a trip to

Ames, Iowa. Recall that I'd been close friends with Dennis's older brother Lee back in Geneseo. Lee was a professor at Iowa State University now, mostly teaching film courses, and he'd gotten me a gig to do a reading, give a talk, and have a conversation with their resident writer, Jane Smiley. Dennis showed up in Ames when I did, crazier than ever. He was traveling across the country in a red drive-away Triumph sports car, with a rough-cut girlfriend in tow.

"I'm gonna get a back-hoe and dig a lagoon in Lee's front yard," Dennis told me. "We'll breed Indonesian land crabs in there. They're carnivorous. They'll eat anything, man! We'll open up a Crab Shack."

On one long night of partying, Dennis and I took off in his borrowed two-seater Triumph, his lumpy girlfriend riding in my lap. We shot along an arrow-straight two-lane country road, searching for city lights—and arrived at a hamlet called Story City. They had one bar, with an accordion band playing polkas.

"We all work at the running board plant," one of the friendly locals told me. I totally couldn't parse what he meant. How could a board run? It turned out he was talking about metal steps to be welded to farm machinery.

On the dance floor, Dennis was—oh God, please no—slam-dancing amid the half dozen locals doing the polka. After Dennis began diving off the accordion band's six inch stage, I got the keys away from him and drove us back to Ames.

The next day, my hosts had scheduled me for my literary lunch with the novelist Jane Smiley, who taught at Iowa State at that time. Our conversation was inconclusive. Neither of us had read any of the other's books, and we had very little in common. Jane used a word-processor and had a literary agent; I was writing on a typewriter and selling my books directly to the publishers. I was an unemployed mathematician; she was an English professor. She was a best-selling novelist; I was a transreal cyberpunk. Talking to Jane, I felt a certain stubborn pride at being an underground figure. But I also felt like I was doing things wrong. I wanted to get a literary agent and a computer, and to start having my novels appear in hardback, too.

Back in Lynchburg from Iowa, at the start of the summer of 1983, I got over my post-partum shock of finishing *The Fourth Dimension* and started a new SF novel, *Master of Space and Time*. In hopes of better sales, I was trying to write this one in something like the Golden Age SF style I'd enjoyed as a boy. It featured my two mad scientist characters, Fletcher and Harry, whom I'd written about in short stories before.

The starting point for my novel was a question I'd been musing over. If you could create a world with any properties whatsoever, what would you ask for?

I'd posed this question to Henry Vaughan one afternoon idling in my office. "There'd be some changes," Henry had said with a laugh, leaving it at that.

As a kind of thought experiment, I set up *Master of Space and Time* so that three people in succession would in fact be able to wish for anything at all—the science gimmick to justify this had to do with a physical constant called the Planck length. But really, it was a classic three-wishes fairy-tale.

At the metalevel, of course, I was also writing about what it's like to be a science fiction writer. For an SF writer is precisely in the position of being able to create a world exactly to his or her liking.

Although I was enjoying my work on *Master of Space and Time*, I was nagged by a sense that, by writing something fairly pleasant and approachable, I was selling out. I mitigated this worry by getting in some good digs at the religious fundamentalists. In my novel, our planet is invaded by alien slugs who control humans by leeching onto their backs—and the slugs' biggest local supporters were, of course, people like Lynchburg's TV evangelist, Jerry Falwell.

O n Halloween of 1983, we went to a memorable costume party with the Vaughans. Sylvia was dressed as a Harlequin clown in a costume she'd sewn, I was a bum in a second-hand suit that I'd cut holes into, Diana had a nurse's outfit, and Henry wore a Ronald Reagan mask in a wheelchair.

"Time for your enema, Mr. President," Diana whooped, wheeling Henry outside for another joint.

When Sylvia and I came home from that party, she started singing *"Au Claire de la Lune."* She'd sung bits of the song while finishing the costume during week, and during the party. Now she stood by our porch steps, sincere and moonlit, singing the whole verse through.

> "Au claire de la lune,
> Mon ami Pierrot,
> Pretez-moi ta plume,
> Pour ecrire un mot.
> Ma chandelle et morte,
> Je n'ai plus de feu.
> Ouvrez moi ta porte,
> Pour l'amour de Dieu."

The words seemed profound: "In the clear moonlight, dear Pierrot, lend me your pen to write a word. My candle is out, I can't light it. Open your door to me, for the love of God."

As I watched her from the steps, it was as if our daytime personalities were blanked out now: we were a bum and a clown, but not just any clown. Pierrot. The song was serious as a sacrament, serious and somehow sad.

Inside the house, we opened beers and sat on the couch. Pierrot fell asleep on the derelict's shoulder; we were extras in a black-and-white movie.

It had been a full year since the big fight that had sent me off to stay at Greg's. I certainly hadn't converted to clean living, but Sylvia and I were having fun. We were lovers and pals.

Some of our new Lynchburg friends invented a semi-imaginary society called the Lynchburg Yacht Club. In the summer of 1984 they organized a big party at the boathouse at Sweetbriar College, about fifteen miles north of Lynchburg.

Sylvia and I were excited about the event, and she even sewed me a new Hawaiian shirt, traffic-yellow with fans and cerise designs, billowing and lovely. At the party we danced to a live jazz band, jabbered, drank and flirted. Some of us rowed in the lake, some jumped in naked.

One of fate's kind gestures had brought my favorite poet Anselm Hollo to the Yacht Club party too. He was in Sweetbriar as a writer-in-residence that year. I'd been reading him for years, but I'd never met him before.

Although he was maybe ten years older than me, we immediately recognized each other as kindred spirits. Fellow beatnik writers.

Anselm had an encyclopedic knowledge of world literature, and an exquisite mastery of the spoken word. He was wonderfully serious about writing. Whenever I was with him, I felt like I was talking to a sage on Mount Olympus, not that there was anything solemn about him. He'd often break into wheezing laughter while we were batting the ideas around. He had a cosmopolitan accent, having grown up Finnish. Anselm once remarked that *every* Finn deserved to have a biography written. He himself accumulated some wonderful memoir materials in a book called *Caws and Casuistries*—although his short, pungent poems are the most accurate memoirs of all, like X-ray snapshots of instantaneous mental states.

We hung out with Anselm and his girlfriend quite a bit over the months to come. And meeting him rekindled my interest in poetry to the point where I put together my Xeroxed chap-book of poems, *Light Fuse and Get Away* in 1984. I called myself Carp Press after a line in Rene Daumal's book, *A Night of Serious Drinking*: "I have forgotten to mention that the only word which can be said by carp is art."

In 1985, I got arrested while slowly piloting Sylvia's Buick back from a poker party with Henry Vaughan and Mike Gambone. I was sentenced to a series of driver education classes. It was a kind of turning point for me—the first time that I really internalized the fact that I had a growing problem with alcohol. Not that I managed to give it up yet—that would take me about ten more years.

In these classes, I sat next to a black guy called Otha Rucker. He wasn't from Lynchburg proper, but from way out in the country. I had a kind of family feeling towards him, and I hung out with him at the breaks. Otha's country accent was so strange that I could hardly understand a word that he said—often I couldn't even discern the general topic he was talking about. But I liked being with him anyway. A little later, in my novel *The Hollow Earth*, I'd write about a white boy from a farm near Lynchburg who makes a fabulous voyage with his black half-brother, Otha.

Cyberpunk

L et me back up a little now, to trace out some parallel literary history.
When Robert Sheckley had visited us in the spring of 1982, his wife Jay
had been telling me about a new writer called William Gibson. Before they left,
she gave me a copy of *Omni* with the story, "Johnny Mnemonic." I was awed by
the Gibson's writing. He, too, was out to change SF. And he wasn't the only one.

I started getting mail from a younger writer in Texas called Bruce Sterling.
He'd written glowing reviews of *Spacetime Donuts* and *White Light* in a
weekly free newspaper in Austin—he was one of the very first critics to
appreciate these books. Soon after this, maybe in 1982, Bruce began
publishing a zine called *Cheap Truth*.

Bruce loved all things Soviet—it wasn't that he was a Communist, it was
more that he dug the parallel world aspect of a superpower totally different
from America. He spoke of *Cheap Truth* as a *samizdat* publication, meaning
that, rather than printing a lot of copies, he encouraged people to Xerox their
copies and pass them from hand to hand.

Reading Bruce's sporadic mailings of *Cheap Truth*, I learned there were
a number of other disgruntled and radicalized new SF writers like me. At
first Bruce Sterling's zine didn't have any particular name for the emerging
new SF movement—it wouldn't be until 1983 that the cyberpunk label
would take hold.

The *Cheap Truth* rants were authored by people with pseudonyms like
Sue Denim and Vincent Omniaveritas. I was too out of the loop to try and
figure out who was who, but I took note of the authors being hyped: Bruce

Sterling, Lew Shiner, William Gibson, Pat Cadigan, John Shirley, Greg Bear and me.

I couldn't actually find books by many of these people in Lynchburg, Virginia, but Bruce did mail me a couple of his own novels, which I greatly enjoyed. I was thrilled to be joining forces with some other writers, it felt like being an early Beat.

*P*hilip K. Dick had died of a stroke in the spring of 1982, during my last semester at R-MWC. By then he'd become one of my favorite authors, and I began thinking about him a lot.

Some writers and editors were organizing an annual literary award honoring the memory of Philip K. Dick—and in the fall of 1982, Susan Allison told me that my novel *Software* had been nominated. I felt like I had a good shot at the award, given that my SF has something of the same off-kilter, subversive quality as Phil's. I began dreaming that my writing income might rise to a sustainable level.

Early in 1983, Henry and Diana Vaughan took Sylvia and me to a party at one of their saleswomen's houses. I didn't know too many of the people, they were country hippie types with long hair. There was plenty of pot and loud music.

At some point I glanced across the room and in walked Phil Dick. He didn't say he was Phil Dick, but I felt sure it was him. He looked to be wearing a replica of his body from some ten years earlier, with a beard and his hair still dark.

At first I just grinned over at him slyly—like Aphid-Jerry eyeing "carrier people" in *Scanner Darkly*. And then I introduced myself and drank beer and whisky with the guy in the kitchen. I was too hip to confront him with my knowledge of his true identity.

The man's cover was that he owned a fleet of trash trucks. He called himself the Garbage King, and said, "I've furnished my whole house with things that people threw out."

I steered the conversation around to science fiction, mentioning *Software*, wanting to put in a plug for my book.

"What's the book about?" asked the Garbage King who housed the soul of Philip K. Dick.

"It's about robots on the Moon. In a way they're black people. The guy who invented them is dying—he's my father, see—and the robots build him a fake robot body and they get his software out of his brain."

"Go on."

"They run the software on a computer, but the computer is big and has to be kept at four degrees Kelvin. It follows the old man around in a Mr. Frostee ice-cream truck. There's a big scene where these robots want to eat the brain of this kid called Sta-Hi."

"Alright!"

In March of 1983, I got the Philip K. Dick award for *Software*. Sylvia and I flew up to New York City for the awards ceremony. Earlier that evening we had dinner with my editor Susan Allison, Phil's editor David Hartwell, a writer friend of Phil's called Ray Faraday Nelson, and the well-known author Tom Disch—who was the one who'd initially proposed starting the award. Disch was a good guy, immensely hip and cultured.

Our whole party walked over to Times Square, where we saw *Bladerunner*, the brand-new movie based on Phil's novel, *Do Androids Dream of Electric Sheep*. On the way over, I talked to Ray Nelson—he was such an in-the-moment guy that later in the evening when he had to make a speech, he just went over the things we'd talked about.

I liked the *Bladerunner* movie a lot, particularly the first part, with the blimps bearing electronic billboards, and the cop smoking pot while he interviewed the android, and the dark futuristic city with the neon lights glinting off pavements slick with rain. The last part of the movie seemed too violent, and inappropriately so, given that Phil's *Androids* novel had largely been about empathy and peace. But that's Hollywood.

At the time I was wondering if Phil's worries about the movie in progress had driven him to his fatal stroke. But those who knew him said he was happy and excited about the film.

"Phil would have loved it," Ray Nelson reassured me after we saw the movie.

The award ceremony was in an artist's loft, with the hallways covered in reflective silver paint. One of the first people I ran into was my artist friend Barry Feldman from college—whom I'd invited. Incredibly, he was wearing a suit, and he looked more like Chico Marx than ever. He seemed just a bit envious of me getting an award—although Barry was a great painter, working all day long in his studio, he wasn't breaking into the gallery scene. On a sudden whim, I told Barry he could pose as me and enjoy the fame.

As I was such an outsider to the SF scene, nobody knew what I looked like, and the substitution worked for about half an hour. Barry stood by the door shaking hands and signing books, twinkling with delight. I stood across the room, drinking and hanging out with Sylvia, our Rutgers friend Eddie Marritz, his wife Hana, and Gerard Vanderleun, who'd edited *The Fourth Dimension* at Houghton Mifflin. In the end it all got sorted out, and I met the people I needed to meet—among them was Susan Protter, who'd end up being my literary agent for the years to come.

Finally I stood on the bar at one end of the silvery room and delivered a short acceptance speech that I'd composed on the plane, thinking about the Garbage King.

> "If I say that Phil Dick is not really dead, then this is what I mean: He was such a powerful writer that his works exercise a sort of hypnotic force. Many of us have been Phil Dick for brief flashes, and these flashes will continue as long as there are readers . . . . I'd like to think that, on some level, Phil and I are just different instances of the same Platonic form—call it the gonzo-philosopher-SF-writer form, if you like . . . . If it is at all possible for a spirit to return from the dead, I would imagine that Phil would be the one to do it. Let's keep our eyes open tonight, he may show up."

The next day we went to visit Barry and his wife Randy Warner at his studio. I'd lifted a bottle of liquor from the awards ceremony to give him. He looked a little embarrassed. It turned out he'd bagged three bottles himself.

I first met my fellow cyberpunks Sterling, Gibson, and Shiner in September of 1983 at a world science fiction convention in Baltimore. They'd all read my new novel *The Sex Sphere*, which had just been published by Ace. They were impressed by how out-there my book was—Sterling compared it J. G. Ballard's *Crash*.

Gibson was a remarkable guy, and I liked him immediately. He was tall, with an unusually thin and somewhat flexible-looking head. At one of the con parties, he told me he was high on some SF-sounding drug I'd never heard of. Perfect. He was bright, funny, intense, and with a comfortable Virginia accent.

Back home in Lynchburg after the convention, I spent a day at my downtown office as usual and drove home in Sylvia's 1956 Buick, feeling resplendent in a Hawaiian shirt that she'd had sewn for me. And there were Gibson, Sterling and Shiner on our front porch, along with Bruce's wife, Nancy, and Lew's friend, Edie. They'd decided to drive down from Baltimore after the convention.

These guys were all a bit younger than me—I was thirty-seven by now. To some extent they looked up to me. And I admired their writing in equal measure. It felt wonderful to hang around together.

I met the other canonical cyberpunk, John Shirley, two years later, in 1985, when he and I were both staying with Bruce and Nancy Sterling in Austin, Texas, in town for the North American science fiction convention, which was featuring a panel on cyberpunk. John was a trip. When I woke up on Sterling's couch in the morning, he'd be leaning over me, staring at my face.

"I'm trying to analyze the master's vibes," he told me.

The antic SF personage Charles Platt was there in spirit; he'd mailed Bruce a primitive Mandelbrot set program that he'd written in Basic. We'd set the program to running on Bruce's crude Amiga computer, and a couple of hours later we'd see a new zoom into the bug-shaped fractal—chunky pixels colored in blue, magenta and cyan.,

As we walked around Austin together talking, John Shirley had a habit of picking up some random large stone from a lawn, lugging it over to me, and putting it into my hands. Sometimes I'd be so into the conversation that I'd just carry the rock along for a few steps before noticing it.

Naturally we'd get high in the evenings. I recall driving a rented Lincoln around town with John. He was riffing off my book *Software*, leaning out of our car window to scream at the Texas drivers, "Y'all ever ate any live brains?"

The writers on that 1985 cyberpunk panel were me, Shirley, Sterling, Lew Shiner, Pat Cadigan, and Greg Bear. Gibson couldn't make it. The moderator—an SF fan whose name I've forgotten or never knew—hadn't read any of my work, and was bursting with venom against all of us. He represented the population of SF fans who are looking for a security blanket rather than for higher consciousness. For his ilk, cyberpunk was an annoyance or even a threat. He'd slid through the 1970s thinking of himself as with-it, and cyberpunk was yanking his covers. And he wasn't the only one who resented us.

To my eyes, the audience began taking on the look of a lynch mob. Here I'm finally asked to join a literary movement, and everyone hates me before I can even open my mouth? Enraged by the moderator's ongoing barrage of insults, John Shirley got up and walked out, followed by Sterling and Shiner. But I stayed up there. I'd traveled a long distance for my moment in the sun.

"So I guess cyberpunk is dead now?" said Shiner afterwards.

I didn't think do. Surely, if we could make plastic people that uptight, we were on the right track. That's what the punk part was all about.

Soon after getting that Philip K. Dick award for *Software* in 1983, I signed on with Susan Protter as my literary agent. Actually I'd met two potential agents at the award ceremony, but it was Susan who followed up and kept phoning me. She was a very talkative woman, with a great New York accent. She said she'd been a Red Diaper baby, that is, her parents had been Communists—indeed her father had been the treasurer of the New York City branch of the Party.

As an author, it's often up to you to find your book deals on your own, although sometimes an agent can turn up a fresh opportunity. The larger part of what agents do is to get you better terms for your deals—an agent has the nerve to tweak the fine print of the standard contracts that publishers offer. Agents also make sure that the publishers actually pay you all the money they owe you. Every now and then payment is an issue, whether the cause is a bureaucratic snafu, deliberate chicanery, or a corporate bankruptcy. And it's useful to have an agent to orchestrate your foreign rights sales. If you leave that to your U. S. publishers, they skim off a full seventy-five percent of the foreign advances.

The best thing of all about having an agent was that now I had someone else on my team, someone just as interested in my book deals as I was.

I was planning for my next book to be something different, a Beat novel and not science fiction at all. I planned to call it *All the Visions*, and saw it as a lightly disguised account of my life thus far, focusing on the more ecstatic and countercultural events.

As I mentioned earlier, I'd always savored the legend of Jack Kerouac writing *On the Road* on a roll of teletype paper—and, emulating the master, I got a roll of copier paper, rigged up a holder for it, and pounded away on my trusty IBM Selectric. In about two weeks, I'd speed-typed the ninety-foot scroll that was *All the Visions*, really more of a memoir than a novel.

To my disappointment, I quickly learned that, at least coming from me, such a book was unmarketable. I'd have to get back to science fiction.

Despite the Dick award and the cyberpunk connection, my sales weren't shooting up to any particularly high levels, and it didn't look like my Ace advances were going to increase. In the fall of 1983, Susan Protter made a contact with a new company called Bluejay Books. In point of fact, this company was just one guy, Jim Frenkel, who'd sunk his life savings into his dream of becoming an SF publisher. But he was willing to pay me considerably more than Ace, he'd publish me in hardback, and he wanted a two-book deal.

Susan and I decided to go for it. My first Bluejay book would be the golden-age-style SF novel *Master of Space and Time* that I'd recently finished. And the second would be a transreal version of my scroll, science fictionalized into a novel called *The Secret of Life*.

It took me about a year to write *The Secret of Life*, from June of 1983 to June of 1984. By my standards of those years, this was a long time. I was hung up on the notion that I needed to write a great SF novel; I wanted to bat this one right out of the ballpark. Since then, I've learned that overly high expectations only drag me down. I write the most fluidly when I write as if it doesn't matter. Trying too hard only hangs me up.

Another thing slowing down my writing—relatively speaking—was that, to some extent, I was running out of steam, scraping the slice of melon right down to rind. I'd been driving myself awfully hard.

But I do like the way *The Secret of Life* came out. As an objective correlative for my ongoing sensation of alienation from mass culture, the

Rudy-like main character actually *is* an alien. He's a flame-creature from a UFO who happens to have his flame-mind embedded into the spine of a human body. I put a lot of my past into the book—my friend Barbie's toy circus, my Beat Chevalier story, the flying wing that Embry and I had seen, my vision of the One with Niles in Louisville, my wild times in college, my courtship of Sylvia—I even included Sartre's *Nausea*, using quotes from it as the section headers.

Whenever I finish writing a novel, I'm homesick for my characters and the little world that I made. And I miss the daily hits of creative bliss. When I finished *The Secret of Life* in the summer of 1984, I took it even harder than usual. I drove up to Charlottesville to attend a talk by a philosopher of mathematics I was interested in, and on the way back home I stopped at a winery and bought a case of wine. For the next week I was guzzling that stuff. My college friend Don Marritz came to visit us, and even when we went for a picnic in the woods, I was doing this Hemingway routine of cooling two bottles in the stream. I was a wreck.

The Secret of Life appeared in hardback from Bluejay in 1985, and got a couple of good reviews. And then Bluejay Books went bankrupt, tangling up the book rights in such a way that no paperback edition of it ever did appear. It took Susan Protter some seven years to collect all of my advance money from Jim Frenkel—but eventually she did. She was like Inspector Javert tracking down Jean Valjean in *Les Miserables*. Let it be said, however, that Frenkel is a good guy.

Feeling temporarily burnt-out and underpaid by SF, in the summer of 1984, I got a deal for another nonfiction book with Houghton Mifflin, a general book about mathematics, with the non-committal title *Mind Tools*. I agonized over what to talk about, and how to slant it.

Around this time I began to sense that I was missing out on a great intellectual revolution: the dawn of computer-aided experimental mathematics. Fractals, chaotic iterations, cellular automata—the images were popping up everywhere. If you're a mathematician, becoming a computer scientist is not so much a matter of new knowledge as a matter of new attitude. Born again. Letting the chip into your heart.

I wasn't sure how far I might go in this direction, but by way of preparation, my new book would survey mathematics from the standpoint that everything is information.

I worked on *Mind Tools* through the fall of 1984 and all of 1985. It turned out to be a lot of fun for me—I organized it in an interesting way, and I did more research into the history of math. It was good to nestle back into the bosom of Mamma Mathematics, and good to be learning a little more about computer science. I invented all sorts of new things for the book and I spent a lot of time making little drawings and models to go with it.

I made a deal with Nancy Blackwell Marion at the Design Group to redraw my images in a uniform way—she was using the latest in graphical technology, an Apple Lisa, the high-priced precursor of the Mac. As Nancy's office was right next door, we had a lot of pleasant back and forth discussions about the results. I spent over a year on the project.

But no matter how fast and well I wrote, the money wasn't coming in fast enough. Yes, my books were getting published and earning good reviews, but none of them were big hits, and my advances were only so-so. The kids needed braces, and their college tuition fees loomed on the horizon.

Professional writers have to spend all too much time worrying about how to sell their work. It's draining. After four years of freelancing, by 1986 I was ready to come in from the cold. And so I started thinking about finding a teaching job again. This time I didn't have to go through the depressing routine of sending out a bunch of job applications to strangers—I lucked into very nice teaching job at San Jose State in California, thanks to a math friend who was working there.

We were in Lynchburg from 1980 through 1986. In some ways these years were hard, and in other ways they were exhilarating. But one of the main things is that these were very close years with my family.

In the mornings, Sylvia and Georgia would head out for Seven Hills, and I'd pack lunches for Isabel and Rudy. Rudy was a crossing-guard and had to leave a little before Isabel. She was a cheerful little thing, with a surprisingly deep voice. I liked singing songs with her at the breakfast table. Combing her hair into ponytails was sometimes an issue, as she didn't like how the brush pulled at her hair. I'd make a game of it by pretending I was talking to someone else about the job while I did it.

"Yes, make this pigtail really tight so she'll squeal!"

In the summers we'd go stay with Mom in the family cabin near Boothbay Harbor—she'd gotten to keep it in the wake of the divorce. Sometimes Embry's two children, Embry III and Siofra, would fly up from Louisville, and the five little cousins would hang out together.

Mom was very capable at running the cabin alone. She kept an easel on the front deck and painted nearly every day—mostly she liked to do landscapes, sometimes incorporating a bit of actual sand from a shoreline she was painting. It was heavenly for all of us in the mornings with the sun slanting through the piney air onto the log porch and the kids in their PJs.

Meals in Maine were big events. One evening, a riot nearly erupted when Mom served an overly small meatloaf—due to her diabetes, she tended to think of meals as coming in precise and delimited portions. Sometimes Sylvia or I would cook, but it was tough to keep Mom out of the kitchen. And I still hadn't outgrown the habit of arguing with her when she'd tell me what to do.

Georgia and her cousin Siofra were around fifteen, and considered themselves a cut above the younger three cousins. They were always designing unsuccessful boy-catching hairdos for themselves. Sometimes they'd put on their best clothes and lug trash bags of our empty beer cans to town for the recycling money, always with the hope of meeting boys, although if that didn't work out, they could buy maple-flavored fudge or cute souvenirs from the Smiling Cow gift shop.

One afternoon, the three younger cousins and I rowed a heavily laden dinghy a short distance across the bay to the deserted, woodsy Cabbage Island, bent on spending the night. Georgia and Siofra were currently too mature for such antics. We sat around a campfire in the dark for awhile—me, little Rudy, little Embry, and Isabel—and then we walked down the sloping rocks to the water to look for phosphorescence in the waves. We couldn't quite see the fire from down there, only the glow. I began telling a scary story.

"What if we when walk back up there, we see a man and three kids sitting around our fire, and the man turns his head and looks at us—and he's *wearing my face*! And then the two boys and the little girl turn and look at us too, and they look exactly like—"

"Don't!" cried little Embry. "I don't want to hear this!"

We'd brought a tiny tent, and the three kids squeezed into it. I was going to be stoic and sleep out under the open sky right outside the tent. But in the middle of the night I had a nightmare that vermin were crawling all over me.

"Rats!" I screamed. "Rats!"

The kids were horrified and delighted. I squeezed into the pup tent with them, and never mind how tight it was. We were mammals in a den, with the kids piled on the downhill side, and Father Pig slightly up-hill.

It was wonderful to awaken on the misty island and explore the rocky shores and the dense woods.

At one point I rigged up a canoe with a sail, and I made a keel by attaching two vertical boards to a board lying across the width of the canoe. One memorable day—this would have been in 1983—Rudy Jr. and I sailed out of our cove, around a point and into Boothbay Harbor itself. We ate a pizza there, bought some maple sugar candy, and sailed back. On the trip home, with the wind rising, we heeled over and cut through the water at a marvelous rate. We felt like Vikings, like spacefarers. An epic journey. Years later, in 2003, this trip would serve as a partial inspiration for my intergalactic quest novel, *Frek and the Elixir*.

In Lynchburg we'd often head out for the boonies too, which weren't at all far away. We liked a wide shallow spot further up the James River, where the clear water danced across round boulders and slick stones. Plants with little yellow flowers grew right in the water—people called them trout lilies. What a wonderful name.

Occasionally nobody would want to go into the boonies except me, and then I could always count on Arf. One day in 1985, he and I floated down the James River from Lynchburg in a rubber raft. Arf spent most of the ride sitting like a person, with his butt down, and with his back leaning against the fat ring of the raft. He raised his noble muzzle to the airs, staring off across the water, cocking his ears, taking everything in, twitching his beautiful black nose. Eventually we fetched up in some shallows and made our way to the highway. An old farmer in a pick-up gave us a ride back into town. This little outing would serve as one of the seeds for my novel, *The Hollow Earth* that I'd write after we moved away from Lynchburg.

The holidays and vacations rolled by. Sylvia's parents would come to us for Christmas, and we'd visit them in the summers. Mom or Pop would visit for holidays, too, but never at the same time. Sometimes we'd have Thanksgiving at Embry's farm, the jolly kids sitting at their own table.

A family's parade of days, with Sylvia and I leading our troupe of three little pigs. It seemed like it would never end, but now, looking back, it didn't last nearly long enough.

At the tail-end of our time in Lynchburg, at the end of 1985, I became stoked about writing more science fiction. I always start missing SF before too long—the funky old-school grooves, the wild thought experiments, the idiosyncratic characters with their warped argot, the eternal pursuit of transcendent truth.

Ace had let *Software* go out of print, so now Susan Protter got me a deal with John Douglas at Avon Books to reissue *Software* along with a projected sequel to be called *Wetware*. Both would appear as mass-market paperbacks. John Douglas proved to be a supportive, companionable editor, and I'd end up selling him several more novels over the coming years.

Odd as it now seems, it was only with *Wetware*—my thirteenth book— that I started writing on a computer. The previous dozen manuscripts were all typed, with much physical cutting and pasting. Sometimes, if I couldn't face typing up a fair copy of the marked-up and glued-together final draft, I'd hire a typist.

But with *Wetware* I was ready to change. Sylvia, the kids and I went up to Charlottesville in November, 1985, and visited the only computer store in central Virginia. I ended up with what was known as a CP/M machine, made by Epson, with Peachtext word-processing software, and a daisy wheel printer. The system came with a Pac-Man-like computer game called Mouse Trap that the kids loved to play.

Although I knew a lot about the abstract computers discussed in mathematical logic, it would be several more years before I grasped how my kludgy, real-world computer worked. The whole schmear about copying software into system memory was a mystery to me. For the moment, all I

213

knew was that I had to run two or three big floppy disks through the machine to start it up.

While I was gearing up for *Wetware*, I'd started what I thought was going to be a short story called "People That Melt," and I sent the story fragment to William Gibson, hoping that he'd help me finish it and, not so incidentally, lend the growing luster of his name.

He said he was too busy to complete such a project, but he did write a couple of pages for me, and said I was free to fold them into my mix in any fashion I pleased. As I continued work on my "People That Melt" story, it got good to me, and it ended up as the first chapter of *Wetware*. As a tip of the hat, I put in a character named Max Yukawa who resembled my notion of Bill Gibson—a reclusive mastermind with a thin, strangely flexible head.

Once I got rolling, I wrote *Wetware* at white heat. I wrote the bulk of the first draft during a six-week period from February to March of 1986, although the full process took about five months. I made a special effort to give the boppers' speech the bizarre Beat rhythms of Kerouac's writing—indeed, I'd sometimes look into his great *Visions of Cody* for inspiration. *Wetware* was insane, mind-boggling, and, in my opinion, a cyberpunk masterpiece.

A couple of years later, in 1989, it would win me a second Philip K. Dick award.

This award ceremony would be at the smallish NorwesCon SF convention in Tacoma, Washington. It wasn't like the artists' loft in New York at all. It was in a windowless hotel ballroom with a dinner of rubber ham and mashed potatoes.

By then I'd be working a day job again, and not having time to write as much as before, which put me into a depressed state of mind. Winning the award, I felt like some ruined Fitzgerald character lolling on a luxury liner in the rain—his inheritance has finally come through, but it's too late. He's a broken man.

In my acceptance speech, I talked about why I'd dedicated *Wetware* to Phil Dick with a quote from Camus, "One must imagine Sisyphus happy." I see Sisyphus as the god of writers or, for that matter, artists in general. You labor for months and years, rolling your thoughts and emotions into a great ball, inching it up to the mountain top. You let it go and—*wheee*! It's gone. Nobody notices. And then Sisyphus walks down the mountain to start again. Here's how Camus puts it in his essay, "The Myth of Sisyphus":

> "Sisyphus, proletarian of the gods, powerless and rebel-
> lious, knows the whole extent of his wretched condition:
> it is what he thinks of during his descent. The lucidity
> that was to constitute his torture at the same time crowns
> his victory. There is no fate that cannot be surmounted by
> scorn."

As so often happens to me, nobody knew what the fuck I was talking about. None of my friends were at the ceremony and, despite the award, I had the impression that nobody who was actually at the con had read any of my books. One of the fans invited me to come to his room and shoot up with ketamine, an offer which I declined. Outside the weather was pearly gray, with uniformed high-school marching bands practicing for something in the empty streets.

One of the last things I did in Lynchburg in 1986 was to join in a river-boat regatta. In 1775, two of my local ancestors, Anthony and Benjamin Rucker, had designed a flat-bottomed wooden boat that could be poled down the James River from Lynchburg to Richmond. They used it to ship hogsheads of tobacco from the local farms to Richmond. In numerous spots, the river becomes a shallow rapids, and you have to slide your boat over stretches of rocks—thus the sturdy, flat bottom. The 1775 Ruckers' boats were called bateaus. With the help of their friend Thomas Jefferson, they patented the design.

In 1986, some people in Lynchburg had the idea of getting a bunch of crews to build their own bateaus, and to have a five-day boat race down the river from Lynchburg to Richmond. Henry Vaughan and I joined the rotating crew of the *Spirit of Lynchburg* for one day—camping out the night before in a pasture by the river.

It was nice out on the James River. Henry and I wore kerchiefs against the sun, and I started calling him Otha. The only hassle was that our so-called captain was a gung-ho jock who was seeing this event as a serious athletic competition, and he kept exhorting us to pole like crazy, push through the wall of pain, put out a hundred and ten percent, bullshit like that. But our home-made boat was so heavy and leaky that after the first hour, we were in last place, with the other boats out of sight far ahead. Maybe the jock thought he was the captain—but, being a Rucker, I figured I was the Shadow Captain. I mocked and chaffed the tyrant, evoking merriment from the crew. At the end of the day, the jock wanted to slug me, but I slipped out of his reach amid my fellows.

Back in my Lynchburg office, three young artists from Richmond came to see me, as if sent by that old Richmond reprobate, Edgar Allan Poe, to meet the Shadow Captain. They'd brought me some beautiful drawings of tesseracts unfolding, and of four-dimensional cubes. It was exhilarating to learn that, bit by bit, my ideas were getting out there.

I'd found my new job in California, and it was time for our family to move. In my rented office, I'd carved into the soft, black, plastic top of my desk the names of the books I'd done over my four years there, along with the dates I'd worked on them and the time I'd spent:

THE FOURTH DIMENSION	9/82 -2/83	5 mos.
MASTER OF SPACE AND TIME	2/83 - 6/83	4 mos.
ALL THE VISIONS	6/83	2 wks.
THE SECRET OF LIFE	6/83 - 6/84	12 mos.
MIND TOOLS	6/84 -12/85	18 mos.
WETWARE	12/85 - 5/86	5 mos.

I'd used my time well.

Moving to California

I got the formal job offer on my fortieth birthday, March 22, 1986. We were going to California, and I was going to teach math and computer science at San Jose State University.

Sylvia was up for it, she'd had it with being poor in a small, Southern town. And the kids, though somewhat anxious, were excited too. They were interested in the California things like skate-boarding, beaches and Valspeak.

We had a huge yard sale. We parted with some big things: the upright piano that we'd tormented our children with lessons on, the slate-bed pool table that I'd bought from Mike Gambone, and, most painful of all, our 1956 Buick. We packed all our remaining goods into a huge rental van.

Arf was worried that we might leave him behind. While we were packing, he spent as much time as possible in the back of the van, lying next to the furniture, as if to say, "Don't forget me!" Isabel and I had a running joke that Arf thought the place were moving was called Cowifornia.

Once we got going, in July, 1986, Sylvia drove our station wagon, known as the Purple Whale, with two of the kids. The third kid would ride in the truck with me and Arf. I rotated to a different kid each day.

On the first day, Isabel was my passenger. We were listening to the truck's feeble AM radio, and as we headed through the overgrown hills of rural Virginia near the North Carolina border, a hillbilly evangelist came on the air, preaching the usual farrago of fear, guilt, and resentment. And then, as if he didn't already sound stupid enough, he began *speaking in tongues*, slobbering and babbling.

217

"I'm so glad to be leaving Virginia," I told Isabel. "I feel like a Jew leaving Hitler's Germany."

The first big stop was Graceland, in Memphis, Tennessee. They had a special parking lot for people driving rental moving vans. We chained Arf in the shade under the van. At Elvis's grave, I got Georgia to pose by the stone and pretend she was crying. The people behind us frowned that we were treating this as a joke.

As we got further out west, Isabel and I noticed something. Whenever cows came into sight, Arf would slide off the van's seat and stand four-legged on the floor next to me.

"Arfie is a cow detector!"

I told the kids about Mountain Cows—I'd read about them in a *Tales of Paul Bunyan* book as a boy. Given that the cows graze so much on steep hills, some of them have evolved to have their left legs shorter than their right legs, so they can comfortably progress along a mountain with the shorter legs uphill. These are the Right-Moving Mountain Cows. There's also a race of Left-Moving Mountain Cows; they have their shorter legs on the right. It's almost impossible for Right-Moving Mountain Cow and a Left-Moving Mountain Cow to mate.

"What happens when they get to the edge of a hill? How can they get back?"

"Well, they only pasture the mountain cows on conical hills. They go around and around."

There were no cell phones in those days, and we didn't have a list of the motels up ahead. In order to meet up at the end of each driving day, Sylvia and I relied on—synchronicity. One of us would pull over at a likely looking spot, and wait for the other one to show up. Somehow it always worked.

It's been my experience that, more often than seems likely, meaningful coincidences do occur, just as if the world were well-written novel. The fact that the world exists at all is already wildly improbable, so why not suppose that some cosmic forces have arranged events in an artistic way?

Along these lines, I sometimes like to suppose that our sheet of reality is rigorously deterministic, but that causes and effects flow backwards as well as forward through time. The start of a novel matches its ending; the past matches the future.

But—and here's my science fiction writer's mind at work—suppose that, up in some higher-level time, some force has worked on successive *drafts* of the novel that is our universe, incrementally nudging it to towards perfection. I like to think that we're the final, published version, the best of all possible worlds. It's no accident at all that everything fits. The outfit that put this whole thing together—they really had the budget.

The trip out West took about a week. Sylvia stopped at each state line and had the kids take her picture under the "Welcome to . . ." sign. We hardly wanted the drive to end. I kept thinking how cool it would be if the Earth were flat and infinitely big, and you could take a road trip that went on forever, always in transit, never having to reach an endpoint and face the music.

I'd found us a house to rent near San Jose, in a village called Los Gatos, at the base of the coastal mountains west of town. Los Gatos was like a river settlement, in a way, except the flowing river was busy Route 17, which led over the mountains to the beach town of Santa Cruz. Los Gatos was prosperous little burg, with a nice shopping street and rich yuppies in its hills. Apple's Steve Wozniak was said to live there.

Sylvia hadn't seen our rental house before we arrived, and initially she was disappointed. It was very large by California standards, but rundown. Another problem with our house was that, for the whole two years that we rented the place, it was continuously for sale, which meant that we had deal with an endless stream of pushy realtors wanting to show the property. I came to think of realtors as terrible people.

But, at that point, buying a house was out of the question for us. We weren't making enough money. The houses in California cost eight times as much as in Lynchburg.

Adjusting took some time. I'd always thought of California as a lush paradise, but it was drier than I'd imagined. For the first seven years we lived there, it hardly rained at all. And you had to get into your car to do almost anything. It seemed like we were constantly driving on parched freeways, baking in the endless sun.

The people we bumped into around Los Gatos itself weren't especially friendly. Everyone seemed to be in a hurry or stand-offish—as if they were worried I might ask them for money or strong-arm them to join a cult.

Los Gatos High School was an impressive place—it looked a lot like the Riverdale High where Archie and Veronica went, an imposing 1940s building with palm trees on the lawn and a big stone staircase. It took the kids almost a year to fit into the intricate social scene—and Georgia never really managed it, as it was her senior year of high school. Imagine emerging into the last fifteen minutes of some California teen movie and trying to make the scene. Impossible.

This said, Georgia did dig up a few bitter outcast punker friends to hang with for that last stretch of school. And the following fall, she was off for college, back East to the same Swarthmore where Sylvia and I had met. Putting Georgia on the plane in the fall of 1987 was one of those threshold moments when I can feel my life change—it was the mirror-image of that moon-silvered night when I'd first fed her a bottle of milk.

Rudy and Isabel got involved with the high-school track team—it was a cozy scene for them, with road trips to meets. And they could hang around in the track shed after school. Pretty soon Rudy had an after-school job putting together computers. And he came to like heavy metal music. He was filled with zest and gusto—as if life were spread out before him like a huge wonderful banquet, endlessly fascinating and filled with unlimited opportunities.

Isabel was learning to play the flute, and getting involved with making bead jewelry to sell to the other students. She formed a partnership with her new friend Camille and founded "Icy Jewelry." Isabel designed and made most of the jewelry, while Camille planned their marketing campaigns. It was a preview for the future—in later years, Isabel would start her own professional jewelry business, and Camille would get a job crafting ads at Google.

The Pacific Ocean was within striking range—amazing. We made weekly family trips to the beaches in Santa Cruz—it was only a half hour's drive over the mountains. I found the California beaches to be nicer than those of the East Coast. The water was cleaner, there weren't so many buildings at the water's edge, and all of the beaches, everywhere, were public, with free access. I particularly liked the wild and pristine beaches bordering the farmlands and nature preserves north of Santa Cruz.

Sylvia's parents came over for our first California Christmas in 1986, and her father, Arpad, gave me the money to buy a used surfboard and a wetsuit from a local surf shop.

"This was Chang's board," said the proprietor, eyeing the battered but attractively priced board I'd selected. "He . . . " The guy's voice trailed off. I never did find out what happened to Chang.

The surfboard was long, robin's egg blue, and with the brand name Haut. I bought a fiberglass repair kit—remembering how brother Embry had used a similar kit to repair the rusted-out spots on his Model A Ford. I laid out my board in our basement and spent a week patching up the gaps in the smooth outer plastic that covered the inner core of plastic foam. And then, finally, it was time to hit the curl.

As I really had no idea at all about how to surf, I decided to have my first session at the obscure Three Mile Beach north of Santa Cruz. We went out there on New Years Day, 1987. The beach was a little hard to access, with a cliff that we had to clamber down. But we made it—Sylvia, the kids and me, also our new science fiction writer friend Marc Laidlaw and his wife Geraldine.

Marc was about ten years younger than us, a California science fiction writer with a skewed sense of humor that I enjoyed. He'd get into riffs where he'd switch from voice to voice, presenting a whole ensemble of characters. Sometimes he'd even provide voices for things like trees and waves. I loved listening to him.

Eventually Marc and I would collaborate on four SF short stories about a pair of surfers called Zep and Del. Although Marc had grown up in Laguna Beach down in SoCal, he didn't seem to know much more about surfing than me.

I dug how crazily chaotic the waves were on the deserted beach that first time. In my thick, cushiony rubber wetsuit, my body felt warm, even cozy, although the touch of the Pacific on my hands and face was stunningly cold. I swam out and rode some tiny waves of foam on my stomach. I quickly came to understand how hard to would be to catch a glassy big wave, let alone stand up.

In the end, I never got very far with surfing, but it came to be a mental metaphor that I liked to use for my activities. Serious surfers are out there nearly every day, year after year, in all kinds of conditions, engaging with the sea—and that's sort of what it's like to be a pro writer.

We met Marc in the fall of 1986 through the young San Francisco SF writers Richard Kadrey and Pat Murphy, who invited Sylvia and me over to the apartment they shared.

Kadrey was at the same time sweet and menacing. He had an ever-expanding collection of tattoos on his body, each one in a different style. He wore shades and black leather. He loved talking about famous mass murderers and about hard-core erotic photographs. His novels were full of blood and gore. But yet, in person, he was one of the nicest people I'd ever met, incredibly sensitive and understanding, a fount of empathy.

Murphy was remarkable as well. She had a goofy, comedic quality, and she liked delving into tiny details about how the world works. She had a job as a staff writer for the Exploratorium science museum in San Francisco, and would craft articles about topics like lenses or pencils or ears of corn. Her SF novels were playful, liberating and radical.

I was thrilled to go to Kadrey and Murphy's apartment. From my years of reading about the Beats and the hippies, I was perhaps a little overexcited about meeting San Francisco writers. Marc Laidlaw's oblique way of expressing himself caused me to jump to the (fallacious) conclusion that he was high on mescaline. And writer Michael Blumlein's recently shaved head led me to deduce (quite incorrectly) that he was a junkie with AIDS! Hardly anyone shaved their heads back then (and now that they do, Blumlein wears a long ponytail).

Blumlein is a fascinating character. I already knew his work because he'd contributed the most disgusting and politically inflammatory story that I'd ever seen, "Shed His Grace," to an underground SF anthology, *Semiotext(e) SF*, which I'd helped edit. Blumlein's story is about a man who castrates himself while watching wall-sized videos of Ronald and Nancy Reagan.

I'd quite accidentally fallen into co-editing *Semiotext(e) SF* with a writer called Peter Lamborn Wilson. He happened to live upstairs from my friend Eddie Marritz in New York. When I'd been visiting Eddie in 1985, I'd asked him if he knew anyone who had some pot. And Peter Lamborn Wilson came downstairs and turned us on—and then Peter was, like, "And by the way, would you help me edit an underground science fiction anthology?" Eventually he got the writer Robert Anton Wilson to participate in the editing too.

It was a very edgy book. By the time I came to California in 1986, we'd pretty much finalized the line-up of stories for the anthology, but it didn't actually appear till 1989—in a small-press blare of no publicity and no reviews.

So anyway, all I knew about Blumlein was that he'd written this shocking but irresistible story, which is why I was so quick to draw unwarranted conclusions from his shaved head! Blumlein seemed very mild-mannered and soulful, and prone to the psychiatric conversational style of asking endless questions. He also worked as a physician, and he knew all sorts of gnarly things. As I got to know him better, I'd realize that Blumlein's mildness was a kind of front, and that under the surface, he seethed with the same kinds of contempt and bitterness that I myself often feel towards the powers that be.

In some ways these writers were more serious than our Lynchburg friends had been. I quickly found that I couldn't run my mouth in quite the same self-aggrandizing way I'd used in Virginia. If I'd start sounding too puffed up, they'd just glance at each other and laugh. I was in a more sophisticated community now, and I had to adapt.

Our children particularly liked Marc Laidlaw—he was as close to them in age as to the ages of Sylvia and me. Marc and Geraldine had cool little statues of the elephant god Ganesh all around their apartment, and they had a pet python who was about eight feet long. Marc fed the python a white mouse now and then, and when telling us about this, he'd act out the mouse's reactions.

Geraldine was an irrepressible loudmouth—when I'd call Marc on the phone, she'd stand near him, interrupting him, even though she couldn't hear what I said. She made a little money telling fortunes with Tarot cards at an occult supplies shop in the Haight Ashbury.

To gear up for "Probability Pipeline," the first of our four collaborative surfing science fiction stories, Marc and I began studying surfing magazines. There was a phrase in one of the ads that Marc particularly liked: "Life on the edge measures seekers, performers, and adventurists." Marc and I deemed this line to be worthy of enshrining as the key text of a new literary movement that we called Freestyle.

"There it is, Rude Dude," Marc once wrote me. "The Freestyle Antifesto. No need to break down the metaphors—an adventurist knows what the Ocean really is. No need to feature matte-black mirrorshades or other emblems of our freestyle culture—hey, dude, we know who we are. No need to either glorify or castrate technology. Nature is the Ultimate. We're skimming the cell-sea, cresting the waves that leap out over the black abyss."

I came up with an even shorter summary of our principles: "Write like yourself, only more so." For about ten minutes Marc and I convinced Richard, Pat and Michael that they were Freestylists too, not that any of them ever took our idea very seriously. The problem with Freestyle, as a movement, was that it really had no prescriptive program. We were all diverging along our own worldlines.

As soon as we moved to California, Sylvia lined up a job teaching French at a public two-year community college, which looked to be a much better career than teaching in high-schools. But it was only a part-time position, as they only had the one introductory French course. So she started to think about teaching community college courses on English as a Second Language (ESL). The catch was that, in order to be certified to teach ESL, she'd have to take two years' worth of courses in linguistics—which seemed like a big hurdle.

A year after we moved to California, in July, 1987, Sylvia's mother died unexpectedly, a terrible shock. Sylvia flew over to Switzerland for the funeral, and I stayed home with the kids. Sylvia was brokenhearted. Partly to take her mind off her grief, she went ahead and started taking courses at San Jose State, picking up the linguistics courses that she needed for certification to teach ESL. Each of us was retooling as fast as possible.

Meanwhile the realtors' efforts bore fruit, and we were evicted from that first rental house. We had very little time to find a new rental, and we ended up in a small beige tract home on a busy street, a road so busy that wrecked vehicles regularly careened into our front yard.

It was an impossible situation. I felt like a plastic bag blowing around in the cheap-ass San Jose maelstrom. But a year later, we found our third rental, this time on a leafy hillside street in Los Gatos, just a block from where we'd rented at the start. The new home was a pleasant house with a large deck overlooking the flatlands of Silicon Valley, twinkling with lights at night.

A surprising individual appeared in our social circle when we moved to San Jose—Dennis Poague, a.k.a. Sta-Hi, my personal Neal Cassady. Dennis was living in a rooming house and working as a cab driver. He was down and out, friendless, maybe a little strung out on speed, and happy to have us in town. By now he thought of us as family.

It was fun to have Dennis come over, up to a point, although he was always one for pushing your hospitality too far, yammering on and on about something until you'd relent and say yes. He'd acquired an ancient old milk-delivery truck that he'd spray-painted in silver, and he got us to let him park it our back yard. It barely ran; it was more like a storage locker for him. The back was stuffed with various treasured bits of junk—parts of motorcycles, broken electric guitars, boxes of old skin magazines, industrial laboratory equipment, mounds of Goodwill clothes—whatever.

One of the greatest nights I had with Dennis was early in 1987, when the newly launched Beastie Boys gave a concert at a small auditorium in San Jose. I'd been reading about the Beasties, so I'd gone ahead and bought three tickets, treating Dennis and my fellow professor Jon Pearce. Sylvia wasn't interested in seeing this particular show, so it was a boys' night out. Dennis showed up his Goodwill finest—he had a giant gold lamé jockey's cap, a leopard print shirt and mauve bell-bottoms. Jon was bemused, but game for the action.

"These guys are—geeks!" Jon happily exclaimed after the Beasties delivered their first song. In other words, they were one with us.

It was one of those rare concerts that was unimaginably better than anything I could have expected in advance. A gift from the gods. I played the songs in my head for months. The Beastie's rap-based technique of sampling snippets from other music seemed like a nice match for the dawning computer age's jumpy modes of thought.

A big upside of being in the Bay area was that we could see great music as often as we wanted to. My favorite punk band, the Ramones, passed through San Jose every year, always playing at the same rudimentary night club, One Step Beyond, a box amid warehouses. Sylvia and I took Georgia there soon after we arrived, and a couple of years later we took Rudy Jr. These were very small shows, like dances at a private high-school. The Ramones weren't all that famous yet.

A couple of years later I took all three kids to see the Ramones at the outdoor Greek Theater in Berkeley. Isabel was young enough that she didn't want to venture into the mosh pit, so she was sitting by me. The lights went down, a fog of dry ice smoke washed across the stage, and two red spotlights silhouetted a pair of figures standing on amps and holding guitars. It was Dee Dee and Johnny Ramone, with Joey center stage.

"Isabel!" I exclaimed happily. "Remember this. *This* is rock and roll."

Joey was an unlikely figure to be a rock star—pale as an alien grub worm, spindly and awkward when he'd menace the crowd with his microphone stand. He had a wonderfully emotive voice—that was always the juicy core of a Ramones song. Joey had feelings, he cared. He wasn't at all like the stereotype of a harshly screaming punk rocker. In concert, I always felt like Joey was talking directly to me, but maybe everyone else thought that too.

I liked the way that the Ramones played straight-on classic rock and roll—and managed to make it new. They amped it up, they made it faster and tighter, they wrote goofy lyrics, and middle-of-the-road people didn't like them. I think of my science fiction as having similar qualities. That is, I write tales with classic SF themes like higher dimensions and aliens, I push my effects to new levels of weirdness, my characters are suffering and realistic humans—and I'm not all that popular among typical SF fans.

The very last time we saw the Ramones was in 1995, with a large crowd at a battered old theater hall on Market Street in San Francisco. It was their last tour. Rudy Jr. got thrown out of the concert during the first song for stage diving. The Ramones had something like an immense Presidential seal on the curtain behind them, edited to be a symbol for the Ramones.

The song that sticks with me from that last concert was their rendition of Bob Dylan's "My Back Pages," with the refrain "Ah but I was so much older then, I'm younger than that now." Being the Ramones, they turned Dylan's folkie, meditative music into a hysterical buzz-saw of guitars played faster than seemed humanly possible. As always, Joey's tuneful, insolent, jaded voice gave the song heart and—above all—made it new. Pretty soon after this, all of the Ramones would be dead.

*I*n addition to the San Francisco SF writers, Sylvia and I found a nice set of friends among the faculty at San Jose State in 1986. Two of them were fellow mathematical logicians who'd also reinvented themselves as computer scientists—Michael Beeson and Jon Pearce. They both said they'd taken a lot of psychedelics in the sixties.

"Computers are the LSD of the 1980s," Michael remarked soon after I arrived. I could see what he meant. These machines were becoming an all-consuming society-wide obsession, and in the process they were changing our self-images and our perceptions of how the world worked.

Michael had a mathematician's trait of being rigorously logical, which gave conversations with him an odd feel. Sometimes I'd derail one his deductions with a completely random remark, which he'd then ponder and decide how to handle. He might shove my interruption out of his way and continue as before, or burst into laughter and request amplification, or start an entirely new line of logical investigation.

Although Michael could be stern when arguing a logical point, he had a very warm and humane side as well. His face would light up with pleasure when we met, and he'd hug me when we parted. He greatly enjoyed the jokes I'd tell him, like when I told him, "Our dog Arf's so smart he can say his own name," and then, several weeks later added, "Arf's so famous that the other dogs talk about him."

Both Michael and Jon were married, each with young children. Jon was California mellowness incarnate. He scattered his speech with words like "groovy," "awesome" and "trippy," and was a master at inserting the word "like" into a sentence. Somehow he could get away with this.

Jon said he required very little sleep. He was constantly mastering great new swaths of computer science and writing up lecture notes on them. At times his notes seemed to bear the imprint of his experiences as a Berkeley logician—for instance he might diverge into a discussion of an imaginary "metalanguage" when an outline of some actual programming language would have been more to the point. But if I mentioned this, Jon would argue that it was a mistake to teach about actual programming languages, since they changed every couple of years anyway, going in and out of fashions like hairstyles. The platonic ideal of the underlying meta-language could serve as a programmers' beacon throughout his or her working life.

227

It was such fun to listen to Jon's slow, oozing voice that he could say almost anything. Like one time, he was talking to me and the kids, and I asked him about the secret of his alleged appeal to our female students, and Jon made a joking remark that the kids and I would repeat to each other for years.

"I tend to dazzle."

Cellular Automata

So how did I get that job in California, and what did I end up doing there?

A year before we left Lynchburg, in 1985, I had become interested in some computer programs called cellular automata, or CAs for short. My first contact with the modern CA mind-virus was through an article by Stephen Wolfram in the *Scientific American*. He was displaying his cellular automata as changing patterns of pixels on the computer screen. The colorful images had an organic, natural look, neither too orderly nor too random. Wolfram seemed to think that CAs were rich enough to emulate anything at all, be it a society, a brain, a pond, or a galaxy.

The patterns spoke to me at a deep level. You might say they were a trigger that sent me into a metamorphosis—like a full moon that changes a werewolf from a man into monster. These fascinating graphics set me on a path to becoming a computer hacker.

Here I need to pause and explain that I use the word "hacker" in its original, positive sense of "clever person who delights in doing complex things with computers." Unfortunately, by the end of the 1980s, our ignorant and hysterical mass media had begun using "hacker" exclusively in the negative sense of "computer intruder, electronic embezzler, or cybercriminal." It's as if the media had arbitrarily decided to begin using "realtor" to mean exactly the same thing as "sleazeball, scam artist, swindler." Well, maybe that's not such a good analogy!

229

But please indulge me, and understand that in the times I'm reminiscing about, computer hackers were good people—and far from dull. Hollywood often depicts computer types as nerdy, inhibited types, but that's not generally accurate. It's more common that hackers are like acid freaks or mad scientists or car mechanics or surrealist artists.

From Wolfram's article, I learned that his CAs, or cellular automata, were based on the idea of dividing a region of space into a grid cells, and then letting a tiny program run inside each of the cells. A CA is a *parallel* computation, in that each of the thousands of cells acts like an independent computer. With each tick of the system clock, the cells look at their nearest neighbors and use their tiny programs to decide what to do next. You can put random starting values into the cells or input some particular pattern. And you can change the little program that goes into each cell. Incredibly rich patterns arise: tapestries, spacetime diagrams, bubble chamber photos, mandalas . . .

As I say, I felt a sense of recognition when seeing these pictures, as if I'd been waiting to see them for my whole life. Come to think of it, I'd actually been writing about these kinds of patterns for several years. In my novels *Software* and *Wetware*, I'd wrapped my bopper robots in colorful plastic that acted as a computational tissue, generating unpredictable patterns. I'd called the stuff flickercladding. In hindsight, I could now see that I'd covered my boppers with CAs.

Early in 1985, I convinced the magazine *Science 85* to pay my expenses for a journalistic trip up the East coast to visit the cellular automata researchers. Wolfram was first on my list. He'd gotten his Ph. D. in physics at age twenty, and now, at the ripe old age of twenty-six, he was a visiting fellow at my grad-school haunt, the fabled Institute for Advanced Study in Princeton.

Wolfram was stocky and tousled, with the directness of a man who knows what he's doing and doesn't much care what others think. I felt a kinship to him right away. We were even wearing the same kind of clothes: oxford cloth button-down shirts and chino pants. I started out by having lunch with him in the good old Institute cafeteria—where I used to eat with Gaisi Takeuti when I was on the path to becoming a set theorist.

One of Wolfram's hopes for CAs was that they could be used to analyze certain kinds of phenomena that resist being reduced to any simple formulas. To get the conversation going, I asked him what engineers thought about modeling air turbulence with CAs.

"Some say it's wrong, and some say it's trivial," said Wolfram in his thoughtful Oxford accent. "If you can get people to say both those things, you're in quite good shape."

We went up to his office and he introduced me to another CA researcher, a cool guy called Norman Packard. They began showing me cellular automata on the computer screen. Some of the patterns were predictable as wallpaper, some were confusingly random, but every now and then we'd hit that pleasing balance between order and chaos that characterizes gnarly CAs. We found one that was shaped like a pyramid, with red and blue lace down the sides, and a symmetrical yellow pattern in the middle—a pattern vaguely like an Indian goddess.

"What's the number on that one?" asked Wolfram.

"398312," answered Packard.

"*This* is the way to do scientific research," I remarked. "Sit and watch patterns, and write down the numbers of the ones you like."

"Oh, this isn't for science," said Wolfram. "This is for art. Usually I just talk to scientists and businessmen, and now I'm trying to meet some artists. Wouldn't that last one make a good poster?"

At this point a small baggie of what appeared to be pot dropped out of Packard's jeans pocket. Wolfram picked it up, impishly sniffed it and raised his eyebrows. "What's this?" he demanded, as if pretending to be an irate schoolmaster. "What's this?"

Packard didn't say a word. After all, he was in the presence of a journalist! Wolfram handed Norman his tiny baggie and he stashed it away.

Over the coming years, I'd learn that computer hackers are very tolerant people. All they really care about is whether you can make machines do interesting things.

I'd also learn that it's common for hackers to begin seeing the entire world in terms of the computer concepts that they're working on. You don't hear carpenters saying that everything is made of lumber—but there's something about computers that gets deep into a hacker's head.

I'm reminded of a guy I'd meet at an IBM research lab later on. We'd been in his office talking about his work, and then we walked outside together and were looking at a range of low, wooded mountains. He began telling me that the ridgeline of the hills—with trees included—was essentially a version of the same exact noise graph that he was studying in his lab. He was saying this with a complete lack of irony. I felt sorry for him then. But later, as I became more of a hacker, I'd often be just as bad off.

On that first journalistic cellular automata tour in 1985, I continued up to Boston and met some more CA hackers. The guys at MIT had built what they called a "cellular automata machine," which was a special board filled with chips. You could insert it into an ordinary PC computer and then watch graphical images of cellular automata rules running really fast—like light-shows.

A Hungarian computer scientist showed me a screen full of boiling red cottage cheese. Despite the boiling, the cheese was staying mostly red. To him, this represented the persistence of memories in the seething human brain.

"With the cellular automaton machine, we can see many very alien scenes," he remarked. "We have a new world to look at, and it may tell us a lot about our world. It is like looking first into a microscope."

Seeing the CAs running in real time fully converted me. These hackers were having so much fun, looking at such neat things, and making up such great theories about what they saw! I started wondering if I might become one of them.

By the way, my editor at *Science 85* didn't get it about cellular automata. He shelved my article—and a few years later it later it appeared in *Isaac Asimov's Science Fiction Magazine*. The science fiction world takes care if its own.

As I mentioned earlier, in Virginia I had been running low on money and getting worn down by the freelance life. In the fall of 1995, I happened to be complaining on the phone to Craig Smorynski, a mathematician friend in California, about how broke I was, and he told me that they had an opening where he worked, and that several of the faculty admired my book *Infinity and the Mind*.

The place was the Department of Mathematics and Computer Science at San Jose State University in San Jose, California—which lies in the heart of Silicon Valley, at the southern end of the San Francisco Bay, some seventy miles south of San Francisco. It had never before occurred to me before that I might possibly move to California. It seemed as unlikely as moving to China, or to Mars.

I flew out to San Jose State for an interview early in 1986, and gave a talk, for which I was very well-prepared, as the ideas were drawn from the book *Mind Tools* that I'd been working on for the past year. My ideas had to do with complexity, computation, and cellular automata.

Mathematicians and philosophers had begun wondering if there might be some precise way to quantify how complex a given pattern is. A blank wall or a checkerboard seems to have very little complexity. A completely random mess of colored dots has complexity of a sort—but in an uninteresting way. What people were after was a measure of complexity that would give the highest ratings to the kinds of things that humans find interesting and beautiful, things like living plants and animals, works of art, or scientific theories.

A cellular automata hacker named Charles H. Bennett was spreading the notion that we'd do well to measure an object's complexity in terms of how much computation goes into generating the object from its shortest possible description. I'd met Bennett by now, and he'd impressed me as a very brilliant man. So I'd worked a lot of his ideas into *Mind Tools*, and into that talk I gave at San Jose.

Bennett used the term "logical depth" for his new measure of complexity. A checkerboard has no real logical depth: you use a short description to make a simple pattern, with no heavy computation involved. Random fuzz doesn't have a big logical depth either—and this is the interesting part. For the shortest description of completely random pattern is simply going to be a listing of the pattern itself: you use a long description to make the complicated pattern, and again no great amount of computation is needed to pass from the description to the object itself.

But a living organism is logically deep. Why? On the one hand, it has a rather simple description: the DNA. But the organism itself is intricate, and it results from a prolonged process of biological growth which, in some sense, uses the DNA as its starting program.

Human-generated bodies of knowledge are also logically deep. Consider, for instance, the collection of all currently known mathematical theorems. There's a simple underlying program; in this case it's the axioms and definitions found in the first chapters of math books. But the computational process that produced our theorems is huge—it's the work carried out by generations of mathematicians, doggedly figuring out proofs.

I think of music as another example of a message with high depth. The musical score and the words of the lyrics might be rudimentary, but performers can make the music deep by practicing a lot and adding mental spin. Along the same lines, you can argue that a novel is logically deep. It has a simple description—in the form of the author's outline. But the work of writing the finished book is very long computation.

In all of these examples of logically deep patterns, we have phenomenon with a rather short description that generates a very intricate pattern. I would of course admit that pushing this kind of reasoning into the worlds of artistic creation is a bit risky. But staring at images of cellular automata makes this kind of mental leap seem increasingly reasonable. You can start up a CA rule with a seed no more complicated than a few dots—and a few minutes later, you're looking at a braided macramé like a valley of rivers, or at nested scrolls resembling a pattern made by a dedicated ivory-carver.

My talk at San Jose State was well received. It was a milestone for me—my re-emergence into academia. The interview committee took me to an inexpensive outdoor cafe and we drank a couple of pitchers of beer, with dappled patches of shade and sun bobbing over us. Everyone was hip and mellow. The San Jose State faculty thought it was great that I wrote science fiction as well as popular science books. Welcome to California.

"If you want, you can teach computer science as well as math," one of the guys told me. "And if you do that, we'll pay you ten percent more."

"I'd like that a lot."

Starting in at San Jose State in the fall of 1986, I was assigned two computer science courses, plus a course on the good old history of mathematics. The department was using IBM-clone machines with Intel microprocessor chips, and I bought myself one of these beige boxes.

The harder of my CS courses was about assembly language. Assembly language is very stark and simple, with about a hundred elementary commands. What makes assembly language tricky is that in order to use it properly, you need to have a very clear image of what's going on inside the specific kind of computer that you're writing your program for. Learning Intel assembly language was a little like learning, say, the complete set of the part numbers for a 1986 Ford Motors Company truck engine.

Fortunately for me, there was another mathematician-turned-computer scientist at San Jose State who was also teaching Assembly Language, a man named William Giles. His class met the period before mine, and he was kind enough to let me attend his lectures. Giles was a good guy who wrote a lot on the blackboard with chalk. By the end of the period the front of his body would be covered with white dust—and his back too, because he liked to lean against the board while he was talking. In a way, it was fun sitting in someone else's class like a student again, soaking up info for free.

I wrote down everything Giles said, and then I would teach that to my students. Not that I understood everything. When my own assembly language students would ask me how to do the homework, I'd tell them the truth.

"Hell, I can't do it either. I only figured out how to find the on/off switch on my computer last week."

For some reason the students liked this. "You're a good guy, Dr. Rucker," they'd say. I got great student evaluation ratings in that course. I was really bringing the material down to their level. And by the second time I taught Assembly Language, I was ready to set the class to writing cellular automata programs.

There was a full spectrum of races among the computer science students, with many Indians and Chinese, a few Filipinos and Latinos, some Iranians and, more populous than any other group, the Vietnamese. San Jose has one of the largest Vietnamese communities of any town in America—the signs in buses and voting booths are in English, Spanish, and Vietnamese.

I really enjoyed hanging around with my students and hearing their offbeat accents. Who needs intergalactic aliens, when you have computer science majors in San Jose? And, by the way, after meeting the Vietnamese, I was gladder than ever that I hadn't gone to fight against them in that crazy war. First of all, I liked them—and second of all, they seemed very tough and tenacious.

In the summer after my first year at San Jose State, in 1987, I persuaded the department to buy me one of the cellular automaton machines that the gonzo MIT hackers had told me about on my journalism run back East. The "machine" turned out to be a memory-chip-laden card you could plug into a slot in an ordinary PC-clone computer. It had the effect of making my new home computer feel as powerful as the high-end Silicon Graphics and Sun machines that Wolfram had been using to look at his CAs.

With my new card, I could watch globs of red and blue oozing around, almost like oil-drops in a light show. And to make it the more geekily titillating, the language for programming the cellular automaton machine was a willfully obscure "Reverse Polish" dialect known as Forth. I soaked it right up. Programming was close enough to mathematical logic to be congenial for me.

In the past, I'd always envied laboratory scientists for having machines to play with. And now I had one too. I relished the hands-on, experimental nature of computer work.

From grad school I knew all too well that if you find a hole in a mathematical proof, you can very well be left with nothing at all. But if a computer program has something only slightly wrong with it, you still might see something interesting on the screen. Hackers have a saying for this: "It's not a bug, it's a feature." In any case, the interactive, iterative process of programming meant that usually I could, in time, get my programs to do what I actually wanted them to.

I took to lugging my heavy PC-clone computer to parties to show cellular automata to whoever was there. Sometimes, if I was sure of finding the right kind of host machine, I'd just bring the bare cellular automata card and a connector cable. Musician-style, I took to calling the CA card my "axe." It was wonderfully science fictional to bring my axe to parties and play symphonies of living colors.

One of the King Kong Original Hackers of the Valley was a guy called Bill Gosper. Back in the 1970s, I'd read about him in a column by Martin Gardner, describing how Gosper had discovered a special pattern called the Glider Gun for an early cellular automaton known as the Game of Life. Gosper and his friends were among the very first computer types at MIT, majoring perforce in mathematics (as there as yet were no computer-science courses). It was they who'd first adopted the word "hacker" as a proud name for their ilk.

One night in 1987 when I was high, I mustered the courage to phone up Gosper, and he cheerfully agreed to have me visit him at his office. Although he was five or ten years older than me, he sounded like an excitable kid.

Gosper was working for a company called Symbolics that made computers the size of refrigerators. His office was filled with beige plastic artifacts: an ellipsoidal electric pencil sharpener, a stack of computer monitors, odd-shaped modern chairs.

So far as I could make out, Gosper's job at Symbolics was to work on a program that could in some sense behave like a mathematician—manipulating such things as algebraic equations, geometrical constructions, matrices and integrals. But he spent most of his time devising weird graphics involving cellular automata, fractals, prime numbers and the like.

At one point he held the world record for computing the most digits of pi. Being Gosper, he didn't compute pi as a series of decimal digits like 3.1415926 . . . Instead he computed it as a so-called continued fraction, that is, as deeply nested expression that has fractions within fractions within fractions.

$3 + 1/(7 + 1/(15 + 1/(1 + 1/(292 + \ldots))))$

Although Gosper didn't have a PC-clone machine, the desk of his absent secretary did, so I opened up her computer case and jacked in my axe, showing Gosper the new wave of East coast cellular automata. He was only mildly impressed. The old Game of Life was world enough for him. He'd recently devised a hack that let him explore spaces with trillions of cells at a time.

I came to love hanging around with the guy, and occasionally he'd join our family for holidays. He always reminded me of a giant prehistoric bird, with his beaky profile, bouncy gait, and discordant voice. About ten percent of Gosper's words weren't standard English. Instead they were odd phrasings peculiar to him. Like he'd use "mumble" as an ordinary word, as shorthand for technical expressions that were too dull to actually say out loud.

"Let's set mumble to mumble," he once remarked to me, leaning over his screen. "Ooh! It's not converging. What the hell's going on? 572??!!! It's supposed to be 570! God help us. It's batshit. Oh, this should be a Taylor series, right? I have to stun it, I have to neutralize it. Now we can crank up the value. And this is the *right* answer." Gosper paused and gave me a sly smile. "Now let's see if I can earn my nerd merit badge."

"How?" I asked, greatly enjoying myself even though I had no idea what he was talking about.

"By typing in this number," answered Gosper, the keyboard clicking. "The nineteen digits of two to the sixty-fourth power."

Eventually he'd tire of discussing computer science with me. "That's enough about *square* things," he'd say. "How about *round* things?"

By this he meant that we should switch to his other obsession: throwing his Aerobie flying rings. He had several hundred of them, each one labeled with a number. Gosper knew the flight characteristics of each Aerobie as if they were cattle in a herd. He liked hacking the physics of toys.

In addition to keeping Aerobies in the trunk of his car, Gosper usually carried a Superball that he'd toss at things, putting some weird spin on the ball that made it bounce right back to his hand.

From time to time I still meet Gosper for lunch. Invariably he insists on the buffet at an Indian restaurant. When I saw him in 2008, he showed up carrying a pizza box, and with a three-foot tall man at his side. The box held a steel packing puzzle of Gosper's design, known as the Twubblesome Twelve. And the little person was a random youth he'd met at a donut shop. Gosper was teaching him math.

My cellular automata machine card took me all kinds of places. I was at the first-ever workshop on artificial life, in Los Alamos, New Mexico, in the fall of 1987. The town of Los Alamos is weird and quiet, like a *Twilight Zone* movie set. No less a man than William Burroughs went to a boarding school there.

The idea behind the a-life conference was: Forget artificial intelligence, let's do artificial life, let's make a pool of simple programs that interbreed and compete and get more interesting as time goes on! It was another of my science fiction dreams coming to life, for in *Software* I'd written about a race of self-replicating, evolving robots who shared and recombined their programs like DNA.

The conference had a relaxed vibe, with a lounge outside the lecture hall where lots of computers—including one the hosts had lent me—were running artificial life and cellular automata demos. I spent most of my time in the lounge, tweaking with the hackers.

A big turning point came when, later in the fall of 1987, I attended an annual Silicon Valley event called the Hackers Conference. As I keep insisting, hacker was still a good word, and these guys were Silicon Valley programmers and hardware tweakers. Some of them were even fans of my books. The fact that I'd written a science fiction novel called *Software* had put me on the hackers' radar.

I brought my computer with its CA axe, and I stayed up all night with the hackers, drinking beer, smoking pot, and admiring the weird things on their computer screens. In the wee hours of the night, they examined my cellular automaton machine card and told me how it worked.

A guy named John Walker remarked that it should in principle be possible to get rid of the card and accelerate the CA programs with pure software.

By way of spreading the word about CAs, I gave a special Christmas talk and demo at the IBM research lab in San Jose in 1987. I plugged my cellular automata card into one of their IBM PCs and connected it to this monster projector that they had. Nobody outside high-end labs had computer projectors back then, so it was incredibly exciting for me to see my images get so big. I would have liked to take off my clothes and let the sparkling little squares of the CA graphics slide across my bare skin.

The guys loved my realtime animated images, and when I was done I got more applause than I'd heard since being on a panel with star writer Larry Niven at a world science fiction convention one time in 1980. But now, after my IBM talk, some execs took me into a conference room and started asking me, "What are CAs good for?"

I kind of hoped they'd offer me a consulting job, but I didn't really have a convincing answer to their question. I mean, yes, I could make promises about CAs eventually being able to simulate air turbulence or the heat flow in a jet engine. But, to me, it was evident that the main thing about

239

CAs was that they were beautiful art that had permanently changed my way of seeing the world. The execs weren't into that.

No matter. As it turned out, John Walker was going to pull me deep into a business project for creating software to look at CAs.

Computer Hacker

My new hacker friend John Walker was a founder and the CEO of a booming Sausalito corporation called Autodesk, and in 1988 he asked me if I'd be interested to come work for him. Autodesk had done very well with their drafting software, and they had a big surplus in the bank. Walker wanted to explore some radically new kinds of software products.

I wasn't sure whether I should accept Walker's offer. But, as it happened, in February, 1988, a computer science student at San Jose State had gone over the edge and had mass-murdered seven people at the lab where he worked. Richard Farley. I'd in fact sat next to Farley in the assembly language class that I'd audited during my first semester of teaching. He was a real asshole, always arguing with the teacher over picayune points that made no sense, and sleazing all over any women students who committed the error of sitting near him. Farley's rampage set me to wondering whether San Jose State was paying me enough to be associating with these kinds of people. If I could go into industry and make some real money—why not?

So when Walker and one of his software engineers, Eric Lyons, showed up at my house in the spring of 1988 with a computer to show me a new Mandelbrot fractal zoom program they'd written, I decided to pursue Walker's suggestion that I find work at Autodesk. The actual job offer came through in the fall of 1988, and I worked at Autodesk until 1992.

Fortunately, San Jose State liked the idea of having faculty go out and work in industry for awhile. It was, after all, by far the best way for a computer science professor to pick up new skills. Whatever you know about computers is continually becoming obsolete, and the only people who stay abreast are the commercial software engineers. So the math and computer science department agreed to let me go on half-time leave, which I later increased to full-time leave.

Autodesk's core business was a product called AutoCAD, an electronic drafting program used worldwide by architects and industrial designers. But Walker didn't want me to work on that. Instead he was starting a small Advanced Technology Division, headed by Eric Lyons, and, for the moment, me and one or two other guys.

My first project was to produce some cellular automata software with Walker. He was an insanely talented programmer. He worked at the level of a grand master in chess, or at the level of a mathematician at the Institute for Advanced Study. Over Autodesk's one-week-long Christmas break, Walker wrote an assembly language program that eliminated any need for a special card such as the so-called cellular automaton machine I'd been carrying around.

My role in this was to create some sample CA rules for our new software to run, and to write a manual explaining it all. I got deeply into the task. Walker and I and finished our project over the course of several months. When we were done, we'd produced a slick, boxed software package called *CA Lab: Rudy Rucker's Cellular Automata Laboratory*, which sold for about $50 and went on the market in 1989. In those pre-Internet days, some people were actually willing to buy software of this kind on disks. I did demos of it at a number of computer trade fairs, always having to parry the same old question.

"What's it good for?"

"You stare CAs for hundreds and hundreds of hours and they eat your brain, okay?"

We sold a decent number of copies, and Walker had the idea that we could develop a whole line of software packages for hackers to enjoy. These packages were meant to be like books, but interactive, illustrating new aspects of science. Walker wanted to call the line the Autodesk Science Series.

The second package in the series was *James Gleick's Chaos: The Software*, designed to let users play with some of the programs mentioned in Gleick's bestselling book *Chaos*.

What was the chaos craze all about? Chaos is another new idea whose true origins lie in computer science. We all know about simple, deterministic processes that do something utterly predictable—like a cannonball flying along a predetermined parabola through the air. We also know about completely messy natural processes, such as the crackling static we might hear on a radio.

Chaotic processes lie midway between the extremes of predictability and randomness. On the one hand, a chaotic process doesn't settle into any kind of dull and simple pattern. On the other hand, a chaotic process isn't actually random. It's generated by some fairly simple and deterministic law of math or physics.

There's a certain overlap here with Bennett's notion of logical depth that I mentioned before. A chaotic pattern is logically deep in that it's generated by a concise rule that uses a long computation in order to produce the patterns that you see.

The hard thing to grasp about a messy-looking chaotic process is that it *is* in fact deterministic. If, for instance, you set about computing the successive digits of pi, you'll always end up with that same number sequence, 3.1415926 . . . So all the digits of pi are in some sense predetermined. But yet—and this is the subtle point—the digits aren't *predictable*, at least not predictable by any rapidly-acting rule of thumb. Yes, someone like Bill Gosper can compute the billionth digit of pi, but he needs to run a powerful computer through quite a few cycles in order to come up with the answer. There *are* some good formulae, but there's no quick and dirty pencil-and-a-scrap-of-paper shortcut for finding the billionth digit of pi. Pi is gnarly, pi is chaotic, pi is logically deep.

In his *Chaos* book, Gleick talked about some mathematical systems that were known to generate chaotic patterns. Among these were the Lorenz attractor and the Mandelbrot set, and we put simulations of these into the Autodesk *Chaos* software, along with some other funky things.

Working on this second Autodesk program all through 1989 and 1990 was a lot harder for me than working on *CA Lab* had been. The big difference was that this time Walker didn't step in and write the bulk of the code. Instead I worked with another Autodesk programmer, a knowledgeable and irascible guy called Josh Gordon. Truth be told, my own programming skills were still pretty rudimentary. I was in over my head.

And Josh was never shy about telling me this. But somehow we struggled to a conclusion and in 1991 we shipped this second product, too.

Later, on my own, I'd write a third science series program called *Artificial Life Lab*, which would be published as a disk with a book in 1993, not by Autodesk, but by the low-end Waite Group Press in the North Bay.

Rather than using my literary agent, Susan Protter, for this minor book project, I pigheadedly made the deal on my own. But then, annoyingly, the Waite Group refused to pay me my royalties on the Japanese edition of the book. And without the relentless force of La Protter by my side, I never did get that money. As I mentioned before, it's not so much that I need an agent for getting deals—it's more that I need the agent for making sure the contract is fair, and for making sure that the publishers honor it.

The three software packages that I worked on, *CA Lab*, *Chaos*, and *Artificial Life Lab*, are all long out of print by now, but you can download them for free from my website, www.rudyrucker.com. In searching my site, note that eventually we had to change the name of *CA Lab* to *Cellab*. The robotic greedheads who run some boring company called Computer Associates were threatening to sue us for infringing on their sacred trademarked initials CA. As if cellular automata hadn't been around much longer than them.

A s Autodesk was located in Sausalito, some seventy miles north of where I lived, I only went there physically about once a week. The rest of the time I'd stay in touch via email, which was something brand new to me.

I quickly learned some painful lessons about email. Never write and send a message when you're angry or, even worse, drunk. And don't send the message to everyone in the company. And especially don't use curse words. Fortunately, hackers tend to be resilient and forgiving types. As Walker once put it, "Don't worry too much about flaming me. I have thick scales."

Going up to Autodesk in person was always a kick. Some days it would feel like grabbing hold of a live electric wire with a million volts coursing through it. They always had the latest software and hardware, and the engineers were weird and smart, with awesomely wild plans.

Sometimes after work I'd visit with some spacey fans who lived in Mill Valley. One day early in 1989 they gave me a large marijuana plant, live and growing in a big pot that I could nurture in my back yard. I'd gotten a maximum new Mac computer from Autodesk that same day as well, along with Stephen Wolfram's brand-new computer algebra software, *Mathematica*. And thanks to my fat new salary, I'd bought myself a peppy red Acura car. Driving home across the Golden Gate Bridge that day with all my goodies, I was, like, "*Yeah!*" It was one of those rare moments when everything seems to come together.

I took to listening to CDs of environmental sounds on the long drives home. I missed rain so much that I'd play a CD of a thunderstorm. I had other nature CDs too: a rain forest, a blizzard with a banging shutter, and a walk along a brook in a meadow followed by a ride in a sailboat. My mind would drift and I'd think about computer programs— not as code, but as patterns of shapes and connections, sort of like the way I'd formerly thought about the mathematics of hyperspace and infinite sets.

*T*hings were always changing at Autodesk. By the time I stopped working there, in 1992, the Advanced Technology division employed about twenty or thirty people. As well as my little Science Series programs, they'd set up a virtual reality lab.

We had sets of Jaron Lanier's new VR goggles, which held a little TV screen for each eye, also his stretchy, optical-fiber-equipped data gloves that tracked the position of each finger joint, creating images of your hands in the virtual world that the goggles were showing you. I wrote a demo that immersed the user in a flock of artificially alive birds that were continually wheeling and regrouping around the user's position in cyberspace. Rather than making them look like actual birds, I made the birds look like three and four dimensional polyhedra that I called topes—and thus my demo was called Flocking Topes.

The lab's goal was to develop a VR operating system to be called Autodesk Cyberspace®. They'd picked this name on their own, and without asking me about it. My old cyberpunk writer friend William Gibson was a little annoyed by this development. After all, he'd *coined* the word cyberspace, and now Autodesk wanted to trademark it? A few months later, when I saw Gibson at a San Francisco virtual reality fair called the Cyberthon. He half-jokingly threatened to trademark the name of Autodesk's original virtual reality programmer, a talkative hipster named Eric Gullichsen.

Although sales of our *Chaos* program were even better than *CA Lab*'s had been, the profits from these relatively low-priced packages were negligible compared to Autodesk's income from their flagship product, AutoCAD. And Autodesk Cyberspace® was shaping up to be a dud. And then the company's stock price dropped.

Autodesk got a new CEO named Carol Bartz, and she closed down the Advanced Technology division. The company offered me the option of moving to Michigan and working on postmodern mathematical methods of describing curves in space, but I couldn't face leaving California. And so, in the fall of 1992, I was out of my software engineering job. I got a good severance package from Autodesk, and I decided to postpone my return to teaching until the fall of 1993.

During the fall of 1992, I worked on my transreal Silicon Valley novel, *The Hacker and the Ants*, and in the spring of 1993, I finished the code and the manual for my *Artificial Life Lab* project. Autodesk had gladly granted me the rights to this package, they didn't care about at all. They were, like, "Don't let the door hit you in the ass on the way out."

I hacked pretty hard that spring to get the *Artificial Life Lab* program working. The best part of it was a colony of virtual ants that I called "boppers," just like the robots in my *Ware* novels. By way of testing out my new software before its publication in the fall of 1983, I gave a talk on my boppers program at a Silicon Valley company called Interval.

The manager who'd issued the invitation struck me as a vain blowhard. He wanted to bend my ear about some fundamental contradiction in mathematics he thought he'd discovered, when all he'd really done was to have a sloppy stab at some of the same old puzzles that occur to everyone who ever writes a thesis in mathematical logic.

"I'm no mathematician," he'd begin his declamations with feigned humility.

"I can see that you're not!" I wanted say.

How is it that guys like that end up being managers, while the smart people are the peons? While we talked, some poor guy who'd applied for a job as an Interval hardware tech was off in a corner assembling a balsa wood model airplane. This was supposed to be a dexterity test to see if the guy was qualified. What an obnoxious thing to do to someone at an interview.

The MacArthur prize-winning chaos theorist Rob Shaw had a research spot at Interval at this time. I'd always admired Shaw, he'd tried to use chaos theory to beat the roulette wheels in Vegas, and, in a more academic vein, he'd written a famous monograph called *The Chaotic Dynamics of a Dripping Faucet.* He looked more like a hippie or a biker.

I knew Shaw from the early cellular automata days. The very first time I'd encountered him, he'd been sitting next to me on a plane to Las Alamos, and I'd thought he was a carpenter. He'd been doing this odd calculation with a pencil on a matchbook cover—it looked like long division, and he seemed to be doing it wrong. Later, when I realized who he was, Shaw had informed me he'd been computing the square root of two in binary notation, to see if the sequence of zeroes and ones in the answer would appear chaotic—and, yes, they did.

After my talk on my virtual ants, I went up to Shaw's office with him to hang out. He showed me a virtual stream of water that he'd designed, and some nice artificially alive insects. He gave my virtual ant program his blessing.

"That's a wild piece of code, Rudy."

*I*n the fall of 1993, I headed back to teaching computer science full-time at San Jose State. I was glad the department had kept my position open for me.

It was little weird to be teaching yet again. Everything felt slow and dull compared to the scene in the Autodesk research labs. I was back to grading tests and homework programs, back to worrying about the ratings the students gave me on their evaluations, back to worrying if I was ever going to get tenure.

Attending a department party, I visualized myself as a rabbit caught in a snare, struggling against a tightening wire noose around my neck. I'd learned from having pet rabbits in Lynchburg that, when frightened or upset, rabbits can in fact make a sound. In my head at the faculty party, I was going, "*Wheenk, wheenk, wheenk!*"

Head trips like that cheer me up. They make the world more like a novel. In fact I became so fond of the word "wheenk," that I began using it a technical lit-crit sense to mean, "strong and touching emotions felt by a character in a work of fiction." And then, if some story I was writing seemed too cold and scientific, I'd give myself the shorthand reminder, "Put in more wheenk."

A couple of months after I returned to teaching, President Bill Clinton passed through Los Gatos—he and Hillary were having dinner with some tech leaders in a restaurant here. My family and I were standing on the sidewalk as the Clintons' limo tooled by—with the Autodesk exec Carol Bartz riding in there with them.

"Carol!" I yelled, leaning out into the street. "I want my job back!"

The people around us laughed. They understood.

A s I became a more established member of the San Jose State Math & CS department, I was expected to teach harder courses, to advise more students, and to attend more committee meetings. With the age of fifty coming up on me, I still didn't have tenure—my checkered career had delayed any decision—and now I wanted finally to close the deal.

I put a lot of energy into learning the object-oriented languages C++ and Java, and into figuring out how to teach Windows programming and the principles of software engineering. All through the decade of 1994 through 2004, I worked on developing a framework of extendible object-oriented code to make it possible for my students to write complete videogames for their semester projects. To my mind, games are one of the most interesting areas in computer science, combining nearly every aspect of the field.

The purpose of writing the framework—which I called the Pop framework after my father—was to make it possible for my students to bypass most of the difficulties in graphics programming, and to quickly achieve a certain level of artistic self-expression. I wrote up a fresh iteration of the Pop framework and the accompanying notes every semester, and sold printed copies of the notes through the campus bookstore. Eventually I ended up publishing a final version of my notes as a textbook called *Software Engineering and Computer Games*, which appeared in 2003.

I'd started out with two dimensional games, but along the way I figured out how to extend my software framework to three-dimensional worlds. I wrote the 3D code over a couple of weeks in June of 2001, in what John Walker would call a "bloodlust hacking frenzy."

At the end of this particular effort, I was so excited and drinking so much coffee that my heart was palpitating in my chest. I considered going to the hospital, but instead I set off to go SCUBA diving with brother Embry on Grand Turk Island instead—after many years in Louisville, Embry and his wife had moved back to the Caribbean. An hour after I left my computer behind, my heart was fine.

It's hard to communicate just how exciting and addictive computer programming can become. It's akin to the experience of playing a videogame, but more intense and creative. As a hacker, you're able to reach down into your artificial worlds at very deep levels. You can add in anything at all if only you can visualize it clearly enough. What makes the work especially fascinating is that unexpected things may emerge, happy accidents of the interacting computations. And you can capitalize on these quirks to create previously undreamed of features.

On the cellular automata front, I somehow talked the Electric Power Research Institute at Palo Alto into a grant that ran from 1993 to 1997, and released me from some of my teaching duties. Each semester I'd work with a small team of students, pressing forward on a new software package for exploring cellular automata. I wanted the colors to be smoother and less blocky, so I was putting a continuous range of values into my cells. I named my new software CAPOW, an acronym for Cellular Automata for POWer simulation.

Our program was never very useful to any electric power engineers, but the images were gorgeous. They were really and truly like oil-glob light-shows now, far more beautiful than anything I'd been able to achieve before. Even better, I found some CA rules that could spontaneously grow screens of lovely, throbbing paisley. These rotating patterns—called

Belousov-Zhabotinsky scrolls among biochemists—resembled lichen on rocks, pairs of eddies behind an oar, cross-sections of mushroom caps, fetuses, and many other naturally occurring shapes. The scrolls have a pleasing way of nesting within each other; think of little whirlpools on the rim of a bigger one.

More and more often, I spent my evenings at my computer screen, eternally tweaking my programs. Over time I learned to see nested scrolls everywhere, even within my thoughts. And that's where the title for my memoir comes from. A life story is made of scrolls within scrolls, divagations within tangential tales within related anecdotes—and all the stories are forever turning and rotating, throbbing with their own kind of life. *Nested Scrolls*, yes.

Remember to Write

I n Silicon Valley, my life was becoming more and more exciting, what with my faculty friends, the Bay Area science fiction writers, and the hackers I was meeting. I was out of the cave and into the marketplace. New opportunities kept cropping up. I was like some Darwin's finch with a beak evolved for cracking open a special kind of seed. There'd been no seeds of the proper type in Lynchburg, but they were all over the place in the California.

A guy called Marty Olsen phoned me at my office at San Jose State, very voluble and friendly. "You sound bummed," said Olsen. "A guy like you shouldn't be bummed. You're a great writer."

I was in fact feeling a little downcast because I wasn't getting much writing done anymore. Olsen had an interesting proposal. He wanted me and my old SF mentor, Robert Sheckley, to write scripts for a TV series about the future. The show would be hosted by no less a figure than the psychedelic pioneer Tim Leary.

Olsen wrote me a couple of letters to set up the visit. He was in Venice, California, trying to make a living as a screenwriter. He had a penchant for pretending he was living in the Venice of the Italian Renaissance. The letters would begin, "Dear Ruckella."

In the spring of 1988, I flew to L.A. and met up with Olsen and Sheckley. It was great to see the Sheck-man again, he was mellow and relaxed. My hero. It was like being with the magic gnome in a fairy tale.

"This is all bullshit down here, Rudy," Sheckley affably told me. "Just get as much money in front as you can. I had a deal here to write a TV series about two robots running a filling station on Mars. We had lots of meetings, everyone acted excited, and the project died."

Tim Leary and his wife were glad to see us. He was friendly and personable, handsome and charismatic. He'd cleared off a dining-table and set out pencils and pads of paper so we could brainstorm and take notes. But first I showed Tim some cellular automata.

I had my cellular automata card with me, my axe, and I took apart his PC-clone box and jacked it in. Tim liked the images, of course, and thereafter he started dropping the phrase "cellular automata" into his diffuse but rewarding essays.

We sat around the table for an hour or so, thinking of good topics for shows—we could do one about virtual reality, one about robots, one about smart drugs, and so on. Tim would be the genial anchorman, reading the scripts that Bob and I would produce. It sounded great to me.

"These are the guys," Leary told Olsen happily. "You found the right guys."

But the show never got funded and none of us got paid.

When Sylvia and I arrived in California in 1986, a couple of Berkeley freaks named Queen Mu and R. U. Sirius were editing a radical magazine called *Mondo 2000*. I saw my first copy of it in a rack of screwball zines at the fabled City Lights Books in San Francisco. The *Mondo* editors were pursuing a weird fusion of computers and psychedelic drugs.

Somehow hearing of my arrival, Queen Mu got in touch with me and asked me to give a talk on cyberpunk at a ratty venue on San Pablo Street in Oakland. She was a fey, breathless woman my age, elegant in a New England kind of way, given to showing all her teeth in the ecstatic rictus of a smile. And R. U. Sirius was a highly educated street hipster with a goofy grin.

I'd asked Mu if she might pay me for my talk—after all, she was charging the public an admission fee to attend. She was somewhat tight-fisted with her workers, and a payment wasn't possible. But she did make me a gift of a flat metal peppermints box filled with buds of pot.

So one evening in the winter of 1986, I went to Berkeley, got high, ranted about cyberpunk, and read some weird scene from *Wetware*. And there with I'd brought the Movement to the Bay Area! Soon fellow cyber-punk John Shirley would be relocating here as well.

After my talk, we had a show and tell session. The evening was more like a soirée than a lecture. Some of the *Mondo* people had brought brain toys that they'd discovered or even made on their own. One that intrigued me was a pair of ping pong ball halves that you wore over your eyes like goggles. The balls were lit in stroboscopic flashes from little diode lights you controlled with a dial on a box.

I donned the device and began tuning it. To my amazement, I started seeing—deeply zoomed images of the Mandelbrot set fractal! Had I discovered the essentially fractal nature of the human sensory system? Or was this just Mu's insanely strong pot?

When I'd experiment with the flicker effect later, I could never see the fractals quite so well as that first time. But I did learn that almost any flashing light source can set off patterns on your closed eyelids, and you don't really need an electronic strobe system. Simplest of all is to lie on your back on the beach with your eyes closed, spread your fingers, and move your hands up and down above your eyes, casting a series of rapidly flick-ering shadows. Of course if you do this, the people walking by think you're weird. . . but in California that's not such a big deal.

In any case, my point is that you do see some nice stuff if you pay atten-tion to your immediate and unfiltered perceptions. We have a tendency to ignore the more subjective aspects of our perceptions in favor of the shared elements that everyone sees at the same time. But at some level there's an equal reality to the things you see with your eyes closed, or to those darting shapes that you sometimes see at the edges of your visual field.

Mondo 2000 magazine would ramp up to national distribution and I'd write a few reviews and short articles for them, but not very many. The problem was that Queen Mu tended to lose whatever I mailed in and to make me send it again. And then when she'd finally read it, she'd demand a complete rewrite, and then she'd lose that, and I'd have to mail in the rewrite again. And after the article came out, she'd never pay me.

Hardly a viable literary market. Nevertheless I valued our relationship. Mu and R. U. were such cool people. It was always a treat to go to the Mondo parties—Mu had rented an immense California Craftsman style house in Berkeley for the magazine's offices, and some of the staffers lived there as well. Everyone there would so frikkin' hip. It was this Kentucky boy's dream come true.

I ran into the intensely charismatic Tim Leary a couple more times at *Mondo 2000* events and parties. Tim would always act like he and I were old pals. I was proud to know him. To Sylvia's surprise, Tim was curious about where she'd gone to high school in DC.

I remember asking Tim a question I'd always wondered about. "Tim, I only took psychedelics, like, two or three times, and that was enough to last me a lifetime. It would always wipe me out. How is that you can keep on tripping year after year and still be able to use your mind?"

Rather than speaking directly to my question, Tim told me about an acid trip he'd taken that week. He'd wandered out into the streets of downtown L.A. and had totally forgotten where he was. He'd ended up sitting on a bench with an old homeless woman, drinking in the cosmic beauty of her face. Listening to him, it almost seemed like he was an indestructible cartoon character. Or maybe a great sage, a con man, a revolutionary leader—or all of the above.

After Georgia finished college as an art history major in 1991, she spent some time working as a temp in the San Francisco offices of Pacific Gas and Electric, known as PG&E. For a while there, she began calling herself GE&O. She was hungry for a more art-related job, and I urged her to ask *Mondo 2000* to hire her to help with the graphics, reminding her that, as *Mondo* was so flaky, she'd need to phone them three or four or five times. And, lo and behold, in 1993, it worked out.

Mu, being fairly paranoid, worried that anyone she hired might be from the CIA, so she felt safer bringing in someone like Georgia, the child of a personal friend. And Georgia had a true flair for graphical design. Her time at *Mondo* was like a postgraduate education for her, readying her for a professional career in the field.

*I*n the end, I did finally score some money from *Mondo*. This was in 1991, when Queen Mu and R. U. Sirius got a contract to do a major book with the full title, *Mondo 2000: A User's Guide to the New Edge : Cyberpunk, Virtual Reality, Wetware, Designer Aphrodisiacs, Artificial Life, Techno-Erotic Paganism, and More*. R. U. phoned me up and asked me to edit the book for them. The idea was to take excerpts of articles that that had appeared in the magazine and somehow arrange them into a book. But neither Mu nor R. U. could quite see how.

"We need a mathematical logician for this, Rudy," said R. U. "You're the man."

I agreed to do it, but only if they'd negotiate a contract through my agent, good old Susan Protter, and only if they'd pay me my share in advance. I knew that otherwise all the money would disappear before I ever saw any.

So we worked out a deal and I organized the book as a kind of encyclopedia, alphabetically arranged by keyword hot topics, with good bits from the magazine pasted in and some additional entries that I made up myself, such as the one on "wetware," which I defined in terms of viewing your DNA as a kind of computer program for constructing your body. As my authority, I quoted Max Yukawa, who was in fact the William-Gibson-based character in my novel *Wetware*, not that anyone picked up on this.

The book hit with a big splash. A photographer from *Time* magazine came to take photos of us—I remember posing in a gully behind the *Mondo* house, along with Mu, R.U., and the *Mondo* art director Bart Nagel. We were dressed like punks or acidheads, and I felt like a member of the Jefferson Airplane. We made the cover of the February 8, 1993, issue of *Time* magazine with an illustration by Bart and and the following text.

CYBERPUNK
Virtual **sex**, smart **drugs**, and synthetic **rock 'n' roll**!
A futuristic subculture erupts from the electronic underground.

Very satisfying.

One might then have expected *Mondo 2000* to become a successful magazine about the emerging computer culture. But it didn't work out. Queen Mu ran the advertising department under the pseudonym of Ann Venable, and she tended to get into crazy arguments with potential advertisers. She was also editor in chief, and *Mondo* was forever off schedule, with the issues coming out at best twice a year.

In short order, some gimlet-eyed yuppies showed up and ate *Mondo's* lunch. Thus was born *Wired* magazine. They covered the same kinds of topics as *Mondo*, but they were tightly organized—and they slanted their articles to appeal to entrepreneurs rather than to stoners.

I remember an epic party from the declining days of *Mondo* in 1994, held in a building called the Brazilian Room, deep in Tilden Park on a hill overlooking Berkeley. Eventually I'd rework this scene for my novel *Saucer Wisdom* of 1999.

The Brazilian Room was a low wooden hall surrounded by a big patio, perched on the brow of a long meadow rolling down to some woods. The theme of the party was the Casbah, and a lot of people were wearing costumes.

Wes Thomas, who'd begun working as the editor at *Mondo*, was dressed as an Arab woman named Amara. The Casbah theme had been Wes's idea. He felt that we should think of the Web as an arabesque labyrinth. The *Mondo* editors were always big on understanding technology as metaphors—instead of actually learning anything hard. Queen Mu was holed up in the kitchen, spaced-out and inaccessible behind starry eyes and rictus-like smile, her voice breathy and brittle. Bart Nagel the art director, a saturnine man with a shaved head, was nicely turned out in a tuxedo and an authentic-looking maroon fez. R. U. Sirius, whose *Mondo* post had changed to "Icon at Large," was slouching around on the patio with his lovably goofy grin, eternally fingering his long hair, simultaneously alert and bemused.

"Hi, R. U.," I said.

"Rudy! What's happening? Hi, Sylvia. Glad you guys could make it."

"This place is magical," said Sylvia. "I never knew it was up here."

"Find your way through the labyrinth," said R. U. "I think I was at an acid test here a really long time ago. Or maybe it was a wedding."

There was a good spread of mid-Eastern food, lots of beer and wine, a fair amount of pot out on the fringes of the patio, and who knew what odd chemicals in some of the people's blood-streams. For entertainment, there was a celestial hippy-dippy storyteller, a cursing poetry performance, and bizarre instrumentless electronic live music.

Among the guests was an astronomer from U.C. Berkeley; it turned out he'd read one of my science books. He was a professor on a sabbatical visit to Berkeley from his native Rome.

"Do you think aliens could travel as cosmic rays?" I asked, getting down to an idea I'd been thinking of using if I ever wrote another of my *Ware* novels.

"That is a genial notion," said the astronomer. "What do you have in mind exactly?"

"Suppose that beings all over the universe code themselves up, both mind and body, and send the coded patterns across space as high-energy electromagnetic signals," I said. "Cosmic rays." I held out my arm and wiggled my fingers, and then drew my fluttering hand down an imaginary line towards my head.

This being a *Mondo* party, the professor was primed for weirdness, and he took this happily in stride. "Like Puck who slides down a moonbeam. A most efficient method for interstellar travel. Some cosmic rays are energetic gamma rays. These are the signals your extraterrestrials can be modulating with information. A fine idea. Life is to make entertainment."

Looking across the patio, I could see an impressive dominatrix-dressed woman named Raven. She looked like a red and black ice-cream sundae.

"Perhaps she offers us a ride in her flying saucer," said the astronomer. "She is very ample."

"I'm not sure she's really a woman," I said. "She's from San Francisco."

"America is the great labyrinth," said the astronomer.

The evening wore on. The air was filled with a combination of licentiousness, California weirdness, and business chatter. There were lots of young gen-Xers, tons of old punks and hippies, and a good sprinkling of new-wave media artists, writers, and scammers from the ages in between. Everyone had the sense that somehow, some way, there was money to be made off the rising tidal wave of electronic information, but nobody was sure how. Above and beyond all that was the joy of being at a big weird party, a feeling of being close to the center of hip.

The oleander bushes at the edge of the patio began to shake—and who should emerge but my California science-writer friend Nick Herbert. Nick had at one time been a physicist working for Memorex to help them design their magnetic memories. But he'd gotten deep into thinking about telepathy and teleportation. He was continually elaborating upon his quantum-mechanical theories about how we might talk directly with Mother Nature.

Nick lived in a tiny cabin in the mountain town of Boulder Creek, and rarely got out. He made a little money by writing popular-science books, by working at a winery, and by carrying out off-beat product promotions. Today he was carrying things like flashlights.

"What are those?" I asked Nick.

"I'm trying to sell Liberty Lights," said Nick. "Tools for enlightenment. Keep an eye on them, would you?" He handed me the three lights and started towards the bar. But then he went briefly into orbit around Raven. Maybe she *was* a woman. Maybe it didn't matter.

"What are Liberty Lights?" asked Sylvia. "Are they ray-guns?"

"I'm not sure." The flashlights had flame-shaped plastic cones glued over their lenses. Sylvia turned one on and so did I. There was a weighted wheel inside the cone that moved as you moved the light; the effect was that the color of the light kept changing. R. U. joined us, and we were waving around the three colored lights and laughing.

"*Far out*," said Sylvia, not quite seriously. "Cosmic!"

"Ten dollars each!" intoned Nick, skipping back with a lit reefer in his mouth. "Yes! All Bezerkistan freaks need Liberty Lights to see God! Test trials are free, but don't be absconding with these carefully tuned devices."

Nick took back the three Liberty Lights and began juggling them, the lights glowing in the dark. He juggled as easily as if he were moving in slow-motion.

"I'm not actually here," he said after a bit, turning out his lights one by one. His joint had gone out as well. "I'm just dreaming that I am."

The bushes shook, and Nick was gone.

*I*nitially I wasn't writing much fiction in California. I had my hands full with my teaching job and with learning computer science.

As a small, initial writing project, I edited an anthology of mathematically-related science fiction stories, *Mathenauts: Tales of Mathematical Wonder*. My inspiration was a pair of such anthologies that the author

Clifton Fadiman had edited when I was in high-school and college: *Fantasia Mathematica* and *The Mathematical Magpie*.

Those two anthologies had gone a long way towards making me want to be a mathematician. I thought it would be nice to have a fresh volume along similar lines, although with a sharper focus on SF. Fadiman's books had included a certain number of classical literary pieces, humorous essays, poems and even cartoons that, in my opinion, weakened the impact of the mix. I was looking for a jolt of real math and real SF.

There was one story in particular that I wanted to include—this was "The Mathenauts," by Norman Kagan, a story that I loved so much that I used its title for the title of my anthology. Kagan's tale is one of the very few that captures the flavor of what it's like to be a mathematician, and it served as an inspiration for my own math-maniac novels *White Light* and *Mathematicians in Love*.

Kagan is by no means a prolific writer of SF—over the years he's spent most of his energy in writing books of film criticism. While editing *Mathenauts*, I was so eager to meet him that I actually organized a day of mathematical SF movies at San Jose State—and had Kagan as a guest speaker. He proved every bit as quirky and funny as I'd hoped.

As these were pre-Internet years, finding the other stories for the volume was a somewhat hit-and-miss affair, largely conducted via the U. S. mail. I got a number of recommendations from my math-columnist mentor Martin Gardner. And once I got the word out, a number of people mailed in suggestions or submissions.

In the end, it was a nice volume, but it was too specialized a book for Avon Books or Houghton Mifflin, who'd been publishing my other books. My agent Susan Protter sent the proposal to the editor David Hartwell at Arbor House, and my anthology came out in 1987. Hartwell really understood the idea behind *Mathenauts*, and he took the trouble of promoting it to mathematics departments across the country. This would prove to be the beginning of a long and pleasant editorial association with him.

But really *Mathenauts* was just a sideshow. For my own peace of mind, I needed to get a novel going.

In my last year at Lynchburg, in 1986, I'd begun thinking about writing a historical SF novel involving one of my favorite notions from fringe science: the Hollow Earth. The idea is that our planet is in fact hollow like a tennis ball or like a fisherman's float. A race of people live inside. But how do we get in there to visit them? Perhaps through holes in the ocean floor, or perhaps via an immense hole at the South Pole.

My special inspiration was Edgar Allen Poe's novel, *The Journey of Arthur Gordon Pym of Nantucket*, which describes a sea voyage to the walls of ice around the Southern pole, with the implication that there is a huge opening to be found there, a great shaft leading into Mother Earth's womb. Wanting this to be true, I reasoned that, even if Poe had erred about the hole being clearly visible, it might still exist, but be hidden beneath a sheet of accumulated snow and ice.

My old friend Gregory Gibson, in his capacity as antiquarian bookseller, sent me some nineteenth century sailing narratives, and a fine twenty-volume edition of the collected works of Poe . I pored over these, coming to identify with Eddie. Poe wrote of being possessed by an imp of the perverse, who impelled him to do deliberately alienating and antisocial things—which described my punk attitude to a tee.

While still in Lynchburg, my expanding researches had led me to the rare book room in the library of the University of Virginia, where I found writings about John Cleves Symmes Jr., who began proselytizing his doctrine of the Hollow Earth in 1818. Symmes lived in Newport, Kentucky, and he styled himself the Newton of the West. He was too busy lecturing—or too sly—to publish any books under his own name, but I found a nonfiction *Symmes' Theory of Concentric Spheres*, and a novel, *Symzonia: A Voyage of Discovery*, which are purportedly written by Symmes' followers. My feeling is that, as the books speak so very highly of Symmes, he either wrote them himself or collaborated heavily.

In California in 1986, I started work on my novel, *The Hollow Earth: The Narrative of Mason Algiers Reynolds of Virginia*. It's about a country boy who leaves his farm and travels down the James River as a stowaway in a bateau, accompanied by his dog Arf and his boyhood companion Otha, who's now an escaped slave. They meet Edgar Allan Poe in Richmond, and they travel onward to Antarctica and to the Hollow Earth.

I wasn't sure how to light up the inside of the Hollow Earth, a land which I called Htrae. If you put an Inner Sun in the center, then it seems like everything would fall up into the sun. One day when I was walking around San Francisco with Marc Laidlaw, I found the solution.

It was a new science toy called a plasma sphere, on display in a new age shop. By now nearly everyone's seen these one of these things—it's a hollow glass ball with an electrode in the center. Branching lines of electrical discharge reach out from the electrode to the outer surface, and if you move your fingertips around on the sphere, the glow lines trail after them. *That's* the way to light up the Hollow Earth! Have titanic aurora-like streamers of light reaching from the Central Anomaly to the inhabited inner surface of Htrae.

The writing went slowly. I find it hard to keep my novelistic momentum if I only have a spare hour here and there in which to write. The only extended patches of free time that I had were during the school vacations—especially in the summer—but often we'd want to take family trips then, making road trips around California or flying to visit Sylvia's father and brother in Geneva.

When my first August in California came to an end and the fall semester loomed, I thought of the early sailing ships trying to reach the fabled southern continent of Antarctica. Sometimes they'd overstay the brief polar summer, become iced in, and spend the dark, howling winter hunkered in their vessels, hunting seals for food.

Repeatedly iced in by my teaching duties, I took nearly three years to finish writing *The Hollow Earth*, which finally appeared in 1990, edited by David Hartwell, who'd moved to William Morrow. At the end of the book, I used the hoaxing Poe-like expedient of writing an afterword to the effect that *The Hollow Earth* was a manuscript that I'd found in the rare books room at the University of Virginia.

To this day, I get occasional emails from readers taken in by this. They wonder why I haven't done anything to help mount an expedition to retrace my hero Mason's steps. One guy even assumed that since *The Hollow Earth* was just an old public-domain manuscript that I'd edited, it was okay to post a page-scan of my book on the web!

My kids liked hearing me talk about the Hollow Earth. Once, while cross-country skiing with Isabel near Lake Tahoe, I pointed out the blueness of the light that seemed to emerge from the holes our ski-poles made in the snow.

"Proof that the Earth is hollow!" I told my daughter.

"As if more proof were needed," she responded cheerfully. "When will they *see*?"

Oh, one more thing. In 1990, there was an article about my novel in the San Jose newspaper, and a bum came by my office to tell me some news.

"The sun is cold and hollow," he said. "That light you see overhead is just the interaction of some special rays from the sun with our upper atmosphere. I used to be a very famous surfer, you know. Look."

He pulled out a page torn from an encyclopedia with a grainy picture of someone on a wave.

"That's me. Inside the Hollow Sun."

I identified with Edgar Allan Poe because of his outré imagination, his difficult career, his connection to Virginia, his love of language, his charlatanism—and for another reason as well. Along with Jack Kerouac, Poe is one of the writers most known for their drinking problems. As I mentioned, Poe once wrote an essay about his inner "imp of the perverse," a force that goaded him to screw things up whenever they were running too smoothly. Poe was said to have a genius for being drunk at the wrong time, and for making the worst possible impression on prospective publishers or employers.

In California, I was smoking more pot than before, and drinking a lot too. I don't think I ever did any serious writing while drinking, although once in a great while I'd write while high. Given that my books are somewhat strange, people sometimes imagine that I was often high while writing, but that's not the case at all. Surrealism, gnarl and odd-ball dialog come naturally to me—they're more or less an automatic default. I've never lacked for wild ideas.

In any case, I was always sober for my teaching job. Having alcohol on my breath would have been out of the question. And I'd learned very early that you never want to be high when you're giving a lecture. Why not? If you're high, then (a) everything seems a lot more important than it really is, and (b) the lecture seems to last for hours.

But just about every evening I'd get into some beer or wine. And, yes, if I had a free afternoon, I was likely to smoke a joint and go for a walk and jot down any ideas about my writing or my programming that happened by. Sober or not, I've always carried a folded-in-four piece of typing paper in my back pocket for this purpose.

262

My drinking and pot-smoking caused some stress in the family, upsetting the children, and leading to quarrels with Sylvia. And often I'd annoy my old friends with late night phone calls—especially the friends who were back on the East coast, three time zones later than California.

One exception was good old Sheckley. He was always glad to talk with me—in fact I remember one time when I phoned him up stoned, and he was like, "Wait a minute," and he quickly lit up some pot so he'd be on the same vibrational level.

I've always been somewhat ambivalent about science fiction conventions. It's exciting to be in a huge crowd of fanatical weirdos—but cons tend to emphasize aspects of SF that don't interest me. The main reason I go to them is to hang out with my fellow writers, to make contacts with editors and publishers, and to meet a few of my readers.

Quite early on, my Ace editor, Susan Allison, had cautioned me about how to behave at SF cons. "They look like parties," she'd told me. "But they're not. They're business meetings."

But I had trouble internalizing this advice. As the years went by, my infrequent trips to the cons became something of a problem for me. I'd go with the best of intentions. But, feeling shy around so many semi-strangers, with free booze on every side, and with louche characters to party with, I'd end up totally wasted, sometimes reaching the point of insulting people who might help my writing career.

It took only a few iterations of this scenario until many of the people in the SF world had gotten the impression that I was obnoxious and blind drunk *all the time*. After all, that's how I'd been the two or three times that they'd seen me! It was a drag. I wanted to clean up, but I didn't know how.

I recall a particularly harrowing evening at the 1993 Worldcon in San Francisco, when I was loudly haranguing the very sweet and likable Ellen Datlow for not buying a story of mine for *Omni*. Ow. I apologized to her and made friends again at the World Fantasy Con in Monterey 1998—my first sober con.

I don't want to overdramatize my problem. On a day to day basis, I was still keeping myself fairly together. I was working and writing, and our family life was generally happy. But I was beginning to understand that I was on a gradual decline, and that one of these days I'd have to change. The change would in fact come in 1996.

While I was still at Autodesk in 1993, I started work on *The Hacker and the Ants*, a transreal novel about my experiences as a software engineer who's working with virtual reality and artificial life programs.

The hero of my tale, a hapless programmer named Jerzy Rugby, becomes embroiled in a plot cooked up by his boss and by an evil realtor. Some virtual ant programs settle into the powerful computer chips embedded in people's TVs, and the ants turn every TV show into computer graphics. Jerzy Rugby is charged with treason. But in the end he wins out—although he loses his wife.

The boss in *The Hacker and the Ants* was loosely inspired by John Walker himself. Fortunately Walker has a good sense of humor. He was quite fond of my book, and like many other hackers, he thought it offered a realistic glimpse into the Silicon Valley of the 1980s.

But Walker didn't like that the boss character dies in my last chapter, so he wrote and posted a phantom extra chapter on his own website, www.fourmilab.ch. In Walker's version, my boss character turns out to have faked his death, and is now free to explain to the awe-struck Jerzy Rugby what my novel's machinations were *really* about. It's pretty funny piece.

Eight years later, in 2002, I had a chance to revise *The Hacker and the Ants* for a second edition, and I brought it into line with the changes in computer science that had taken place in the intervening years. Although I didn't include Walker's version of the ending, I did have my main character, Jerzy Rugby, get back together with his wife.

Due in part to my consuming obsession with computer programming—and due in part to my drinking and pot-smoking—I hadn't been getting along with Sylvia very well when *The Hacker and the Ants* first appeared in 1994. But by 2002, we were happy together again.

Reset

One by one our children finished high school and went off to college. When we drove Isabel to the University of Oregon for her freshman year in 1992, we felt the full impact of the empty nest.

On the drive home, Sylvia and I reflexively stopped for a hamburger in a fast food place. It was a custom we'd picked up from all those years with the kids. But now it was just the two of us, so what the hell were we doing in a McDonald's? We realized we were done with that kind of food for good.

Sylvia and I soon found that, as empty nesters, we tended to be nicer to each other. With nobody else to turn to, it became very important to get along.

And, by now, there weren't so many things to argue about. We had enough money, and Sylvia had found a good job teaching English as a Second Language at Evergreen Community College in San Jose. Over the coming years she moved up the ladder there to the point where her salary was about the same as mine—and she even became the head of her department. She was happy to have a career, and she loved working with her students.

Sylvia and I got to go to Japan with Isabel in August of 1993, when some Tokyo marketing guys set up a tour of paid lectures and bookstore signings for me. My science fiction books were very popular in Japan just then—they were all reading *The Sex Sphere* that year.

One night we went to Roppongi, a hip district of Tokyo, and had dinner with our guides. The meal featured a nice soup of *frofuki daikon*, which means "steambath radish." Outside some street repairs were going on. The workers wore white gloves and tidy uniforms. The wall across the street bore a giant video screen showing—Billy Idol's video of his song, "Cyberpunk." Billy chest burst open, revealing wires. The men in white gloves gestured, waving us on by. My kind of SF was out in the world for real.

Isabel and I liked playing pachinko in Japan. We'd put a few bills into a machine and get a basket of ball bearings, and then dump them in a hopper and rapidly fire them into a steep, nearly vertical play area studded with nails and with high-scoring input hoppers here and there, and with a zillion lights and sounds. Going into a pachinko parlors was like getting inside a machine. Isabel scored big on a machine named Fever Powerful, and we whooped and yelled.

"Fever Powerful! All right!"

Some of the players looked at us with disapproval—we were noisy people of the wrong race. But most of them didn't hear us, or didn't care. The Japanese are into their pachinko machines like Vegas gambling addicts are into the slots.

Another day, the three of us had lunch in a teahouse near the famous Zen rock garden in Kyoto. The lunch was a pot of warm water with slabs of tofu, and a strainer for lifting them out. To spice it up we had a few beans, a piece of eggplant, and a pickled pepper. We sat on cushions on the tatami mat floor by an open paper door. Outside the door was a tiny pond with miniature trees and big carp in the pond. One of the carp jumped halfway out of the water.

"Yes!" said Isabel. "That right there happening was a haiku!"

Even though none of the kids lived at home anymore, they were still around. Georgia had graduated from college in 1991, and she was sharing a San Francisco apartment with three other women. Rudy was still studying engineering at nearby Berkeley. Sometimes we'd be included in the kids' activities—they might invite us to one of their parties, or take us on an outing.

266

I recall a Halloween in 1994 when we went to San Francisco's legendary Castro Street Parade with Georgia and her college friend Bethany. It was epic, with a vast crowd that surged and rippled like the contour lines of a cubic Mandelbrot set fractal. I saw bevies of tall, honking-voiced brides, and a reveler wearing a toilet seat for a necklace.

Georgia, always one for fanciful costumes, was dressed as a supermarket checker. She'd made herself a name tag saying "Lynne. Welcome to Happy Dollar." Her hairdo included a wide bandeau and a lank pony tail. She'd crafted a little cardboard checkout counter to wear around her waist, complete with a plastic window in the cardboard to represent the scanner. Random boxes of merchandise were glued to the counter: cereal, Tampax, plastic knives, ramen noodles, and a bottle of beer. The cops took the beer away.

Sylvia was a prosperous witch in a pointed velvet hat, and I was a mountain climber from the Hollow Earth, dressed in my old knickers from the Zermatt days, with my face painted green and yellow. Rudy was there too, wearing slitted sunglasses, his yellow Mohawk hairdo, and a fireman's reflective silver protective jacket.

Rudy had progressed from heavy metal to punk rock, and in those days, you never knew from one time to next what his hair color or style would be. To some extent we'd stopped commenting on it, although every now and then he'd still get a rise out of us—like when he mowed three bald lanes onto his head to create a double Mohawk with blue-dyed clown puffs on the sides.

The night of that Halloween parade in the Castro, Sylvia and I slept on the living room floor of Georgia's apartment. I'd brought our carved pumpkin along from home, and it was lit on the floor next to us, bathing the room in throbbing orange light. It was a cozy scene. And then Rudy showed up to sleep there too. By now it seemed like a rare and exciting jamboree to have several family members sleeping under one roof.

I'd taken up backpacking, and sometimes Rudy or Isabel would go camping with me, usually in the hills above the Big Sur coast. Rudy and I would conduct intricate, ramifying negotiations—not exactly arguments—about which path to take or where to pitch the tent or how to build the fire. The old father-son thing, and now I was on the other side. I enjoyed the action.

Our family had been admiring some photo books by the artist Andy Goldsworthy, who goes into fields and arranges natural objects into fleeting works of art. On one spring campout, Rudy and I created a two-part Goldsworthy.

Part 1. We pitched our tent on a hilltop with no running water, next to a patch of snow. Rudy made a huge ball out of the snow and flipped it off a cliff, putting a wild spin on the ball that sent fragments of snow flying from its equator.

Part 2. We trekked to a campsite where the Big Sur River runs into the Pacific. We gathered a lot of driftwood beside the river, made a Buddha-sized campfire and we flung a blazing log high into the air above the river. The rapidly twirling log spat off sparks—a perfect match for the spinning snowball.

My parents were on their way out.

A couple of years after we'd moved to California, in 1989, my mother had a stroke while riding up to Maine with a woman friend of hers. Not knowing what else to do, Mom's friend had left her in a hospital in Hartford, Connecticut.

I flew out to be with Mom for a few days, spending my nights in a room the size of a closet at a nearby hotel. It was oddly relaxing to be there, with nothing to do but care for my mother. I'd sit by her bed, and accompany her to physical therapy. She was somewhat paralyzed on one side.

The other people getting rehab were in terrible shape—a boy with a fresh bandage where his foot had been, a woman learning to walk with an artificial leg, and a man with a cut in his head like the gash of an axe, learning to stand. All of them moved at a snail's pace—but the human life force was there, never giving up, taking steps to recover from the most devastating wounds.

On my last morning, I was supposed to be at the airport by 6:30, so I got up extra early to see Mom one more time. She was awake, lying there in the faint dawn light, her head on her pillow, her hair just like always, smiling up at me, her face webbed with fine wrinkles. She looked so beautiful, like a Rembrandt, but incalculably more precious.

Pop and I didn't discuss Mom's stroke. I think he felt too guilty about the divorce to discuss her. And I was reluctant to start up a conversation that might end with me berating him. I was still angry at him for leaving her. But at the same time, I continued to love and admire him. In short, I was conflicted.

Pop showed up to visit us in California in 1990, and we two went to play golf at Pebble Beach—the first and probably the only time I'll play there. I paid for it, wanting to give the old man a treat. He was pretty broke by now, and he loved golf.

At first we were grouped as a foursome with a couple of gung-ho pseudo-jocks who'd yell curses whenever they hit the ball and it didn't fly two hundred yards and land on the green. As if normally that's what *did* happen on their first drive off the tee. And they had a caddy who said snotty things to me, duffer that I am.

"Oops, sir, you hooked that ball into the water hazard." Pause. "The Pacific Ocean, sir."

I told Pop I didn't want to play with those three guys, and good old Pop walked over and told them to go ahead without us. It was nice, for that moment, to be a boy again, to have my father protecting me. That was just about the very last time he was able to do that for me.

And then it was just Pop and me on the Pebble Beach course. The rest of our round was all fun. A day to remember. Pop was talking about the meaning of life in the same eager interested way as always, like an overgrown boy.

Mom had some more strokes in 1990 and she had to go around in a wheelchair. And then she went into a nursing home, and in 1991, a final stroke put her into a coma. We flew out there and sat with her for a few days. For awhile she was in the hospital, but there wasn't much hope of her ever waking up. She'd always said she didn't want to be kept on life support indefinitely, so we brought her back to the nursing home to die. It was hard.

We'd sit with her and talk to her, not that she was responding. But it seemed like the flow of our voices might comfort her. I remembered being a kid sleeping in the back seat of the family car, with the peaceful murmur of my parents in front.

The last night of Mom's life, a Saturday night, July 13, 1991, her breathing was irregular. She'd take five or twelve regular breaths and then not breathe for a beat and then take a deep breath and let out a long exhale. Like a big sigh—heartbreaking. She died a few hours later, alone in the middle of the night.

Embry and I went to the funeral home to have a final look at her. We didn't want to at first, but we realized that we needed to. After some formalities, the funeral director led us downstairs. Mom was on a narrow roller bed that was at an angle to the wall, with a sheet pulled up to her chin. She was so very white. I, the younger boy, the more spontaneous one, stepped forward and touched her cheek and her forehead. Her skin was cold; no living person is ever that cold. She had funny kind of expression on her face, like "See?" or "I told you so."

"It just ends in tears," is what Mom used to say when we boys would do something reckless. Life ends in tears.

Her ashes went into an octagonal cherrywood box that we buried in a little corner by two low brick walls right in the lawn of St. Francis in the Fields, the church I grew up in, the church where Mom took me to nursery school, kindergarten, and grades one through three, the church where I was confirmed and Pop was ordained, the church Embry still goes to. A little corner of the churchyard. Mom's Louisville friends were at the funeral, aged and decrepit.

"Your mother was such an elegant woman," Niles's mother told me. "So warm and real." Niles himself was living in Alabama.

I felt a weariness with being the head of a family. It was so much easier those many years ago when it was only me and Mom, and I would sit on her lap and she would hug me after lunch.

Pop's health declined over the next three years. He was still with that same woman, Priscilla. He had a couple of strokes and in 1993 he ended up in a nursing home near where he lived in Reston, Virginia. The very last time I saw him, early in July, 1994, we quarreled. He was nagging me to quit drinking, and I got mad at him, pointing out that he'd ruined his marriage with his drinking and unfaithfulness, and he started crying.

And then, on August 1, 1994, he was dead too.

A number of strangers made speeches at Pop's funeral, but the words went past Embry and me. The people speaking were local politicians, all of them praising Pop, but not the sandy, freckly Pop we knew as our father. No priest officiated, and there were no real prayers. At some point, two undertakers in suits rolled back a piece of Astroturf and they put the box with Pop's ashes down into a pre-dug hole with a dry clayey pile of Virginia dirt next to it. There were two worn planks by the hole to keep it from crumbling. A little ant was on one plank moving around. A leafy stem of chickweed was waving at the edge of the hole. Then a white woman sang "Amazing Grace" and it was over.

My feelings were all in tangle. I felt lonely, afraid and overshadowed by doom. I felt sorrow over Pop's mistakes, and regret for my impatience with him. I felt tenderness towards his eternally boyish self, and nostalgia for our happy times.

I remembered Pop having told me that when his own father died, he felt overcome by anger—and now I understood. Anger at who? At the ruthless, invisible reaper who'd taken my parents away—and who'd be back one day for me.

A couple of months after Pop's funeral, our dog Arf got hit by a car and I buried him in our back yard. While I was digging the four-foot-deep hole I cried a lot. Somehow I hadn't been able to get the tears out when Pop died, but now I could.

As I buried Arf, at some level, I had to smile too, as I was remembering a story that Pop liked to tell.

One day a little boy comes home from school, and his mother tells him, "Pop's dead."

And the boy is crying and crying, and his mother says, "Oh, you poor dear. Just remember this: even though your father's gone, he's looking down on us from heaven."

The boy glances up. "*Pop's* dead? I thought you said *Pup's* dead! The boy laughs and dries his eyes. "Can Pup and I go out and play?"

For years it bothered me that Priscilla hadn't arranged to give Pop a proper burial service out of the Episcopal Book of Common Prayer—even though he'd been a minister. Embry and I had been too dazed to think of talking this over with her before the burial.

Finally, twelve years later, in 2006, Embry and I would make a pilgrimage to the gravestone and read the service.

"You were right, Pop," I'd say after that reading, and Embry would echo me.

"Right about everything, Pop."

I n June of 1995, I got tenure at San Jose State, and was promoted to full professor. It's too bad Pop didn't live to see it. All my adult life he'd wistfully been asking me when I was going to get tenure. He'd always ask me that, and whether I was as well-known as Michael Dorris, my high-school friend who'd also become a writer.

I could never quite tell if Pop kept asking about Dorris to bug me, or if he just couldn't understand how our old driving-group partner had managed to pull ahead of me. Another unanswered question: Could I have gone back to being Mike's best pal, if only we'd been thrown together more? Could I have possibly cheered Mike up enough to prevent him from killing himself? Some things never get resolved. Life and death roll on.

Anyway—I was really happy about being a professor with tenure. When I was starting out at Rutgers, I'd never expected it would take me nearly thirty years.

For that matter, I'd never imagined how long and arduous my writing career would be. No matter what I tried, my books remained in the so-called midlist zone—they didn't bomb in such a way as to make me unpublishable, but I wasn't writing best-sellers. Still, I kept at it. Writing was my first love and my true career.

And what about my other occupations? I'd say mathematics was my higher knowledge, my inspiration. Programming was a hobby or maybe a vice. And teaching was a day job.

In 1995, a year had gone by with no novel even started, and now it was time to get back on the path. I decided to return to the world of *Software* and *Wetware*, and began working on *Freeware*, which would eventually appear in 1997.

I sometimes write the best stuff when I don't feel particularly creative. On a given day, it's good if I'm just doggedly trying to finish the next scene of another goddamn novel. If I feel like I'm crafting a masterwork, the language is more likely to get away from me. When nothing is at stake, I'm free to go wild with the effects and have my characters say brutally honest things—without losing control. I develop a deadpan, surreal tone that I think of as writing degree zero.

I felt *Freeware* turned out really well, but I tend to think that about all of my books. The meaning of the title is that, throughout the universe, alien minds are traveling from world to world in the form of compressed information files—akin to the files you might download from the web. The alien minds piggyback onto high-energy radiation such as cosmic rays or the signals emitted by solar flares. When these rays strike a sufficiently rich computational object, the object may wake up—and begin emulating the alien mind.

In *Freeware* there are indeed a lot of computationally dense objects on Earth—these are descendants of the *Software* robots, whose minds now inhabit soft bodies made of gnarly, mold-infested piezoplastic.

My old character Sta-Hi is an ex-senator in *Freeware*. Due to various mishaps, Sta-Hi's wife Wendy has her personality living in a piezoplastic ruff that she wears on her neck—as opposed to using her meat brain. She becomes infected with a computer virus called the Stairway to Heaven that opens her up to one of those compressed alien minds zipping around, and she becomes the avatar of a being called Quuz—who lives within the vortex tubes of our own sun. And that's just the start.

Another element in *Freeware* is that Sta-Hi's drug and alcohol problems are seriously messing him up. He's finally thinking about getting sober.

While I was writing *Freeware* in 1995, I was seeing a lot of my artist and cartoonist friend Paul Mavrides. Mavrides had created a number of images for a parodistic cult called the Church of the SubGenius, which had a not-quite-divinity called "Bob," always spelled with the quotes. The Church, which managed to get some people to mail in donations, was a complex, interactive bit of dada art—or rather "bulldada," as they put it. Walker and I had included an image of "Bob" with our CA Lab software so that the sacred visage could be nibbled by CA rules like the Zhabotinsky scrolls. Art patron that I am, I'd even paid Ivan Stang, the Church's main man, for the rights—two hundred dollars out of my own pocket.

More recently, Mavrides had taken to painting on black velvet. But he wasn't painting Elvis, the Virgin of Guadalupe, or dogs playing cards. He was painting the Kennedy assassination, the bodies at Jonestown, the Challenger explosion, the AIDS virus, and cockroaches.

I really liked the black velvet painting of the cockroaches—called *Victors*. The chartreuse and magenta glow from its background reminded me of a computer screen full of cellular automata. When I read a big article about Mavrides in *Mondo 2000*, I got stoked enough to buy the cockroach painting—and never mind that it was me who'd written that article!

Mavrides was a saturnine, puckish character, a little younger than me. I thought of him as an old-school beatnik, with his finely honed sense of the absurd and his espresso-dark cynicism. I liked taking a day off and driving up to San Francisco to hang in his studio, later going out with him for coffee or tapas on nearby Valencia Street. During those peaceful after-noons, if we were in the mood, I'd read him the latest chapter of my novel-in-progress while he painted. Paul's cartoonist fellow roomer, Hal Robbins, would often join us. A writer reading new work to his artist pals—that felt like the way life should be.

I was still having fun some of the time, but by 1995, alcohol and pot were taking an increasing toll. What had once seemed to be a path to bohemian adventure had become a ball and chain. I'd often wake up in the middle of the night and lie there wishing that I was dead. As for the future—I imagined ending up like a shabby animal in a concrete zoo pen, blank and weary, forever waiting for my next trough of slop.

Kerouac and Poe don't work as role models when you're pushing fifty.

At first I thought I could quit beer and keep smoking pot, but that only worked for a couple of weeks. The pot led me back to the beer. I needed to get past the habit of taking stuff in order to feel different. So I tried giving up pot too—but I found I couldn't keep it up on my own.

Reluctantly I began going to the meetings of a mutual-support group for people with the same kinds of problems. I fully expected to find a bunch of evangelical, goody-goody squares at the meetings. But of course they were drunks and stoners, sober now, but still crazy—definitely the kind of people I might have hung with in the past. Their stories were twisted and darkly funny.

Even though I liked the group and I knew I wanted to quit, it took me about six months to make it stick. The turning point came in June, 1996, three months after I turned fifty.

I'd gone backpacking alone near Cone Peak in Big Sur. The first night, I made a camp by a stream in a redwood grove six miles in from the road, and on the second day, I hiked a big loop, leaving my stuff at the camp.

On the steep grassy hills overlooking the ocean, I savored the mind-opening feeling of the vast space around me. I felt embedded in the natural world. The hills were dotted with yucca plants: batches of big spiky leaves with giant phallic stalks shooting up ten or twelve feet, huge and covered with white flowers smelling of magnolia. Everything was placed in just the right spot—the yuccas, the slopes, the oaks and redwoods, Cone Peak in the background, and the foggy curve of the coast.

Back at my tent, I went to sleep early, and awoke in middle of the night feeling fully rested. The half moon was high overhead. I got up and strolled around, wanting to savor this rare moment of being alone in the wilderness, beneath the redwoods by a stream.

At the sight of some spooky, dead branches hanging down I began to be a little scared. To push that away, I expanded my awareness to have a sense of the cosmos all around and within everything, a sense of the universe as being filled with love. I saw the world as a single fabric that I was a pattern in. And then, alone in the dark woods, I felt as safe as if I were at home. I sat by the inky, silvery stream, its gurgles and splashes like musical notes—chaotic and beautiful.

Something about this experience made it possible for me to begin mentally reaching out for help at crucial times—for instance when I was about to take a drink. I'd feel like the help came right away—and I'd be able to resist the drinks. Amazing.

Although I've always believed in a mystical overarching cosmic mind, I've never been conventionally religious. Yes, I've gone to church on an occasional basis for my whole life, and I enjoy the service—but I don't take the prayers and hymns to be literally true. I see a church service as a social bonding ritual and a form of communal meditation. It wouldn't be at all accurate to say that I'm a born-again convert.

For me, asking for help can be as simple as getting into the moment, taking a few breaths, and wishing to be a calmer, more loving person. And I don't feel that it's necessarily true that I'm getting help from the outside.

It could be, that when I'm asking for help, it's a way of saying, "My usual logical mode of thought isn't working, and I need to jump off my gerbil-wheel." In more exalted terms, it might be that, if I view myself as part of a cosmic web of existence, it's easier to rise above my personal fears and resentments—and those are the feelings that made me want to drink and get high.

Staying sober requires a certain amount of ongoing effort, although over the years it's gotten easier. I like it. I feel more comfortable in my own skin. I'm less tormented, and I don't want to die. And I have better relationships with the most important people in my life: Sylvia and the children.

I had a slight worry that giving up pot and alcohol might impair my courage to write or lessen my flow of inspiration, but far from it. The pace of my writing production picked up, and I went on to write four novels and two anthologies in the ensuing five years, a run as good as any I've ever had.

I seem to have more time available for work now, and I'm better able to plan and control my projects. It's easier than ever to relax and to proceed at writing degree zero, telling my version of the truth.

One thing I'd always liked about drinking or smoking pot was that it tended to alter my usual trains of thought. It's always unpleasant when I get into a mode of endlessly replaying certain mental tapes— rehashing an argument, say, or obsessing over some fears or resentments. Sometimes I long to turn off my inner monologue. And getting zonked is one way to do this.

But I'd always known there are other paths to liberation. Somehow I've never had the patience for prolonged bouts of sitting meditation. But exercise has a way of emptying out the mind as well. I like the stretching and bending of yoga. And mountain-biking around my village and the nearby hills is a wonderful way to get out of my head and into my body.

Writing is a kind of spitiual practice as well. When I'm actively writing, I forget about myself. I get drawn into the craft and into the play of ideas. As the John Malkovich character in the movie *Art School Confidential* puts it, doing my work provides me with a "narcotic moment of creative bliss."

The first book I wrote after getting sober was, perhaps thanks to my own imp of the perverse, one of my oddest books of all: *Saucer Wisdom*. I wanted to do something special for the Millennium.

The book evolved in a strange way. In 1997, *Wired* magazine had decided to start a line of books. I'd done a couple of journalistic pieces for *Wired* over the years—for one article I went into the Intel chip-fabrication plant; for another I went to the secret storeroom at Skywalker Ranch where they have Yoda, R2D2, and the Lost Ark. And in 1997, one of my old friends, Mark Frauenfelder, had become a new editor at *Wired*.

Mark was a fan of my writing and a thoroughly likable guy. In the late 1980s and early 1990s, I'd written some ephemeral pieces for Mark's print zine *Boing Boing*—which would, in 2000, evolve into the most popular blog in the world.

Mark suggested that I write a work of speculative futurology to be a *Wired* book. I sent him some ideas that he liked, but then his fellow editors wondered if I could find a thread to tie my disparate predictions together. I proposed that I frame my book as if I'd learned my facts about the future from a man who'd actually been there. My time-traveler was to be Frank Shook, a crackpot UFO abductee who's been given a tour of the next three thousand years by the aliens.

My old pal Gregory Gibson was visiting me at the time, and I took him along to the pitch meeting with the *Wired* editors in February, 1997. On the drive from San Jose to San Francisco, Greg and I cooked up the scheme that he would present himself as actually *being* Frank Shook, the saucer nut. Greg has a piercing glare, and was then wearing a full beard, with his hair very long. He looked like a homeless Viet vet. At the pitch meeting, with four editors present, Greg made a few tense, distracted remarks, and then stalked out, muttering that it was too painful to be talking about his experiences to so many of us at once.

There was a stunned silence. After a bit, I let on that Greg had been hoaxing them, but the editors didn't quite want to let go of the illusion. It was decided they'd present the book as a factual true-life adventure starring the characters Rudy Rucker and Frank Shook. And they'd market it as it were a book akin to Whitley Strieber's UFO abduction book, *Communion*.

I was a little worried about what this might do to whatever slight credibility my name has, but I was willing to grit my teeth and go through with it—not only in hopes of sales, but also as a way of thumbing my nose at conventional notions of respectability. Eddie Poe the hoaxer would have done no less.

The guys at *Wired* were fond of me, and relatively new to book-publishing. My agent Susan Protter hit them for an advance about five times as large as I was usually getting. They didn't realize how cheaply I could be had. Or maybe they did, but they wanted to do me a favor.

I had a bit of trouble writing the book. The big advance made me nervous—I felt like I had to come up with something unusually good. And, as I got deeper into the project, I started being paranoid that the aliens—if they existed—might show up to harass me.

In April, 1997, for instance, I went on a road-trip with Sylvia and Georgia. We hit Las Vegas, the Grand Canyon and Zion national park in Utah. At Zion I had a very frightening dream.

In my dream, the aliens are high over me, in a long-legged Dr. Seuss-style walking-machine that's also a bulldozer, and it's rocking *uhhnnnm, uhhnnnm, uhmmmmn*, the way machines do when they're trying to push something. I protest, and the aliens shine a laser down into my mouth. The laser is etching my teeth as if they were computer chips in a fabrication lab—*ZZZZT ZZZTTT*. It's incredibly painful, and it's happening way too fast . . .

I woke myself up and felt that dark, helpless paranoia of the real UFO nuts who think the aliens have already taken over the world and that we're just their cattle, their lab rats, controlled by our etched-in implants. I felt doomed.

The next morning the newspapers were filled with news of a mass UFO cult suicide. And when we got home, we found our house flooded with five hundred gallons of raw sewage. The main line had clogged up while we were gone, and the neighbors' crap had backed up through our toilet. Was this the revenge of the aliens? Was the sewage the objective correlative of UFOlogy?

Walking the hills above Los Gatos a few weeks later, I lay down in a grassy little meadow and looked up. I was wondering how it would be to see a classic flying saucer up there, drawn in lines of pale light against the blue sky. The noises in the woods began to take on an alien cast, sticking together to form higher-order mental forms.

To further roil my psyche, Greg kept leaving me crackpot voice-mail messages in the persona of Frank Shook. And I was arguing with him about whether I was going to give him a percentage of my book advance. On our way into the *Wired* pitch meeting, I'd in fact told him that I'd cut him in, but once I had the deal, I didn't feel like paying him after all. And then I did give Greg some money, but I grew so resentful about it that, for the sake of our friendship, he agreed to give the money back. It was a mess. I was going nuts.

Transrealism was the only way out. I put all my fears and misgivings into the book. I even wrote a scene where my character Frank Shook robs the home of my character Rudy Rucker. Frank steals Rudy's book manuscript and his computer.

In search of a big third act for the novel, I flew to Spearfish, North Dakota, in June, 1997, to meet up with an artist friend of mine who lives there. His name is Dick Termes, and he paints primarily on spheres. He says that right after Christmas is the best time for gathering "canvases" to paint on, he picks up lawn-scale ball ornaments on sale at K-Mart, covers them in gesso and paints marvelous scenes using his own method of "six-point perspective." What's six-point perspective? Well, you can look it up—Termes has a video explaining it on the Web.

When I visited, Termes lent me his car, and I drove across the state line into Wyoming to visit the Devil's Tower—which appears in the classic UFO film, *Close Encounters of the Third Kind*. The Tower was even more alien and inspiring than I'd imagined it would be. My characters Rudy Rucker and Frank Shook had their final meeting there, and Rudy took a ride in an alien-filled saucer.

I ran this long, strange trip to the end and mailed the final manuscript to *Wired* in the summer of 1997—whereupon they told me they'd canceled their whole line of books. Susan Protter went after them and made them pay most of that fat advance they'd promised. Like I always say, it's times like that when you really need an agent. And then Susan sold the book again to Tor Books—for a more modest sum.

I was happy to be selling a book to Tor—they're the largest publisher of fantasy and science fiction in the world. And I'd be working with the editor

David Hartwell, who'd moved to Tor as well. As it turned out, I'd continue selling books to Hartwell at Tor for some years to come.

I find Hartwell enjoyable to work with. He's an old-school kind of editor, highly educated, and sensitive to the subtlest literary references. He has an encyclopedic familiarity of the existing SF and fantasy literature, a far broader knowledge than mine. He tends to understand what I'm writing about and what I'm trying to do—which isn't always a given. And he tends to give me good advice on my manuscripts without over-doing it.

With all this said, I should mention that, in the isolated case of *Saucer Wisdom*, it was actually Dave's wife, Katherine Cramer, who did the lion's share of the editing. The book came to Dave's desk when he was overburdened with multiple deadlines, so Katherine stepped in. And, as it happened, she gave me some very good advice about kicking the book's ending up a notch.

I'd made a bunch of drawings to go with *Saucer Wisdom*, supposedly Frank Shook himself had drawn these figures. There was some question as to whether we'd need to have them redrawn by a professional artist. But Dave Hartwell made the call that we could just use my drawings as is.

As he put it, "If they're supposed to be drawn by a UFO nut while he's in a flying saucer, how polished do they have to be?"

To my relief, Tor didn't have the stomach for mounting a campaign to promote *Saucer Wisdom* as being literally true. Instead we marketed *Saucer Wisdom* as a playful and visionary science book about our possible futures—which, to some extent, the book is. Possibly it might have worked better to describe the book as a transreal science fiction novel—which is a more accurate description of its nature.

Like Vladimir Nabokov's novel *Pale Fire*—which initially appears to be a long poem accompanied by extensive footnotes—*Saucer Wisdom* is deceptive. It doesn't look like a novel, but a novel is what it actually is.

Saucer Wisdom didn't sell particularly well. Saucer true believers were offended by my irreverent novelistic tone, while science buffs were put off by the presence of any UFOs at all. Some people didn't seem able to figure out which parts of the book were serious and which parts were funny—and the uncertainty made them uptight.

A Way Out?

For the years 1990–2001, my novel *Software* was under option to a series of film companies, ending up at Phoenix Pictures. Every year someone would renew the option, and I'd get a few thousand more bucks. It was an exciting run, with dozens of ups and downs, and I went to a bunch of meetings with Hollywood people. For awhile I felt quite sure that my books would start being movies—and everything would change.

I took Rudy Jr. down to Hollywood with me one time in March, 1997, to see Scott Billups, who was for a time slated to direct the film. Scott kept telling us about a helicopter skiing trip he'd taken, going on and on about the "long lines of powder," which seemed like a bad sign. He had a connection with Mike Medavoy, the studio head at Phoenix Pictures.

"Mike's got a new wife, and she's running him ragged," Billups told us.

"Is she beautiful?" I asked.

"Whatever she didn't have, Mike bought her," said Billups.

Medavoy wasn't liking the script that Billups's writer had come up with, so Phoenix hired the screenwriters from *Toy Story*, and gave them strict instructions *not* to read my book, but to work only from the existing scripts—there were four prior scripts by now, one of them by my cyberpunk friend John Shirley.

The fifth script was horrible, and they kept getting worse—soon we were up to version eight. By now Billups was being edged out, but Medavoy stayed active. I went down for another meeting in January, 1999, and everyone was really encouraging. For a day or two, I actually thought I was going to get a lot of money.

One of the assistant producers and I went to strip club after that meeting. Sylvia couldn't believe it, me in a strip club with a producer.

"What a *sleaze-bag* that guy must be!"

Actually, if the truth be told, it was *my* idea to go see the strippers. To my tiny mind, this seemed like a reasonable way to celebrate my (imagined) big score in Hollywood. And it was convenient to hit the club, as it was right next to the LAX airport. It was a well-lit airy place. Naturally the women were hard, robotic, and street wise. They seemed more like social workers or dental hygienists than like prostitutes.

I didn't want to dive into the gutter and go mad with guilt. So rather than getting a lap dance for myself, I paid a woman to take my assistant producer upstairs and give *him* a lap dance. Even though I'm sober, I still know how to throw out money in a bar. Especially when I think Hollywood's about to shovel hundreds of thousands of bucks into my lap.

The illusion of getting a big payday went away and the scripts kept getting worse—we were up to version ten before long. The film agent I was using then, Steve Freedman, told me that by now Phoenix had spent over a million dollars on discarded screenplays. I was alarmed that they'd thrown out so much money on such shit. But Steve said it was all good.

"The million dollars makes Medavoy pregnant," insisted Steve. "If he tries to back out, I say—No, you're pregnant, you've got to make the film."

I had one last meeting with Mike Medavoy in August, 2000. He finally wanted my advice on how to doctor the script. They flew me to LA first class, and a limo picked me up at the airport. Like so many people in LA, the driver was talking about the Business, and she was happy to hear I was going to a script meeting.

Outside the Phoenix building, I met Steve Freedman. He wasn't a big-time agent by any means. I'd hired him more or less at random. He looked more feral and weasel-like than I'd remembered from our earlier meetings. He was wearing a Mexican wedding shirt with the tail hanging out. I was wearing black silk pants, black silk sport shirt, black silk jacket and wraparound black shades. Mr. Cyberpunk.

Steve had been somewhat manic during our recent phone conversations, so I warned him not to be throwing in extra story ideas of his own. He agreed readily, and claimed that at the end of the meeting he'd corner Medavoy and get us our final deal.

We cooled our heels in a side room for a half hour, chatting with an assistant producer. Medavoy was stuck in a meeting, running a little late.

"So who's he meeting with?" I asked the assistant producer.

"Arnold Schwarzenegger."

The Terminator! Right here! Arnold was starring in film called *The Sixth Day* that Phoenix was to release in a few months. Soon Arnold walked by with his body guard, coming out of his meeting. He was short, as the big stars so often are. He glanced over, checking us out.

And now it was our turn with Mike Medavoy. It was him, me, Steve, and a couple of assistant producer guys. One of these two appeared to be wearing foundation makeup and lipstick. Or maybe he was made of plastic. My focus was on Medavoy. He was an Irish-looking guy, in preppy clothes.

He said he was worried about the project, and that he was embarrassed to have spent over a million dollars. He longed to hear a decent plot line, clearly broken into three acts.

I'd been preparing for this. By now I understood the Hollywood obsession with three acts. I began pitching my version, talking for five or ten minutes, but I went too slow.

Medavoy interrupted, weary and impatient. "Tell me the second act before I have to kill myself."

Flop sweat. I rushed through the second act, but I only got in a few words about my third act before Medavoy cut me off.

"Hard to make all that work," he said, dismissing my ideas.

And then he told how he envisioned the movie. A thriller. Lots of chase scenes. An epic battle for the spaceport, with American soldiers against robots. A general and a colonel for the lead characters.

"Big base on the Moon," continued Medavoy. "It's called, I dunno, why not the Octagon?"

I was flabbergasted, horrified, uncomprehending. "Octagon?"

"Like the Pentagon where the military is. I was just there on a tour last week. They have two war rooms now. It's great."

I glanced over at Steve Freedman. He was grinning ear to ear with his head nodding *Yes* like a plaster dog with its head on a spring. He'd never actually seen Medavoy before. He was in paradise just sitting at this meeting. There was no way Freedman was going to corner this studio head and tell him he was pregnant.

And then Medavoy's underlings were hustling us out. Steve and I walked across the street and had lunch in the SONY cafeteria, a couple of Hollywood losers, cheering ourselves with thick sandwiches and staircase wisdom. I started rapping about pumping up the third act with a flying robot mosquito loaded with a mind-virus to sting the President. I picked up the frilly toothpick from my sandwich and zoomed it around, menacing Steve with it, and he was laughing. He told me his father had been a Hollywood agent too.

The *Software* project was dead. A couple of months later, in the fall of 2000, Phoenix Pictures sent the new Schwarzenegger movie, *The 6th Day*, into the theaters.

The 6th Day carries strong echoes of my *Ware* books. The two central idea in the movie are to record someone's brain software and to load this digitized personality onto a tank-grown clone of that person.

These happen to be a pair of ideas that appeared, arguably for the very first time, in my novels *Software* (1982) and *Wetware* (1988). It took me some years of thought and effort to come up with these twists. They hadn't been at all obvious or "in the air." But by the year 2000, cyberpunk was old news, and my books had been kicking around the Phoenix offices for a decade.

The villain in *The 6th Day* wears horn-rimmed glasses just like mine and is called "Drucker." Might the film-makers have been driven by a Raskolnikov-like compulsion to confess their crime?

"Yes, I killed the old woman with an axe! Yes, I stole Dr. Rucker's ideas!"

So did I sue? Well, Mom always said it's tacky to sue. I'm a writer, not a lawyer. And, after all, I had picked up a fair amount of money from Hollywood by repeatedly rolling over those option agreements for ten years. Why bite a hand that might feed me again?

Hollywood did indeed come back to me a couple more times—the most exciting was when *Master and Space of Time* was under option to the director Michel Gondry, who'd recently scored a hit with *The Eternal Sunshine of the Spotless Mind*. The cartoonist and screenwriter Daniel Clowes, known for *Ghost World*, was working on a script of my novel for Gondry. Jack Black and Jim Carrey were going to play my characters Fletcher and Harry. But apparently Gondry couldn't get the necessary funding.

In an interview I saw on the web, Gondry gave a kind of explanation, speaking for himself and Clowes: "It's very hard, because all of the reasons why we both like the book are reasons why the studio would not do a movie. It's quirky, it's unpredictable, it's absurd, it's funny, and it's not slick at all. It's rough and grotesque."

When I got my first Philip K. Dick award, I felt sure they'd be making movies of my novels. Now I'm not so sure. It could be that the window for that has closed for good. I don't put much emotional energy into speculating about Hollywood anymore. If a film is ever made, great, but there's no point letting a long-shot dream dominate my thought. Just staying in print is hard enough.

The summer after I turned fifty, in 1996, Sylvia and I took a trip to the Kingdom of Tonga in the South Pacific. Why Tonga? I was looking for a way to get off the grid. And my Autodesk cyberspace programmer friend, Eric Gullichsen, happened to be living in Tonga. He'd ingratiated himself with the Crown Prince there, and he promised we'd be given a royal welcome.

To some extent, this came true. We were met at the airport by a chauffeur-driven limousine, which was ours to use during the time we were on the main island of the Tongan archipelago. The driver was a burly guy called Whitten, nearly six and a half feet tall. He wore a straw skirt.

Tonga was more primitive than I'd imagined possible. Most of the roads were dirt or gravel. Now and then you'd see something like a fireworks stand, an open-air counter with a few shelves. Turned out those were the food stores. There were any number of rangy, irritable pigs roaming free. The outer walls of all the little houses were muddy to a height of three feet—due to the pigs rubbing against the houses to scratch themselves. In the evenings, we'd hear the *thock* of axes as pig-owners split coconuts to feed their herds. Due to the coconut diet, the pigs' flesh was watery and oily.

On the first day, we had to get a visa, so we proceeded to the two-story Foreign Ministry building. The elevator had a marble floor. It was the only elevator in Tonga, manned by a man in a tie and a blue serge skirt.

"Hello," I said.

"*Malo e lelei*," said the elevator operator firmly. "You must learn to say hello in the Tongan way. *Malo e lelei*."

Later we found Gullichsen asleep in a hammock on a porch. He was proud of the bicycle he'd brought to Tonga—all the parts were stainless steel to resist the sea air. He got us invited to the Crown Prince's house—which was the only big suburban-style home around. It was guarded by guys with machine-guns.

Prince Tupou was an eccentric, plump man with a British accent. He'd studied at Oxford, and had brought an English taxicab back with him to serve as his limo. He showed us his computers—the desktop bore an image of the actress Gong Li. He'd tried to get in touch with her, but she wasn't interested. He offered me a job tutoring Tongan high-school students in the use of computers.

"We would not provide a salary," said Prince Tupou. "Perhaps I could eventually reward you with Tongan citizenship."

I politely said I'd think about it. Leaving his house I had a paranoid moment that we were about to be cut down by a hail of gunfire.

Sylvia and I settled in, drifting from island to island in the Tongan archipelago. One day on Vava'u we set out to climb the highest peak in the kingdom—Mount Talau, a hill some four hundred feet tall. On the way, we encountered an old man walking down the dirt street. His shirt had several buttons missing, many of his teeth were gone, and he was carrying a small aluminum tub holding a big steak of fish flesh.

He struck up a cheerful conversation with us, very much at his ease, talking about his sister in California. His name was Lata Toumolupe. He invited us into his home to look at his shells. We took off our shoes, sat on his couch, and he brought out his treasure, a little plastic bag with tied handles and some paper in it wrapped around the nice, shiny shells that he'd gathered and had played with for years. He insisted that we take some. We selected a big whelk, two brown cowries and two tooth cowries.

"It was so touching, him offering us his prize possessions," said Sylvia outside. "You should send him something nice." When we got home I mailed him a diode flashlight, a Swiss knife, and some Pop Rocks candy.

Atop Mount Talau, I found a giant bean pod, pale green and easily three feet long, dangling from an overhead vine. I picked it, and then wondered if it was wrong to make off with the giant bean. I tried to hide it in my knapsack, but it wouldn't fit completely—it peeked out at the top.

When we got back to the tiny village center and sat in a snack bar, I put my hat atop the knapsack, and the waitress thought the pack, bean and hat were a baby. Odd, that. Was the bean coming to life?

Sylvia's personal supplies were in the knapsack too, so she borrowed it to take to the post office while I relaxed in the shade of the snack bar.

"That bean is getting us into trouble," she told me when she came back.

"What do you mean?"

"A woman asked me where I'd gotten it."

"Was she mad that we took it?"

"No, she just wanted to know where we got it, so she could find one. She said it was used for Tongan ceremonies."

"I stole the ceremonial bean?"

At the hotel desk a woman told us more. "It is called a lofa bean. If you let it ripen and get brown, the lofa bean seeds can be used for—dancing." She made a gesture, miming castanets.

Back in the room I continued to admire the bean. I wondered out loud if it might be the larva of an alien centipede. After all, the bean's vine had seemed to hang down from nowhere.

"What if it splits open and eats my brain tonight, Sylvia?"

"It would get a small meal."

Diving along the plunging undersea walls beyond the Pacific island reefs was like dream-flying across the steep mountain meadows of Zermatt. The walls were covered with chubby coral that was rubbery instead of hard. This soft coral was chartreuse, lavender, and pink. It came in a wondrous range of shapes, as if Mother Nature were diddling the parameter dials on a fractal generator.

Once I went down a wall covered with hard and soft coral and drifted with the current. Out in the open sea were big sharks, considerably larger than me, some of them. Not all that far away. I was about seventy feet deep. About fifty or a hundred feet below us was a swirling whirlpool of big-eyed trevalleys, each of them trying not to be out on the edge where the sharks were. The school was like a slow cyclone, making a shape like a nest, with every now and then a bright flash as one of the large fish turned onto his side to wriggle deeper into the core.

On another dive I saw some very fine manta rays. We dropped down to a sandy crushed-coral bottom at about fifty feet, crept up near some coral, and there they were, two large mantas, twelve feet across, one of them dark all over, and the other one light on the top. They were hovering over the coral heads to be cleaned by some wriggly finger-sized fish called wrasses—this spot was called a cleaning station.

The mantas were just as alien as I might have hoped, incredibly stream-lined, with a geometry determined by curvature and flow and torsion. They had oval bodies, and the classic meaty triangular wings, with a rudder fin and a long spike in back. They were close enough to me that I could have touched them, had my arm been twice as long.

Their eyes were in protruding knobs at either side of their heads, not that they really have a separate head. They had slit mouths that opened up big and round when they sucked in water—I think they feed by filtering out plankton and other little things. The mantas had pairs of little steering appendages sticking out of the sides of their heads, fleshy and oar-like, rather than fin-like.

Truly these dives were visits to alien worlds, and I'd use these scenes in my novels such as *Spaceland* and *Hylozoic*.

Sylvia and I snorkeled as well as doing SCUBA. Around us were clouds of little butterfly-like fish, yellow and white and fluttering like confetti. Over and over, looking ahead, we'd barely notice things disappearing—*zip!*—into hidey-holes. Eventually, with much patience, we were able to see that the little phantoms were bright-colored, fringed cones—like tiny, spiral feather-dusters. A local told us these were the feeding organs of creatures called Christmas tree worms. They lived in the coral, and they grew themselves hinged trapdoors like thumbnails to cover their holes.

I thought once again of my old idea of there being forms of life that move so fast that we never quite see them. Why not? Only a few centuries ago, we were unaware of the microscopic creatures that are invisible to the naked eye.

*I*n January, 1997, I decided to write another *Ware* book, this one to be called *Realware*, with much of it set in Tonga. *Realware* continues along a path I followed throughout the *Ware* series, that is, the process of expanding the range of things that we might regard as being patterns of information.

To recapitulate: *Software* (1982) suggests that your mind as a software pattern that could run on a robot body, *Wetware* (1988) points out that DNA is a tweakable program so you can in fact grow a new meat body for your software to live in, and *Freeware* (1997) proposes that aliens travel as radio signals coding up the software for both their minds and their bodies. As a final step, in *Realware* (2000), the characters obtain a device which creates arbitrary physical objects from their descriptions. In 2010, the four novels would be reissued in a single volume called *The Ware Tetralogy*.

I structured *Realware* as a love story—over the years I'd come to understand that it's almost always good idea to have romance at the heart of a novel. And I included a scene with my main character hugging his estranged father and seeing him off to something like Heaven. At the end of the novel, my character Cobb Anderson achieves an apotheosis as well. In writing these two scenes, I felt as if I were laying to rest the specter of my last painful argument with Pop in 1994. One of the virtues of writing is that you get to revise your past.

By the way, in *Realware*, my old stoner hero Sta-Hi, although crazy as ever, is sober. This annoyed a few of my fans. In my later books I'd lighten up and let some of my characters get high again. Or maybe even—what a concept—not be addicts at all.

*A*t school I was still teaching software engineering and working on my textbook. More and more, I wanted to break out of my usual routines. When I finished *Realware* in 1998, I started thinking I might write a historical novel about the sixteenth century Flemish painter Peter Bruegel.

I'd loved Bruegel's work ever since that year I'd spent in Germany as a boy, when my grandmother had shown me that book of his paintings. I'd been naively pleased by the Bruegel's hundred-in-one pictures like *Netherlands Proverbs*, and fascinated by his apocalyptic paintings like *The Fall of the Rebel Angels*, with its wriggling mask of chimerical creatures. In later years I became fonder of Bruegel's mature, naturalistic paintings such as *Peasant Dance* or *Hunters in the Snow*. With their deep, detailed pictorial space, these late works are like windows into other worlds.

Bruegel's paintings are like novels, so filled are they with character, landscape and incident. I feel a pang when I stop looking at one of them, akin to the sadness I feel when reading the last page of a great book. It occurred to me that if I were to write a novelistic narrative of the man's life, I could hang out with him for a quite a long time.

Now that I had tenure, I was able to score for a sabbatical. In the fall of 1998, Sylvia and I took a long trip around Europe, and on our trip, we made a point of swinging through Bruegel-related towns: Antwerp, where he worked as apprentice; Brussels, where he had his studio; Vienna, where the bulk of his paintings hang; and Naples, where two of his sardonic final works can be found.

We felt at home in Belgium. Some of Sylvia's ancestors were from the lowlands—her maiden name is in fact a variant of Bosch. My ancestor Peter Rucker, who came ashore at the mouth of the James River in Virginia in 1690, was from a family of harpsichord makers in Antwerp. The best known of these craftsmen was Andreas Ruckers, who, as it happened, was in the same guild as Bruegel. Painters, instrument makers, and cabinet makers were lumped together in those early times.

Walking down the streets of Antwerp with Sylvia, I was thinking that the genes around us were much the same as the genes in Bruegel's time—as if Antwerp were an isolated pond of fish. And surely some of the genes were ours as well. The mouths and noses looked familiar.

Sylvia was going to stop by and visit her father in Geneva, but I'd head straight to Vienna to look at the twelve Bruegel paintings there. When I went to catch my train, I got into this science fictional mind-trip that Bruegel was alive inside me. And I started seeing things as if I were Bruegel, looking with his eyes around the station, like, wondering about those diabolical magic moving stairs over there—was this Hell? A beggar girl was sitting and singing—beautifully—she was only lovely thing in this subterranean ants-nest of lost souls. I followed signs for my track—and I ended up outdoors, amid half-finished construction. The sun was setting, light glared from a glass building, I saw no sign of green, just pipes and stone and pavement, and for a minute I was so into being Bruegel that I felt utterly lost and confused. Yeah, baby!

In the Vienna museum, their amazing trove of Bruegel paintings is hung in a single high-ceilinged room. Entering this divine space I felt a sense of urgency, as if the paintings and the beings within them were calling out to me.

I visited the Bruegels on four different days. Coming back to the same paintings over and over, I was struck by the obvious yet transcendental fact that the images were always the same. Everyone in these little worlds is frozen forever in time, living a day like any other day, a day that lasts forever. Another thing that struck me was the fractal nature of the paintings: when I looked twice as hard, I'd see *three* times as much. This property of having "too many details" is precisely how mathematicians formally characterize fractal shapes such as the famous Mandelbrot set.

Sylvia met up with me in Vienna. It was late September in 1998. One Sunday afternoon we went to a circus in a tent on one of the squares, a lovely show, bright with color and laughter. When we went outside , there was a chill in the air and low gray clouds with scraps of blue showing through. Most of the leaves on the trees were yellow. All of a sudden it was fall. Summer had been fading gradually, but we'd been too busy with our fun to notice. It occurred to me that I myself, at 52, was entering the autumn of my life. A heavy thought. *It turned to fall while we were at the circus.*

When we got back to California in October, 1998, I began trying to write my Bruegel novel. I wanted to make it a straight historical novel, with no science fiction, but I felt a little skittish about tackling a new genre.

To help get into the right frame of mind, Sylvia and I took an oil painting class at the San Jose art museum early in 1999. My idea was to get a sensual feel for the craft that I'd be describing. As it happened, I really took to painting, and I've gotten more and more into it over time. I enjoy how non-digital and sensual it is to paint, and how different it is from my usual keyboard-based activities.

It would take me until February of 2002 to finish my Bruegel book. I stuck to my plan of making it a historical novel, and I ended up running it through several extensive revisions. When people asked me why this wasn't going to be an SF novel, I'd say, "I don't want to drag Bruegel into the mud." Not that I truly think of SF as inferior. But I felt that the paintings and the turbulent history of Bruegel's times provided more than enough material to work with.

Very little is known about the great man's life, so I was free to invent most of it. I used a kind of inverse transreal method, that is, I studied his paintings and then dreamed up what might have been happening in his life when he painted them. Some of the paintings might depict things that Bruegel saw, while others may symbolize things that were going on in his family. Each chapter of my book is named after one of the paintings, and with a little effort I got the museums' permissions to print black and white images of the works.

I came to identify very deeply with Bruegel as a man. He loved both the fantastic and the literal, that is, he depicted otherworldly drolleries and everyday life. His work was often viewed as vulgar or incomprehensible. And he had only a modest success in his lifetime. None of his works ever ended up on the altar of a church.

I gave my book a dreamy, mysterious title with an explanatory subtitle. *As Above, So Below: A Novel of Peter Bruegel.* The title phrase is a traditional occult saying meaning something like, "On Earth as it is in Heaven." I felt that the motto captured Bruegel's stylistic habit of representing specific human activities in the context of a broad and even cosmic landscape—which is precisely what I like to do.

I Retire

I'd dreamed of breaking out of the science fiction ghetto with *Above, So Below: A Novel of Peter Bruegel*—after all, it's a historical novel about a painter, and a similarly themed novel, *Girl With Pearl Earring*, was a bestseller just then. But none of the mainstream literary publishers seemed interested in my book. Perhaps people had me pegged as a cyberpunk SF writer, and that was that.

My new editor David Hartwell at Tor Books published the Bruegel novel in 2002. Although mainly known for science fiction and fantasy books, Tor has a mainstream imprint called Forge. The novel did pretty well after all, and over the years, I've heard from a number of people, particularly artists, who love the book.

As part of my deal with Tor, I also sold them a new SF novel called *Spaceland* which I'd written rather quickly between September, 2000, and April, 2001, as a break from the Bruegel project.

Spaceland was a contemporary Silicon Valley novel, similar in that respect to *The Hacker and the Ants*. The story was loosely inspired by Edwin Abbott's *Flatland*. I'd happened to notice that the *Flatland* character A Square mentions, almost as an aside, that his adventures start on December 31, 1999. So I set *Spaceland* on that day as well, which seemed fitting, as everyone was so frantic about the Millennium just then. In *Flatland*, A Square is visited by a sphere from the third dimension. In *Spaceland*, Joe Cube, a middle manager at a San Jose computer company, receives a millennial visit from a denizen of the fourth dimension. This book was very easy for me to write, like falling off a log.

I even designed a bunch of illustrations for *Spaceland*, to make it easier for people to understand. Not that everyone *did* understand it—some people resist making the mental leap that's needed to understand the fourth dimension. Like infinity, the fourth dimension is a genuinely new and different idea that can't be dismissed or explained away. And this can be a little scary.

As things worked out, when my Bruegel novel appeared in 2002, I was back in Belgium, living in Brussels for a semester, as a guest of the Flemish Academy of Arts and Sciences, temporarily alone. I had a grant from the Academy to do research on "the philosophy of computer science"—a new topic that hardly anyone's talked about yet.

My apartment in Brussels was near the Marolles district, the raffish old neighborhood where Bruegel's three-story stone house still stands. He lived and worked there for most of his adult life. I liked going by Bruegel's house, and now that I'd written my novel about him, the house meant that much more to me. Bruegel's church is in the same neighborhood, it's where he was married and buried.

I felt a nostalgia for my imagined years of living in Bruegel's house with him—I'd seen him shake fruit-tree petals onto his wife Mayken beneath a tree in the yard, I'd seen him painting his masterpieces in the attic, I'd witnessed the births of his sons Jan and Peter, and I'd attended his death. It's funny how my fictional characters get so mixed in with my own life's memories.

On October 3, 2002, shortly before I got my hardback copy of *As Above, So Below: A Novel of Peter Bruegel* in the mail, I went out to look for a meal. It was just starting to rain, but I had a good coat. I went down into Bruegel's neighborhood, and it started pouring. My pants were getting wet and some rain was trickling in through my coat's buttoned collar. I cut through the arcades in some housing projects, running in and out of the buildings' arches and terraces. And then it was me alone in the night, on the wet cobblestones. I felt Bruegel's ghost come up and walk along beside me, very casually. He'd already read my book of course, and he liked it. What a trip.

For my first six weeks in Brussels, I was living alone, as Sylvia couldn't get away from her teaching job yet. It was strange to be on my own—this was the first time I'd lived alone in my whole life, given that I got married about a week after graduating from college.

Settling into my apartment, I bought a couple of Frank Zappa CDs and a portable CD player with good speakers. Hungry as I was for the sound of a human voice, it was wonderful to hear warm, friendly, mellifluous Zappa and his soaring, lush, romantic guitar solos. In the mornings, I'd do yoga to his CDs. A high point of each day.

As well as doing research, I was giving a course of lectures in the philosophy department at the ancient University of Leuven, which is about an hour from Brussels. Leuven is the university where the medieval thinker Erasmus hung out. The philosophers there in 2002 liked me, they were the ones who'd helped me get the grant.

The one question philosophers always want to ask me is what it was like to meet Kurt Gödel. Really, I pretty much put everything I remember about him into my book *Infinity and the Mind*, with maybe a bit more here in *Nested Scrolls*. But people hunger for that extra bit that I never told before.

"He took off his clothes and stood on his head and wrote GOD = DOG on the blackboard with the chalk held in his toes. I was surprised."

I always took the train to get to Leuven. Train travel perfectly instantiates quite a few of my neuroses. It's archetypal, like the fabric of a dream.

The old-style dangerous metal wheels and gears of the train itself are a nice match for the giant analog clocks they always have in train stations. The Industrial Age! The train leaves at 9:48. The clock says 9:46. The big clock's minute hand moves forward in an abrupt tick. 9:47! Horrors, I'll be late! Running up the stairs, down the long platforms, I begin to sweat, dreading the very real possibility of getting on the *wrong train*.

And once I'm on the European train, for the final nightmare touch, I meet the menacing authority figure, the smiling conductor whose smile is only skin deep, the father who doesn't really like me, and *I can't communicate with him*, thanks to the language barrier! I begin trying to explain myself to my father, but a chill wind tears my words away. My lips move but my voice is inaudible, at the very most I emit a gibbering squeak.

For my research project in Brussels, I was reading Stephen Wolfram's magnum opus of 2002, *A New Kind of Science*, and starting work on a nonfiction book of my own, about similar topics. Remember that Wolfram was the guy who'd gotten me into cellular automata. He'd been working on his big book about computation and reality for over a decade and now it was done and he'd sent me a copy.

The physical weight of Wolfram's book felt like an imposition—it was wearing out my wrists and it was a literal drag to carry around Brussels. So I found a big carving knife in my apartment's kitchen—the knife had those tiny nicks in the blade like you see on the knives in Bosch paintings—and I cut the book into slices of a reasonable size. As I was slicing loose the first three chapters, I noticed that the copy was in fact inscribed to me by Wolfram himself, and I felt a little abashed.

In reality, I would become a strong advocate for *A New Kind of Science*—I discussed and extended Wolfram's ideas in my book about computation, *The Lifebox, the Seashell and the Soul*, and I wrote a long and positive review of Wolfram's book that appeared in the *American Mathematical Monthly* in November, 2003. I regularly took flak on Wolfram's behalf whenever I'd lecture on his teachings.

Very many people indeed opposed *A New Kind of Science*. To me, having known Wolfram for so long, his ideas seemed obviously true. But others found them to be—as Wolfram might put it—either trivial or wrong. When a set of ideas provokes such a firestorm, it's a sign of an impending paradigm shift.

So what was Wolfram saying?

First of all, he was arguing that we can think of any natural process as a computation, that is, you can see anything as a deterministic procedure that works out the consequences of some initial conditions. Fine. Instead of saying the world is made of atoms or of curved space or of natural laws, let's see what happens if we say it's made of computations. This notion gets some people's goat, but if you've hung around computers a lot, it seems semi-reasonable.

Secondly, Wolfram made the point that, by studying cellular automata, he'd learned that there are basically three kinds of computations. The simple ones peter out or repeat themselves. The pseudorandom ones generate a seething mess. And the interesting computations lie in between.

They generate patterns that seem to have some kind of structure to them, but they don't repeat themselves or turn boring.

This second idea is simply a taxonomic observation about the kinds of things we find in the world. The in-between computations are akin to what we might earlier have called chaotic processes. I myself came to call them "gnarly computations." So, if everything is to be a computation, then pretty much all of the interesting patterns in nature and biology are gnarly computations. Fine.

Thirdly, Wolfram argued that all gnarly computations are in some sense equally powerful, that is, given enough time and space, any given gnarly computation can in fact emulate any of the others. If everything is an equally-powerful computation, then we're all in some sense the same.

Note that a computer doesn't have to be made of wires and silicon chips in a box. A cloud can emulate an oak tree, a flickering flame can model a human mind, a dripping faucet can behave like the stock market. And we're not talking about vague, metaphorical resemblances here, we're talking about mathematically precise bit-for-bit representations.

For someone who'd become as steeped in computer science as I had, this third point also seemed reasonable, but outsiders had trouble making sense of it—and in their confusion, many of them grew angry.

Fourthly, Wolfram said that gnarly computations are unpredictable in the specific sense that there are no quick short-cut methods for finding out what these kinds of computations will do. The only way, for instance, to really find out what the weather is going to be like tomorrow is to wait twenty-four hours and see. The only way for me to find out what I'm going to put into the final paragraph-sized "scroll" of *Nested Scrolls* is to finish writing the book.

Wolfram's fourth point is very nearly provable on the basis of some well-known theorems from computer science but, again, many scientists don't like it. They still subscribe to the pipedream of finding some magical tiny theory that will allow them to make quick pencil-and-paper calculations about every aspect of the future. They haven't taken to heart the essentially chaotic nature of the world. We can't control; we can't predict—but even so we can hope to ride the waves.

I gave what may have been the least successful talk of my career when I tried to explain Wolfram's ideas to the computer science department at the University of Leuven near the end of November, 2002. I'd organized some snappy computer demos and slick slides, but the faculty met the new ideas with extreme hostility and complete incomprehension. It was like a classic scene from the history of science.

At the end of my talk, the only comment from the gathered audience was from some old fart (well, he was younger than me, but older) who said, "I hated the beginning of your talk and the end of the talk, it's all completely wrong."

"How about the middle," I snapped back, feeling like Johnny Rotten ducking his shoulder to avoid an incoming beer bottle. "How did you like that?"

I was close to walking out, but my host dragged me up to the computer science faculty lounge for a cup of tea. Several people came up to me and they wanted to argue about every little thing I'd said. But these guys weren't programmers from Silicon Valley. My sense was that they didn't know squat. They hadn't spent years of their lives staring at cellular automata simulations, or worked at companies shipping commercial software. Hell, they were so out of it that they couldn't see why I was teaching my software engineering students how to write programs for video games. They were like stuffy English professors angered that someone might discuss a science fiction novel in a literature course.

I took a lot of photos in Brussels. When I'm alone, having a camera along is sort of like having a friend. I show what I'm seeing to the camera, and the camera remembers it. I also see photography as a kind of sensory amplification. When I'm amped up to spot possible photos, I see my surroundings more clearly, and I become more aware of the visual patterns and of the contrasting collages of content within a street scene.

For many years I'd been using a Leica M4 and then a single-lens-reflex Leica R3 camera. In Brussels I switched to a compact high-quality Contax camera, still based on film. The upside with a smaller camera is that I tend to carry it around more, and I pick up accordingly more shots. The downside is that the images aren't as sharp and richly shaded.

In Brussels, I found that the photo processing shop was willing to copy my film pictures onto a disk as electronic image files. This intrigued me, although at this point I didn't have much use for the files. At this time, it wasn't practical to email pictures as attachments, I didn't have any decent image-processing software, and I wasn't yet posting images on the web. I didn't realize how very soon the mass changeover to digital photography would arrive, carrying me with it. Another wave. I'll say more about this in the next chapter.

Touring around Brussels, I revisited the Atomium that I'd seen at the 1958 World's Fair with my kind Uncle Conrad, now dead. The Atomium's huge linked spheres had been shiny forty-four years ago, but now they were tarnished and even rusty. And all the bright pavilion buildings of the fair were gone.

"They should really keep the place up," I told Sylvia on the phone later that day.

"It's Europe, Rudy," she replied. "Everything's old, it's hopeless."

Inside the Atomium were a series of exhibits relating to the 1958 Worlds' Fair. Seeing them was a knife in my heart. Outside the structure I was filled with the tragic sense of life. Looking at a tree, it seemed the saddest, most wretched thing I've ever seen. But I wasn't really and truly depressed, this was more of a ham-bone, operatic kind of feeling. I was kind of wallowing in it, enjoying the intensity of my emotions.

To cheer up, I bought myself the most expensive beret I could find. They cost according to how big of a diameter they have. I'm not talking about the headband size, mind you, I'm talking about the floppiness, droopiness and zootiness of the thing. My big beret looked very "original," the haberdasher assured me. I took to wearing it all the time, with a striped silk scarf and a long wool topcoat, imagining that I looked vaguely like the medieval philosopher Erasmus.

During this stay, I was also working on a science fiction novel. I'd decided to write a fat novel for once, an epic galaxy-spanning adventure. I felt like I'd never tried to hit the long ball before. To get in the spirit, I read Tolkien's *Lord of the Rings*—somehow I'd never gotten around to reading it before. I enjoyed the series, it has this funny quirk that, if a character is going to walk a hundred miles, Tolkien is going to tell you something about what the character saw during each one of those miles.

I wanted to write something that I could have read aloud to my own kids when they were young, so I made my hero a twelve-year-old boy named Frek. It's 3003 and the biotech tweaked plants and animals are quite wonderful—but there are only a few dozen of the old species left. Nature has been denatured by profiteers. It's up to Frek Huggins to venture out into the galaxy to fetch an elixir to restore Earth's lost species. At least that's what a friendly alien cuttlefish tells him the elixir will do. But can you really trust aliens?

I went with a simple title, *Frek and the Elixir*, not-so-coincidentally echoing titles like *Harry Potter and the Enormous Royalty Check*. In order to organize my long book, I decided to base my outline on a well-tested pattern, as well. I turned to Joseph Campbell's, *The Hero With a Thousand Faces*.

Campbell identifies seventeen typical stages in the universally recurring monomyth, and I decided to write one chapter for each stage—The Call to Adventure, The Refusal of the Call, the Helper, Crossing the Threshold, the Belly of the Whale, and so on.

The Belly of the Whale? At first this Campbellian stage struck me as odd, but, come to think of it, a "whale" that swallows you might any type of transport craft. In many of my own books, a character does get inside something and go somewhere. In *Freeware*, Sta-Hi is carried away from earth inside a flying plastic robot; in *The Hollow Earth*, Mason stows away inside a riverboat; in *Realware*, Willy ends up inside a hyperspherical being called On; in *Spaceland*, Joe is carried to the higher dimensions inside a cuttlefish named Kangy.

And in *Frek and the Elixir*, Frek travels to the center of the galaxy inside a creature that once again resembles a cuttlefish. I have a thing for cuttlefish. Their facial tentacle-bunches strike me as so bizarre and science fictional. I named Frek's alien cuttlefish after a memorably weird math professor I'd had in grad school: Professor Bumby.

When my alien cuttlefish, Professor Bumby, appears on stage, digging his way out of the ground where he'd been buried, he quotes one of my favorite remarks from the history of mathematics, "*Eadem mutata resurgo!*" This means, "The same, yet altered, I arise again."

The mathematician Jakob Bernoulli had this inscribed on his tombstone along with a picture of a spiral—and to me it expresses a certain feeling that I get whenever I manage to start another book. When I'm not writing, I'm dead and dry, but when the words start to flow I'm living again.

During my stay in Brussels I also had the opportunity to perform some real-time video displays as an accompaniment to a piece of electronic music written by the composer Gerard Pape. Pape was the director of a small institute in Paris devoted to the music of the avant-garde composer Iannis Xenakis. Sylvia and I took the train down to Paris a few times, and I'd spend the day at Pape's offices, sometimes working with a Turkish student of his named Sinan Bokevoy.

One afternoon, Sinan was playing his latest electronic composition for me, and I was struck by how well this situation matched *Frek and the Elixir*. I'd just been writing a scene where Frek is in a windowless reality-generating room with alien lampreys. And here I was in the windowless electronic music studio, with a pile of big fat lamprey-like cables behind me, each of them holding about a dozen lines with individual jacks, just perfect for plugging into my spine.

Sinan's piece started with the dilated sound of a hammer pounding, weirdly stretched in time. A single voice began to sing, then decomposed into a choir of reedy wails, deconstructed by Fourier analysis software. It was like an acid trip where a conversation shatters into droplets of sound.

"Why does electronic music always sound so sinister?" I asked Sinan.

"Because these are sounds we're not used to hearing, and anything strange is a possible menace," he answered readily. "Also these sounds are deep, like big things. Also they're dissonant, like unpredictable disorganized things. And they seem to come from every side, like things you can't get away from." He patted his laptop. "Polyphony is a creation not by God, so we think of it as Satanic."

My concert with Gerard Pape was early in December, 2002, at a Paris event called *"Recontres 2002: Musique et Arts Visuels."* Gerard had written a twelve-minute electronic music piece called "Clouds," using samples based on tympani crossed with storm sounds. While it played on the eight speakers in the room, Gerard twiddled dials to continuously adjust the mix. At the same time, I was working my laptop's mouse and keyboard to project a flow of graphics onto a wall-sized screen. There was an audience of about a hundred people.

Although Gerard's tracks were pre-recorded, my programs were generating the graphics live, that is, computing the moving images in real time. That's always been a touchstone goal for me in my computer programming—to create graphics programs that run fast enough to be useable as light-shows. I was excited to be performing at this event.

I started with a two-dimensional cellular automaton cloud in black and white, perturbing it by mouse clicks that made blotches like exploding H-bombs. I switched into some artificial life-forms that flew about like insects, leaving twisty trails in a virtual three-dimensional space. And then I went with a smooth and undulating two-dimensional cellular automaton wave, luminous with a ramped palette of color. I conceptualized this sequence as being a storm with black and white clouds, followed by a scene in the woods where some gnats buzz around each other—above a peaceful puddle, rippled by the winds.

The other composers quietly, earnestly, said, "Bravo," to me as I sat back down. It was very satisfying. Gerard said nothing quite like our collaboration had ever been presented in Paris.

Although Gerard and I had dreamed of using algorithms to connect my graphics to his sounds, we'd ended up just using our brains. Gerard made what he considered to be sonic equivalents of the kinds of chaotic visual effects I'd shown him. And then I listened to a preview tape of his composition a number of times until I thought of a sequence of moving graphical displays that would fit.

The week of that concert I'd been thinking a lot about quantum mechanics, both because I wanted to lecture about quantum computation at Leuven, and because I wanted to use some quantum mechanical gimmicks in *Frek and the Elixir*. One of the interesting problems in the philosophy of quantum mechanics has to do with whether or not you become inextricably entangled with the things that you look at.

Walking in the Latin Quarter, looking at some smoke from a chimney against the sky, not naming it, just seeing it, letting its motions move within my mind, I struck me that I was no different than a mouse cursor moving across the screen of a two-dimensional cellular automaton. I was entangled with the smoke, and in a very real sense, I was the cursor dragging the smoke across the sky.

At this moment I had a strong sense of *aha*. A satori in Paris. I realize that this account will make little sense to most people. But I strongly remember the feeling.

At the time I thought of my experience in terms of a classic koan, momentarily understanding it in a very personal and experiential way.

Q: I see a flag is blowing in wind: Is the flag moving or is the wind moving?

A: Mind is moving.

B ack home in Los Gatos, I stayed on leave during the spring of 2003 so that I could finish writing *Frek and the Elixir*, which ended up being my longest novel yet. I'd had some hopes of selling it to the publishers of the Harry Potter books—after all, my hero was 12, just like Harry—but we ended up selling *Frek* to Tor Books. They did a nice job with it and it sold quite well.

When I went back to teaching at San Jose State in the fall of 2003, I felt like A Square from the book *Flatland*, returning from his trip into the higher dimensions, settling back into the dull level wilderness of his old world.

I no longer felt willing to stay in academic harness. The endless hours of keyboarding and mousing were getting to my hands and my back. We had really uncomfortable office furniture. A state directive specified that any new desk chairs for the California State University faculty had to be purchased from the California Prison Industry Authority, and these prison-made chairs were cheap junk snapped together from kits made in China. Very 1984.

Overall, the California state budget was a mess, and our teaching loads and committee obligations were going up. I felt like I was beginning to repeat myself in my lectures. And I longed to spend my remaining years on what I love most: writing and traveling.

So in the spring of 2004, urged on by a golden handshake offer issued to the faculty by Arnold Schwarzenegger himself, I retired from teaching. I was fifty-eight.

My last day as a professor, I sat at the outdoor coffee bar under my office building where the baristas were playing a Ramones CD, including the songs "Rock N' Roll High-School" and "I Wanted Everything." My favorite musicians had come to sing me goodbye. Joey was dead, but he was still my friend.

I sat for awhile in the sun, drinking tea and listening to the Ramones. No rush. "The KKK Took My Baby Away" was on, one of my faves. What if I got up and started dancing? All around me students were studying, as if there were no music.

I went in for my very last class meeting. My graduate Software Project students demonstrated the final versions of their computer programs, mostly video games. I liked these kids, they were smart and eager. They gave me a farewell card, brought in a pizza, took some pictures. It was touching.

In my office I erased the sign I'd made on my whiteboard, preparatory to retiring.

"Look homeward angel and melt with ruth."
Teaching Assistant 1967–Professor Emeritus 2004.

Thirty-seven years of teaching, off and on. I was ready to be done. Leaving the building, I felt light as a feather.

Old Master

The big project I wanted to tackle in the fall of 2004 was to finish writing my tome about the meaning of computers. I already had some rough draft material that I'd used as the notes I handed out for my philosophy of computer science lectures at the University of Leuven. I'd jokingly entitled my lecture notes *Early Geek Philosophy*—meaning that, yes, we computer types are starting to philosophize about what we do, but we're only the *early* geeks, and more wisdom will eventually be revealed. But really I was really quite serious about the project.

I wanted to understand what computation means. I'd meant to nail this much earlier on—when I'd moved to Silicon Valley in 1986. At that time, my old friend Greg Gibson had said, "Imagine if William Blake had worked in a textile mill. What might he have written then?"

Initially I'd thought I'd get into the scene, figure out what was happening, get out, and write my book on computers and reality. But somewhere along the line I went native. My cover story ate my personality.

I had a mental image of a Soviet jeep driving up to a barbed wire fence like they used to have between West Germany and East Germany. Some East German soldiers carry a struggling figure wrapped in canvas to the fence and throw him over to the Western side. Inside the bundle is a double agent who forgot his old life. That was me—covered in a thick blanket of computer code. But now I was free. I was ready to tell the world what I'd learned during my twenty year stretch in the dark Satanic mills of Silicon Valley.

Hoping for a better-than-usual advance for my book on the philosophy of computer science, I engaged the prominent science-book agent John Brockman. He helped me work out the proposal, and we adopted the title, *The Lifebox, the Seashell, and the Soul*. And then, as seemed to be the fashion, I added a long, explanatory subtitle: *What Gnarly Computation Taught Me About Ultimate Reality, the Meaning of Life, and How To Be Happy*.

Brockman sent my proposal to about thirty publishers, but in the end, we ended up selling the book for a mid-range advance to my editor friend John Oakes, then at Avalon Publishing. Ironically, Oakes had wanted to buy the book before I even got involved with Brockman. In the past he'd been publishing some of my reprints and anthologies at his own house, Four Walls Eight Windows—which had recently been bought out by Avalon, who would in turn be bought out by Perseus Books a few years later. For a writer, it's a little unnerving how chaotic the publishing business is these days.

My book title, *The Lifebox, the Seashell, and the Soul*, was meant to be a kind of dialectic triad, that is, a pattern of the form, *The Thesis, the Synthesis, and the Antithesis*.

With the thesis word, "lifebox," I meant a large database that might include, in my case, my books, my journals, my interviews, my photographs and perhaps an overarching memoir—with the various pieces connected by hyperlinks. A lifebox might resemble a large website.

Some fairly simple programming could endow a lifebox with interactive abilities—to start with, a search engine might be enough. And then people could pose questions to the lifebox, and it would answer with appropriate links and excerpts of text. The result might be a construct that would function as a simulacrum of the lifebox's author.

"What was great-grandfather like?"

"Go online and talk to rudy-the-elder. He'll tell you all about himself."

Could a lifebox become conscious and alive? Initially, the notion of an intelligent lifebox seems quite absurd—which is why we might think of "soul" as being the antithesis of "lifebox."

But maybe someday, a lifebox *could* have something like a soul—if you were to equip it with the right kind of software and run it on the right kind of hardware. Computer scientists have amply shown that simple computations can in fact generate a wide range of natural patterns. The fabulously gnarly Mandelbrot fractal's basic algorithm is little more than a rudimentary equation.

The point is that we may not need a huge intellectual breakthrough in order to create something as florid as artificial intelligence. It may be that a very simple program can do the job, provided we feed the program enough data and run it on fast processors with large amounts of system memory.

As a simple example, Wolfram had noticed that a tiny cellular automaton program can produce the intricate triangular lattices seen on the cone shells of the South Pacific. And this where the synthesis-word "seashell" of my book title comes in.

Thus, *The Lifebox, the Seashell, and the Soul*. As well as talking about artificial intelligence, I'd also be looking at the wider questions of what it means if we try to look at everything in the world as a computation: physics, biology, psychology, society, and philosophy.

I worked on *The Lifebox, the Seashell, and the Soul* very intensely. By the start of 2005, I was almost done. But by this point a reaction had set in. Throughout the book, I'd been arguing that every natural process can be regarded as a computation—and by now I'd started doubting this. After all, at the immediate, emotional level, life doesn't feel like a computation at all.

In February, 2005, to celebrate my retirement, I went on a South Pacific diving trip with my brother Embry. We went to the islands of Palau and Micronesia, an archipelago which dots the seas between the Philippines and Indochina.

On a kayaking-and-snorkeling outing near Palau, I regained my faith in the usefulness of thinking of things as computations. My moment of insight came at our last snorkeling spot of the day, where I swam among lovely pale blue and pink soft corals. These organisms were branching broccolis on the sandy bottom of an archway connecting two bays—and I noted that they were akin to computer-graphical fractals.

Swimming through the arch, I encountered a shoal of perhaps ten thousand tiny tropical fish, not unlike the fish you'd see in someone's home aquarium, little zebras or tetras. Marveling at the scarves of density emerging from the fish's motions, I considered that the schooling was really a kind of parallel computation, with each fish a processor.

The turbulent water currents were computing as well, I mused, and so were the ever-changing clouds in the sky, and the living splotchy patterns on the mantles of the giant clams, and the nested scrolls of the shelf corals, and the gnarly roots of plants on the land. The world was a network of computations, and computing was a metaphor for the dance of natural law.

And what about my thoughts? They could be computations too—deterministic but unpredictable processes akin to fractal broccoli, flocking fish, fluid turbulence, and nested coral scrolls. My thoughts were really no richer than the mass of life forms in these lagoons. My mind could be a naturally occurring computation.

And with this experience in mind, when I got home, I was able to write a satisfactory ending to *The Lifebox, the Seashell, and the Soul.*

For me, each book is in some sense a thought-experiment along the lines of, "What might happen if such and such were the case?" For the purposes of my book-length experiment, I'll adopt some outré idea and psych myself into believing it deep down—and then I proceed to work out the consequences.

This is very much a style of thought that I learned as a mathematician. You start with a set of axioms and see what you can deduce. Software engineering proceeds in somewhat the same way. You create a little program and see what appears on the screen when the program runs. My SF writing is like this too. I make some unusual assumptions about my imagined world, put in a few characters, and see what happens in the story that I write.

Once I'm done writing a given book, I move on. Although the *Lifebox* tome gave me great fodder for future SF novels, on a day-to-day basis, I don't think that the world is made of computations—any more than I think that it's made of atoms or of curved space. These are all just useful modes of thought.

Over the long term, I have more of a pluralist attitude. The world isn't one particular thing, it's all sorts of different things. If I focus on my immediate experience, I'd be inclined to say the world is made of shapes, sounds, emotions—and the ubiquitous white light.

There aren't any simple answers. And we'll never know what it's all about.

On the Micronesian island of Pohnpei, in late February, 2005, Embry and I rented a car and drove to a spot called Liduduhniap Falls. It was up a long dirt road that was hard for us to find—none of the roads had signs. A pamphlet from the tourist office said there was a store at the end of the road by the falls, and that one should pay a dollar to the storekeeper to visit the falls. When we got up there, we saw only a pair of rudimentary Micronesian buildings, basically tin roofs on posts, and neither of them looked particularly like a store.

We heard the sound of a radio from one of the buildings. Peering behind a low fence in front of it, we observed a stocky, bare-breasted brown-skinned woman asleep on the ground, wearing a bright flower-printed skirt with an elastic waistband. No matter how low you set your expectations of formality, the Micronesians always slip beneath it.

Embry and I went ahead to the waterfall, which was a classic tall cataract surrounded by green jungle plants. The two of us went wading and swimming in the waterfall pool. It was exciting to have the falls beat down on us; it gave me a magical feeling of healing.

Looking over at my pale-skinned, gangly big brother, I felt a great tenderness towards him. We were still two boys in a swimming hole.

But, I also thought, perhaps this might be the last time Embry and I would take a trip of this kind. I imagined one of us in the hospital, and the other one talking about our moments of shared tropical joy.

The past never really goes away. The perfect and the imperfect moments always stand.

Life in my own little family rolled on. Sylvia and I came to enjoy our cozy times in our empty nest—it's like a return to the early days of our marriage. I enjoy that Sylvia remembers all the old times, and that we have a long, shared history. We still seem beautiful to each other. I love to hear her voice, and to see her smile.

As Sylvia and I edged into geezerhood, we began fretting that our children might never marry. But then it was time. In the space of the four years

2003 to 2006, Georgia, Rudy Jr. and Isabel all had weddings—Georgia with her husband Courtney, Rudy with his wife Penny, and Isabel with her husband Gus. These were wonderful and deeply emotional events. And it's been nice getting to know the three new in-law children.

At our reunions, I like the moments when Sylvia and I get into the same old cozy give and take with our three kids. For a minute or two we'll once again be rolling on the ground in a heap with our three clever piglets, all of us squealing and nipping at each other—I speak figuratively, of course. Not that we can do this for very long, as the kids do have their own families now. It's amazing to see our children growing up and taking their places in the world.

Our family's size kicked up another notch when Georgia and Courtney had their daughter Althea in 2005, a tender little bud, perfect in every detail. And in 2007, Rudy and Penny had twin girls, Zimry and Jasper, followed by Georgia and Courtney's son Desmond. As I write this in 2009, when we manage a full reunion, there's twelve of us.

I've found that being with our grandchildren is even more pleasant than I'd expected. The biological drive for reproduction is one of those things, like empathy, that's wired in at a very deep level. When I'm watching over the little ones, my face sometimes gets tired—from smiling so much.

And how odd it is to have our own children age towards their forties, to remember how I myself had been at that age, and to realize that the children have ongoing interior lives as rich as mine ever was. Many of their thoughts will forever remain unknown to me.

Georgia shares my raucous sense of humor and my self-driven ability to finish creative projects. She's a graphic designer, and a master at assembling unusual outfits for herself and her children. She's grown into motherhood, becoming gentle and warm. Rudy Jr. has Sylvia's kind nature and my rebellious qualities. He loves to tinker with things and to make them work. He's a cheerful, joking father to his twin girls. Isabel is a jeweler, an artist, a Wyoming outdoorswoman, and the most stylish among us. She's intensely loyal to her family and friends. She's playful and she loves a good laugh.

With five generations to think about, I can shuffle among all sorts of viewpoints. I might compare a memory of my grandmother playing with me to Sylvia playing with one of our grandchildren. Or I might compare my daughter looking at her son to my mother looking at me. Or I might think of how my children's conversations with me echo my conversations with my father.

Life is an endless cascade, a hall of mirrors, a forest with new trees replacing the old.

*I*n the fall of 2004, I started blogging regularly on a site I call *Rudy's Blog*, with the address www.rudyrucker.com/blog. Rudy Jr. runs an internet service provider business called Monkeybrains, and he gives me the server bandwidth for free.

By 2010, after five and a half years of blogging, I'd put up some seven hundred posts which, taken as a whole, bulk to a word count comparable to that of three medium-sized novels.

Am I wasting my time? What's the point of a blog?

The issue of wasting time is a straw man. A big part of being a writer is finding harmless things to do when you aren't writing. To finish a novel in a year, I only have to average a page a day, and writing any given page can take less than an hour. So I do in fact have quite a bit of spare time. Of course a lot of that time goes into getting my head into the right place for the day's writing—and then contemplating and revising what I wrote. But blogging isn't a bad thing to do while I'm hanging around waiting for the muse.

I often post thoughts and links that relate to whatever writing project I'm currently working on. And my readers post comments and further links which can be useful. To some extent my blog acts as a research tool.

Another thing about a blog is that it's a means for self-promotion. By now, my blog has picked up a certain following, and every month it receives about a hundred thousand visits. The only ads I run are for my own books.

But my blog isn't really about research or commerce. The main reason I keep doing it is that the form provides a creative outlet. I like editing and tweaking my posts, and I like illustrating them. I alternate text and pictures, usually putting a photo between every few paragraphs.

I switched over to digital photography around the time when I started my blog in 2004. I've used a series of pocket-sized models—they only tend to last for a year or maybe two, but that's okay as they're relatively cheap

311

and the technology is always improving. I also have a heavy-duty Canon 5D digital reflex camera with several lenses.

I carry one or another camera with me much of the time, and I'm often on the lookout for photographs. I sometimes think of photography as instant transrealism. When it goes well, I'm appropriating something from my immediate surroundings and turning it into a loaded, fantastic image.

When incorporating my photos into my blog, I don't worry much about whether the images have any obvious relevance to the texts that I pair them with. As I mentioned earlier, the human mind is capable of seeing any random set of things as going well together. So any picture can go into any post. The Surrealists called this practice juxtaposition, and it's akin to our Sixties game of listening to music while you watch a TV show with the sound off. Our perceptual system is all about perceiving patterns—even if they're not there.

This said, if I have enough images on hand, I do what I can to bring out harmonies and contrasts among the words and the pictures. Subconscious and subtextual links come into play. Assembling each blog post becomes a satisfying work of craftsmanship.

Having the blog and the digital cameras has revitalized my practice of photography. With the blog as my outlet, I know that my photos will be seen and appreciated. It's not like I'm just throwing endless packs of photo prints into a drawer. For many years, Sylvia assembled our photos into yearly family albums, but now, with the children gone, she's let this drop. "The kids don't want to see albums of us two taking trips," she points out.

I like how my digital cameras give me immediate feedback—I don't have to wait for a week or a month to learn if my pictures were in focus. And I like using my image-editing software. I crop my pictures, tweak the contrast, mute or intensify the colors, and so on. It's like being back in the darkroom with, wonderfully, an "Undo" control.

I mentioned before that having a camera along for a walk is a bit like having a companion. Now that I have my photo-illustrated blog, this is even more the case. When I'm out on the street, I'll sometimes slip into a photojournalist mode of searching out apt images while making mental or written notes for a post.

An interesting effect of the internet is that, if you're a heavy user, your consciousness and sense of self become more distributed and less localized. Even when I don't have the camera along, the blog is a virtual presence at my side. My old sense of self used to include my home, my workplace and the coffee shops I frequent—but now it includes my blog, my email, and the online social networks. As Bill Gibson puts it, cyberspace has become a part of daily life.

As I briefly remarked in the first chapter, *The Lifebox, the Seashell and the Soul* gave me so many ideas that I ended up using them in my next three science fiction novels. In *Mathematicians in Love*, which I wrote from 2004 to 2005, I took up the idea of imagining a world in which nature is in fact predictable, a world in which, for some reason, it's possible to foretell the results of computations in advance.

The book plays out around contemporary Silicon Valley, and it features a couple of punk math grad students who repeatedly alter reality while competing for the same woman—which is how they happen to end up in an offbeat sheet of reality in which, unlike in our actual world, the future is predictable.

In order to give some coherence to the notion of multiple sheets of reality, I used the notion—which I mentioned earlier—that there might be a god-like being who keeps designing fresh drafts of our universe, like a novelist would do.

My specific image of the world-building divinity in *Mathematicians in Love* was based upon a memorable day when my brother Embry and I visited Jellyfish Lake on an atoll near Palau during our epic dive trip of 2005. The unique species of golden jellyfish in this lake barely sting, they don't eat anything, and they get their nourishment from algae cultures that live inside their bodies. All they do all day is pulse their bells so as to move themselves into the sunniest part of the lake to make the algae in their tissues grow. Our guide said that visiting ctenophorologists studying this lake's population had estimated it to be fifteen million strong.

We swam a hundred yards out into the wide lake, wearing masks, snorkels and fins. The jellyfish were of every size. Each of them was pulsing with a repetitive beat, the little ones pulsing faster than the big ones. They seemed to have no inkling of up or down, although once they'd pulsed down to about twenty feet or so, they'd vaguely notice the darkness and bumble back towards the surface.

It was like space-travel to sink into the water staring at them. I saw nothing but the greenish-yellow sunlit water and the endlessly many jelly-fish. A couple of times I dove down to twenty feet, then floated up with the jellyfish all around me. If I relaxed, I could share a sense of there being no special location or direction.

In the more densely packed regions, there might have been sixty of the jellyfish touching my body at any one time, maybe four big guys, eight small ones, sixteen still smaller jellyfish, thirty-two tiny ones, like that.

The jellyfish stung ever so slightly, and the longer I stayed in, the more I could feel the venom. Particularly when I was free-diving down through them, I'd feel tingles on my lips. A couple of them even drifted inside my trunks and touched my private parts. I thought of a line from William Burroughs's novel, *The Ticket That Exploded*.

"Skin like that very hot for three weeks, and then—wearing the Happy Cloak."

Years earlier, I'd used Burroughs's notion of a Happy Cloak in my novel *Software*, where the Happy Cloak takes the form of a jellyfish-like cape of intelligent plastic that sends probes into your spine when you throw it over your back.

In *Mathematicians in Love*, the designer-god of our universe is in fact a very large jellyfish in Jellyfish Lake. This jellyfish-god makes a new version of our universe every Friday.

Sometimes I get a little tired of being cast as a science fiction writer. In my mind, I see my novels as surreal, postmodern literature. I just so happen to couch my works in the vernacular genre form of SF because the field's tropes appeal to me. The downside is that, since my books have that SF label on them, many people don't realize that I'm writing literature.

In academic philosophy, they use the phrase "category mistake" to refer to a situation where one tries to apply a property to something that cannot possibly have this property. The classic example of a category mistake is the question, "Is virtue triangular?"

Sometimes I feel like my whole career of writing literary SF is a category mistake, and I wonder if there might be a way to get my work relabeled.

As Kurt Vonnegut famously put it in 1974, "I have been a soreheaded occupant of a file drawer labeled 'Science Fiction' . . . and I would like out, particularly since so many serious critics regularly mistake the drawer for a urinal." Not too long after this, Vonnegut did make it out of the drawer. Although he never stopped writing SF, he got people to start viewing his works as literature.

More recently, Jonathan Lethem is a strong example of a former SF writer who's managed the escape-from-the-ghetto move. He's a high-lit writer now, but in some sense his books are still SF, or at least fantasy-tinged. In terms of crossover, others start out as a literary writers, and then begin adding SF elements to their novels—Margaret Atwood comes to mind. These kinds of books tend to be called speculative or imaginative fiction rather than SF.

When I gripe about my SF-label to Sylvia, she laughs at me. "Not science fiction? You're writing about robots and talking cuttlefish and flying saucers and trips into the fourth dimension! What do you expect people to call your books?"

So be it.

A year after I'd retired, I had a fleeting nostalgia for professorship, and in the fall of 2005, I went back to San Jose State for one semester to teach a graduate philosophy course on "Philosophy and Computers." I had an interesting bunch of people in my class. I mostly talked about *The Lifebox, the Seashell and the Soul*, but I also wrote two linked short stories that I read aloud to the students.

After the semester ended, I kept thinking about those two stories, and I ramped them into my next novel, *Postsingular*, which I worked on all through 2006. The title plays off the then-popular notion of an impending technological singularity after which computers are intelligent and every-thing is changed. The idea had first been proposed by the SF writer and computer science professor Vernor Vinge back in 1993, but over time, some people had taken it up with a nearly religious fervor—there was a Singularity Institute, a Singularity University and an annual Singularity

Conference. Some of these people seemed to imagine that taking a lot of vitamins would make them into geniuses who lived forever. I was mildly annoyed by the hype, and I liked the idea of leapfrogging past it—thus my title, *Postsingular*.

It wasn't easy for me to write that book. For a time, we SF writers had been resisting the singularity. But Charles Stross had shown us the way in his superb novel *Accelerando*. Once I read Stross, I realized that writing about postsingular worlds only requires a straight face and a little practice. Earlier SF writers learned to write about starships, telepathy, robots, and aliens. It's really no harder for us to write about worlds where a toothpick might be as smart as Albert Einstein. Just start pitching the bull—and keep it consistent.

Although I'm often able to sell my short stories to science fiction magazines, it's a fair amount of trouble for very little pay, and my stories do sometimes bounce back. In the fall of 2006 I hit upon the idea of starting my own online science fiction magazine.

I'd recently written a story with my old SF pal Paul Di Filippo, a tale called, "Elves of the Subdimensions." I was in a rush to get the story published so that I could put it into an upcoming anthology of my stories. Although some will argue that it's a good policy to have at least one brand-new story in each anthology, my feeling at the time was that I wanted to publish "Elves of the Subdimensions" in a magazine as well.

There wasn't time to get "Elves of the Subdimensions" into one of the major print magazines, so I tried one of the existing online SF webzines—and they had the temerity to turn our story down. And that's when I decided to start my own webzine. I mean—why should I court rejection from strangers who weren't even going to pay me, just in the hopes that they might post my story online?

Thanks to working on *Rudy's Blog*, I knew enough about the web to be quite sure that I could design and organize an online magazine. And given that my blog was getting quite a few hits, I'd be able to steer a respectably large audience to the webzine. There'd be no expense, as my son Rudy's internet business, Monkeybrains, was willing to host my webzine as well as my blog.

What to call the webzine? The name jumped out at me from a line Paul had written in our joint story. The elves, who live in the subdimensions (whatever the heck that means), are discussing the oddities of our human world.

"The high-planers ingest sweet chunks of their worldstuff!"
"They use picture boxes to learn their hive mind's mood!"
"Of flurbing, they know not!"

Yes, my webzine's title had to be *Flurb*. I liked the *Mad Magazine* sound of the word, and its vague feel of stumble-bum incompetence. If pressed, I might define "flurb" as a verb meaning "to carry out a complex, non-commercial artistic activity," and "flurb" as a noun could mean "a gnarly artwork that's incomprehensible to the average person."

Rudy Jr. helped me register a domain name for my webzine, www.flurb.net.

I started by asking my SF writer friends for stories, and, as the issues went on, I branched out from there, first turning to writers that I knew less well, and then starting to read contributions sent in by strangers.

I have a fairly clean design for the zine, running a colorful border down along the left side of each story. For the borders, I use patterns that I create with *CAPOW*, the cellular automata software that I'd developed on with my students at San Jose State—I use a fresh pattern for each story.

And, just as on my blog, I illustrate the stories with photographs that I've taken, although for *Flurb*, I cast the photos into a slightly larger format. I only do a new issue every six months, so I have a large number of photos to choose from. I make a pool of the best ones, and I choose the individual illustrations from the pool fairly quickly, almost at random, depending on the gods of synchronicity and on the pattern-creating qualities of the readers' minds.

I've come to enjoy the interactions with my *Flurb* authors, and in the fall of 2010, I reached issue #10. At this point, we get in excess of sixty thousand visitors per issue. And no money at all is involved. I don't charge people to read *Flurb*, nor do we carry any advertising, nor do I pay my authors. I try to treat them well, they get a little publicity out of it, and they get to keep all rights. It's a sideline for all of us.

317

I like to think that *Flurb* is a kind of clear-channel border-radio station for SF. As a personal matter, having *Flurb* as an outlet has freed me to write some stories that are so quirky and non-commercial that I wouldn't have done them otherwise. For instance I wrote a story called "Tangier Routines," about William Burroughs having sex with—and being in some sense eaten by—the early computer scientist Alan Turing. A lot of people liked this gnarly tale. But I could never ever have published it for a large audience in any locale other than *Flurb*.

Editing an issue of *Flurb* twice a year is a slight distraction from my writing—but writers are always looking for distractions. You get distracted until you miss writing enough to want to do it again.

Another thing I like to do these days is to paint. As I mentioned earlier, I took up painting when I was working on my Bruegel novel in 1999. And over the last decade, I've been painting more and more.

I have a visual imagination. For me writing is a like dreaming while I'm awake. That is, I see the scene in my mind's eye before I write it. Sometimes I'll nurse an image of a place or a situation for quite some time before I write about it, in fact I sometimes write a book simply to be able to mentally visit certain locales that I've dreamed up. I pretty much can't write a novel unless I have an image of a fabulous place where I want to go. By writing about these scenes, I make them more real to myself. And painting is another way to layer on more details.

All along, I'd been making little pen and paper drawings of fictional scenes before writing about them. But now I have the more heavy-duty option of breaking out my tubes of paint. I smear things around, I drool over the pretty colors, and nothing is perfectly neat. A painting takes longer than a drawing, and I get more deeply into it.

My level of manual control is low enough that I tend to surprise myself with what I end up painting. Sometimes these surprises show me things that are a good fit for my current novel or story—you might say that I'm channeling information from another part of my brain. But it's fine if I don't use the images in my fiction. The main thing is that I'm feeding my soul and getting into the moment and, if I'm lucky, turning off my inner

318

monologue. Given that painting doesn't involve words at all, it's even more meditative than writing.

Painting has, however, taught me a few practical things about writing. When I'm doing a painting, for instance, it's not unusual to completely paint over some screwed-up patch and do that part over. I think this has made me feel more relaxed about revising my fiction. And I've also noticed that the details that I haven't yet visualized are the ones that give me the most trouble. But the only way to proceed is to put it down wrong, and then keep changing it until it works.

I've done about seventy paintings over the years 1999 to 2010, and I've even sold a few. I maintain a website for them, and I also have it set up so that people can buy prints. But I haven't gotten heavily into the marketing aspects of being a painter. As my painter friend COOP remarked, "It's a whole new way to break your heart." For now I'm content to have painting be something that I do for fun.

This said, when *Postsingular* came out in November 2007, I did manage to have a gallery show in San Francisco. Sylvia and I went to a painting workshop in the South of France the previous summer—which had been a really wonderful time. In our class we'd met a character called Kevin Brown who runs a little gallery called Live Worms in the North Beach area of San Francisco.

Kevin uses his gallery mainly as his studio, but he's willing to rent it out for a weekend to artists who want to put on a show. I was able to talk the Tor Books publicity department into paying the rent, so the *Postsingular* launch ended up being a three day North Beach party in an art gallery filled with my paintings.

It was great to my pictures all hanging together, with friends and fans milling around. Another dream come true.

After writing *Postsingular*, I launched into a sequel, a novel called *Hylozoic*, which I worked on from March, 2007, though June, 2008. "Hylozoic" is an actual dictionary word that means "pertaining to the philosophical doctrine that matter is intrinsically alive." And that's the theme of the book.

Humans—and some invading aliens—have learned how to tweak the quantum computations that are inherent in ordinary matter, and while they're at it, they've developed telepathy. Human-level artificial intelligence is ubiquitous—a stone has a mind now, and you can talk to it. Every object is conscious and alive.

This was a situation I'd always wanted to write about—and my work on the *Lifebox, the Seashell and the Soul* had shown me the way. If a fluttering leaf can emulate my brain, then the leaf itself can be conscious. Why not? After all, we're talking science fiction here.

As another feature for *Hylozoic*, I used the artist Hieronymus Bosch as a character. At one point, I'd thought I might write a historical novel about Bosch—like I'd done with Bruegel. But somehow I didn't feel enough empathy with the man to want to carry out such a project. It felt okay to put him into a science fiction novel.

I'd often wondered what kind of person Bosch was—some passages in his pictures seem rather cruel, in other spots you pick up a feeling of ecstasy, and then again there's often a feeling of mockery and satire. I enjoyed combining these hints into the character that I developed for *Hylozoic*, where Bosch comes across as a genius, a devoted artist, a sarcastic mystic, and something of a prick.

As yet another element in *Hylozoic*, I included some aliens called Hrulls who resemble flying manta rays—this harked back to the mantas I'd seen while SCUBA diving some years before.

As I mentioned in the first chapter, on July 1, 2008—the day after finishing my final revision of *Hylozoic*, as a matter of fact—I had that brain hemorrhage.

One realization I had in the hospital was that I'm not really so scared of death anymore. At some point, it'll be time, and it's going to be okay. It happens to everyone. And I've had a nice long run.

Over the coming weeks, thanks to numerous brain scans, we learned that my burst vein had been something in the nature of an isolated birth defect—a malformed vein that had been lurking in my brain for sixty-two years. And, so far as the doctors could tell, there weren't any more spots like this to worry about. So now it was time to get back to my life.

In the fall and winter of 2008, I wrote the first draft of this, my autobiography, *Nested Scrolls*. I let it sit for about nine months and then, in the fall of 2009, I came back to the work to revise it and complete it. I'd been almost scared to reread it, given that I started it so soon after my brain event. But now I think it seems good.

At the same time that I started thinking about this autobiography, I was thinking about a somewhat fantasy-like SF novel, a book called *Jim and the Flims*, about a young man who nearly dies and then, although still living and fully recovered, travels into the afterworld to deal with some potentially Earth-destroying beings called flims. The story arc of the book involves Jim's mission to bring his dead wife back from the underworld as well—it's kind of an Orpheus and Eurydice tale, only, given my penchant for happy endings, I'm planning to let Eurydice actually return.

I worked on *Jim and the Flims* all through 2009, and I'll finish it in 2010.

Not that there's any rush. At this point in my career, I worry a little about repeating myself, and about adjusting my work to appeal to the public's changing tastes. After seeing the 2009 traveling King Tut show, I decided to add a gold sarcophagus and the reanimated mummy of Amenhotep to *Jim and the Flims*. And I'm thinking that next I might do a whole novel about William Burroughs and Alan Turing. Yeah, baby. Keep it bouncing.

Recently I was talking to the lordly old SF master Robert Silverberg about the ever-changing cast of SF writers. "When I go to a convention I don't know anyone anymore," he griped, exaggerating for effect. "I feel like Chaucer."

When my father was on his last legs, around 1992, he said, "What was I so worried about all those years? What difference did any of it make?"

I felt both liberated and undermined by this remark.

Liberated—because Pop was reminding me that, in the end, my creative turmoil and business deals and emotional adjustments would come, in the end, to nothing. I was going to die just the same. So why spend my whole life tying myself knots trying to make things right?

Undermined—because, after all, the emotions, the creativity and the deals are the things that make my life interesting and pleasant. And if these things are for nothing, then my life is for nothing.

Ultimately I decided not to internalize Pop's late, despairing views. Even if my struggles lead only to the grave, they mean something day to day. I'm keeping myself amused and happy. I'm helping Sylvia and the children make their ways through life. And I'll be leaving some readable books behind.

Like many writers, I spend an inordinate amount of time fretting about the relative success of my works. But I also work at being grateful for what I have. After all, the vast majority of people don't get published at all. My books are printed and find substantial audiences; I get money and respect for my work. I'm lucky to have the ability to write.

My book, *The Lifebox, the Seashell and the Soul*, includes a chapter on viewing society as a computation. Thanks to researching this topic, I've finally came to accept that writers' sales obey a scaling law that's technically known as an inverse power law distribution. You're not getting lackluster book advances because someone is actively screwing you. It's the scaling law.

The scaling law applies across the board—to the populations of cities, the number of hits on websites, the heights of mountains, the number of friends that people have, the areas of lakes, and the sales of books. There's no getting around it. The graph of size versus rank isn't a down-slanting straight line, it's a curve that swoops down fast and hugs the horizontal axis like a graph of $1/x$. Thus, if you're the hundredth-most popular writer, you earn a hundredth as much as the most popular one. Instead of a million dollars, you get ten thousand bucks. That's how nature is. It's not anyone's fault.

Even though my financial rewards are modest, I revel in the craft of writing. I like being able to control these little realities where things work out the way I want. It's no accident that so many of my heroes leave the ordinary world for adventures in fabulous other lands. In just the same way, I move my mind from the day-to-day world into the fantastic worlds of my books. I make art because it feels good.

Writing is hard, and after each book is finished, I wonder if I'll be able to write another. But I keep coming back. And I've got painting as well— another path to creative bliss.

———

I'll end with one last Micronesia story. While touring around that obscure South Pacific island of Pohnpei in February, 2005, Embry and I found our way to an enormous petroglyph rock. It was smooth to the touch, a hundred feet long, resting in the jungle beside an open field with green interior mountains beyond the field, and with heartbreakingly beautiful tree crowns waving against the pale blue sky.

The petroglyph designs carved into the rock were quite old—we saw images of paddles or knives, of woman's vaginas or shields, some bow-tie shapes, and the outline of a whole woman.

To find this site we'd asked at a house near it and a betel-nut-chewing guy offered to guide us. We were glad to have him along for a few bucks. Wiley. He banged one spot on the big rock and it sounded a bit hollow and he said, "There is a door in the rock here, and the brothers went inside."

"What brothers?"

"Two brothers came from far away—" Wiley pointed towards the other side of the island, across the interior mountains, it was maybe ten miles distant, as remote a spot as he knew. "From Kiti. They made these carvings. A giant came, and the brothers hid inside the rock. See here, it's a picture of a lock and a key."

I told Wiley that Embry and I were brothers, and then a little later I told him we were from Kiti, which got a good laugh out of him. It was fun to think of Embry and myself as archetypes, brothers from a legend.

In a field nearby, Wiley showed us a "woman rock" which had a crotch and a slit, really quite graphic. He touched the slit for good luck, and so did my brother and I, all of us hoping to see our women soon.

There were other boulders in the field, and Wiley said they were people as well. He said this field was his land, and that the land was a storyboard, which is a kind of wooden bas-relief that Micronesians carve to preserve their legends.

Wiley's rocky field was a storyboard.

I loved that. He was living mythically and in depth. And that's how I'd like to think I've lived too. It's been deep and intense, here inside this cosmic novel.

———

Back in the first chapter, I mentioned that I wondered what my life has meant. But now I see that's not a question I'm in a position to analyze. I'm inside my story, not outside of it. What does a flower mean? A waterfall?

This said, as a writer, I *can* think about my life's structure, about the story arc. I see a few obvious themes.

I searched for ultimate reality, and I found contentment in creativity. I tried to scale the heights of science, and I found my calling in mathematics and in science fiction. I drank and smoked pot, and then I stopped. I was a loner, I found love, I became a family man. I was a rebel and I became a helpful professor. And I never stopped seeing the world in my own special way.

When I was a kid, I felt like an ugly duckling. I'm a once-awkward outcast who grew into grace—thanks in large measure to dear Sylvia.

Thanks for everything, world.

It's been a wonderful trip.

—Los Gatos, California, January 30, 2010

Bibliograpghy

BOOKS

Jim and the Flims, SF novel, Night Shade Books, 2011.

Nested Scrolls: A Writer's Life, autobiography, PS Publishing and Forge Books, 2011.

The Ware Tetralogy, omnibus edition of *Software, Wetware, Freeware* and *Realware*, Prime Books 2010.

Hylozoic, SF novel (sequel to *Postsingular*), Tor Books 2009.

Postsingular, SF novel, Tor Books 2007.

Mad Professor, collected SF stories, Thunder's Mouth Press 2007.

Mathematicians in Love, SF novel, Tor Books, 2006.

The Lifebox, the Seashell, and the Soul, nonfiction on computers and reality, Thunder's Mouth Press 2005, Basic Books 2006.

Frek and the Elixir, SF novel, Tor Books, 2004.

Software Engineering and Computer Games, textbook, Addison-Wesley, 2003.

Spaceland, SF novel, Tor Books, 2002.

As Above, So Below: A Novel of Peter Bruegel, historical novel, Forge Books, 2002.

Gnarl!, collected SF stories, Four Walls Eight Windows, 2000.

Realware, SF novel, Avon Books, 2000.

Saucer Wisdom, SF novel, Forge Books, 1999.

Seek!, collected essays, Four Walls Eight Windows, 1999.

Freeware, SF novel, Avon Books 1997.

The Hacker and the Ants, SF novel, Avon Books 1994, Four Walls Eight Windows 2002.

Transreal!, collected poems, SF stories and essays, WCS Books 1991.

The Hollow Earth, SF novel, William Morrow & Co. 1990, Avon Books 1992, Monkeybrain Books 2008.

All The Visions, memoir, Ocean View Books, 1991.

Wetware, SF novel, Avon Books 1988, Avon Books 1997.

Mind Tools, nonfiction on mathematics and information, Houghton Mifflin 1987.

The Secret of Life, SF novel, Bluejay Books 1985, ElectricStory 2001.

Master of Space and Time, SF novel, Bluejay Books 1984, Baen Books 1985, Running Press, 2005.

The Fourth Dimension, nonfiction, Houghton Mifflin 1984.

Light Fuse and Get Away, self-published poetry chapbook, Carp Press 1983.

The Sex Sphere, SF novel, Ace Books 1983, E-Reads 2008.

The Fifty-Seventh Franz Kafka, collected SF stories, Ace Books 1983.

Software, SF novel, Ace Books 1982, Avon Books 1987, Avon Books 1997.

Infinity and the Mind, nonfiction, Birkhäuser 1982, Bantam 1983, Princeton University Press 1995, 2005.

White Light, SF novel, Ace Books 1980, Wired Books 1997, Four Walls Eight Windows 2001.

Spacetime Donuts, SF novel, Ace Books 1981, E-Reads 2008.

Geometry, Relativity and the Fourth Dimension, nonfiction, Dover 1977.

BOOKS EDITED

MONDO 2000: A User's Guide to the New Edge, HarperCollins 1992, (with R. U. Sirius and Queen Mu).

Semiotext(e) SF, Autonomedia 1989, (with Peter Wilson and Robert Anton Wilson).

Mathenauts: Tales of Mathematical Wonder, Arbor House 1987.

Speculations on the Fourth Dimension: Selected Writings of Charles Howard Hinton, Dover 1983.

SOFTWARE PACKAGES

The Pop Game Framework, San Jose State University 2003.

CAPOW, San Jose State University 1998, (with a team of students).

Artificial Life Lab, Waite Group Press 1993.

CHAOS: James Gleick's Chaos Software, Autodesk 1990, (with Josh Gordon and John Walker).

CA Lab: Rudy Rucker's Cellular Automata Laboratory, Autodesk 1989, (with John Walker).

Software downloads, writing notes, links to art pages and more are available at the book's website, www.rudyrucker.com/nestedscrolls.
<http://www.rudyrucker.com/nestedscrolls>